WHAT
HAPPENED
TO
YOU?

*Hippies, Gospel Outreach
and the Jesus People Revival*

CHARISSE !
GOD BLESS you for
your faithful work for
Him + His people !
MARC

D1616190

WHAT
HAPPENED
TO
YOU?

*Hippies, Gospel Outreach
and the Jesus People Revival*

MARC S. ALLAN

REDEMPTION
PRESS

© 2016 by Marc Allan. All rights reserved.

Published by Redemption Press, PO Box 427, Enumclaw, WA 98022. Toll Free (844) 2REDEEM (273-3336)

Redemption Press is honored to present this title in partnership with the author. The views expressed or implied in this work are those of the author. Redemption Press provides our imprint seal representing design excellence, creative content and high quality production.

No part of this publication may be reproduced, stored in a retrieval system, or transmitted in any way by any means—electronic, mechanical, photocopy, recording, or otherwise—without the prior permission of the copyright holder, except as provided by USA copyright law.

Scripture verses marked "KJV" are from the King James Version of the Bible.

Scripture quotations marked "NKJV" are taken from the New King James Version. Copyright © 1982 by Thomas Nelson, Inc. Used by permission. All rights reserved.

Cover photo by Gary Todoroff: The Lighthouse Ranch Cross at Sunset

ISBN 13: 978-1-63232-548-8 (Print)
       978-1-63232-549-5 (ePub)
       978-1-63232-553-2 (Mobi)

Library of Congress Catalog Card Number: 2016942985

Dedication

This book is dedicated to my brothers and sisters in
Gospel Outreach.
"By this all will know that you are My disciples, if
you have love for one another."
(John 13:35 NKJV)

Contents

Acknowledgments

'M TEMPTED TO say, "You can't imagine how much fun it's been to talk to all these people," but I think a lot of you can. Many conversations led to a familiar sensation—we had to catch our breath as excitement stirred within when we talked about what Jesus did in our lives. We could feel his presence, and I'm pretty sure he enjoyed our talks too.

I've tried to faithfully record the recollections of those I spoke with. Any mistakes are wholly mine. Opinions that are not directly attributed are mine also.

The following people graciously gave of their time and thoughts: Jim and Celeste Durkin, John and Wendy Langsev, Linda Allan, Frank and Pam Lagielski, Terri Schrater, Laurie Baca, Tim and Anne Nabakowski, Paul and Maureen LaVanway, Bob Doerr, David Sczepanski, Bernie Heraldson, Scott and Elly Snedeker, David and Harriet Bye, Gary Todoroff, John and Judi Jordan, Steve and Irene Barney, Peter van der Gugten, Steve and Susan Insko, Bob and Carolyn Smith, Peter DePalmo, Ron Juncal, Larry Johnson, Bill Ireland, Mike Turner, Elly Conroy, Rob

Anderson, Leslie Dixon, Paul Johnson, Rebecca Muller, Walter and Susie Burbank, Kristine van Dooren, Jane Tuck, Jim and Sue Wall, Steve and Layne Fish, Larry and Claudia Jamison, Travis, Chris Pritchard, Chris Noonan Funnell, Sam Griffith, Edward Blume, Rense Miller, David Hatton, Harry and Sandy Hewat, Dick Benjamin, Richard Benjamin, Lambert and Marnie Hazelaar, Kersti Buchanan-Stoen, Naomi van Dooren Appel, Alex and Renie Elsaesser, Jim and Diane Boutcher, Harold Bailey, James Jankowiak, Joe and Patty Esposito, Andy Costa, Linda Costa, Tom Kennedy, Steve Tipton, Miro Carminati, Catherine Vinci Carminati, Linda Davidsson, Chuck Coleman, and Katherine Twiss. "Let's do this again!"

David Sczepanski excused himself from my interview with him and ran up to his office to retrieve a file box of old Radiance photos and negatives. I was very touched and thankful and able to use some of them. Other photos helped to provide context to the stories in the book.

Gary Todoroff generously allowed me to search through a book of hundreds of photo negatives he made of those times. Just like any family photo album, it was hard to make progress as I saw the images of so many beloved brothers and sisters. Gary scanned the negatives and digitalized them so they could be used.

Special thanks to my wife, Linda, who worked hard to enhance the quality of several old photos so they could be used.

Many thanks also to my editor Inger Logelin and publisher Athena Dean Holtz. This book wouldn't have been what the Lord or I wanted without their help.

Introduction

I FINISHED HIGH SCHOOL in June of 1968, and two friends and I loaded my VW bus with clothes, food and camping gear and hit the road. Starting on Route 66, we headed east from Southern California. Before the end of summer, we had set foot (or at least car tires) in all the lower forty-eight states. We saw the Grand Canyon, the Everglades, Washington D.C., New York City, Yellowstone National Park, the Pacific Northwest and a lot in between.

We had a great time and when we returned, I prepared to enter college. I knew my life was entering a new phase, but I didn't realize the whole world around me was changing.

The 1960s and '70s were a time in America when trusted institutions were weakened and collapsing. Family, country, and especially religion lost their hold on many young people.

This is the story of a group of individuals who became a family called Gospel Outreach—thousands of people who were touched by God during what has been called the Jesus People Revival. The Lord put us together and we called ourselves "brothers and sisters." For the most part, in the early years, we lived on communes with names like the Lighthouse Ranch, the Carlotta Mansion, Living Waters and the Lord's Land.

With a policy of "whosoever will, may come" thousands of young people—and some older—were welcomed. They dedicated themselves to God and one another to become not just Christians, but disciples.

South of Eureka, California, in the town of Carlotta, was an old house called the Carlotta Mansion. It was leased by Gospel Outreach to accommodate the overflow of new converts at the Lighthouse Ranch and it was there I became a Christian in June of 1973. The change God produced in me "in the twinkling of an eye" was profound, and I jumped wholeheartedly into the new life he had given me. I participated in the Bible studies, evangelistic outreaches, worked at Split Stuff, delivered the *Tri-City Advertiser*, planted and thinned trees, picked apples and finally, became a part of the Germany team. My wife Linda and I ministered in Germany from 1976 to 1989 when we returned to the city of my birth, Seattle, Washington, and joined the local Gospel Outreach (G. O.) church.

Like any family, Gospel Outreach had its high points and low points—sometimes very high and sometimes very low. You'll notice I don't spend much time on the low points. Fortunately, time tends to soften those experiences. I have no desire or ability to sort out or correct the past. I hope I've learned my lessons and know that God used even (especially) hurts and trials to help me focus on what is really important—that Jesus be shared through my life in the whole world.

I've put a lot of names in here—as many as I could while hoping to keep it from becoming too much. I want my G. O. family to see themselves and be reminded of what Jesus did in our lives. I would have loved to include everyone in this story! There are many people, extraordinary events and experiences that, only because of space and time, aren't here. All of us had remarkable life-changing experiences. Your friends and family will be amazed at what God did in your life. Maybe they will want to experience the same.

This story is more a collage than a straight chronological retelling, so some events and people may appear out of order. Think of it as a family photo album where pictures of Christmas, summer vacations, and birthdays are all mixed together. If a memorable story or person is missing—well, it's because Uncle Chuck took the photo out of the album and hasn't returned it yet. (My apologies!)

The first time I include the names of some of the women, I use their maiden names together with their present names. This is to help those who knew them then, but may not be aware of their new status. After that, I just use their present last name.

Talk to most people from Gospel Outreach and ask them for a Bible verse, and they'll probably have to run it through the King James Version. That's what we mostly read, and it remains the concordance in our brains. Some verses quoted here are New King James. In other cases, I use King James because at times, it can't be beat for clarity and beauty.

In keeping with the "whosoever will" motto of the Gospel Outreach ranches, I invite everyone who "wills" to join me and the G. O. family in remembering how God saved us and brought us into his kingdom.

I hope anyone who wasn't a member of the G. O. family doesn't feel left out. If you do and somehow wish you could have experienced what we did, I have an idea about how you can have it too. Be a whole-hearted follower of Jesus.

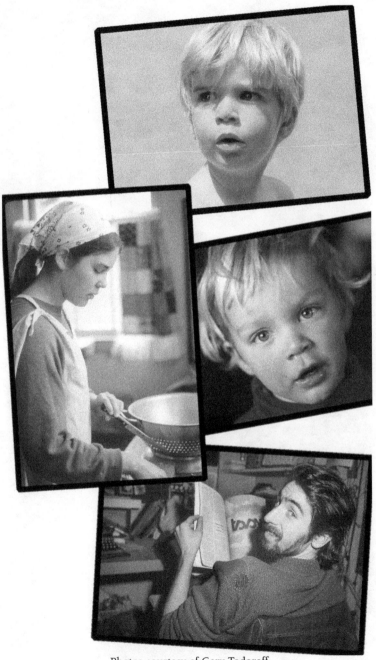

Photos courtesy of Gary Todoroff

CHAPTER ONE

If the Foundations Be Destroyed

WHEN THE CALIFORNIA Highway Patrol car passed Don, heading north, the patrolman turned and looked back at him. *"Oh, great!"* he moaned. *"If he turns around and comes back, I might be sleeping in jail tonight!* He knew the police had questions about some activities in his recent past.

It was the summer of 1974 and Don was trying to hitch a ride south to San Francisco on Highway 101. He had just crossed the one-lane bridge on Hookton Road about ten miles south of Eureka and walked the last hundred feet to the side of the freeway. There he dropped his backpack on the gravel, faced the oncoming cars and stuck out his thumb. That's when he saw the cop.

Don watched intently as the patrol car got smaller in the distance. His eyes narrowed as it slowed, then crossed the freeway median and started coming back his way. He now focused all his energy on his thumb as if, metaphysically, he could send a beam to passing drivers and make them stop.

It seemed to have worked as a car screeched to a halt on the gravel behind him. He grabbed his backpack, turned and stopped. Idling quietly, the offered ride was a faded, yellow VW Bug with Christian bumper stickers plastered all over the back.

He knew where it was headed—to the Lighthouse Ranch, just a few miles off the highway, back down Hookton Road. He stayed there the night before and had no desire to return.

This was his moment of decision. One last look back at the approaching highway patrol car convinced him he had only one choice. He got in.

Don knew what he was going back to. The previous day, a ride offered him a meal and a bed—the kind of offer a hitchhiker wouldn't turn down. This landed him at the Lighthouse Ranch, a Christian commune run by the Gospel Outreach Church of Humboldt Country, California. He got the promised food and bed all right, together with a barrage of Scriptures from the Bible and a smiling invitation to "ask Jesus into your heart."

Sitting in the large dining room of the main building, Don listened as a young man and woman told him of Jesus' love for him and God's plan for his life. He looked around and saw other earnest Christians reading and discussing the Bible or sharing the salvation message with hitchhikers who, in his opinion, had the same mixed luck as he had: free food and a bed if you could stomach listening to these Jesus Freaks. It was just like being in some Gospel mission in Portland or San Francisco. There, you could get a warm meal if you listened to the sermon and even better treatment if you faked sincere faith. Except their food was better than this mostly vegetarian diet.

He'd heard enough of the Jesus stuff. Rather than wait for a ride the next morning, Don walked the five miles back to Highway 101 and stuck his thumb out again. Now, with a cop bearing down on him, he was heading back to the "second to last place" he wanted to be.

But when he made that decision to come back, something happened inside. This time when he heard it, the story of God's love and Jesus' sacrifice for his sins made sense at a deeper level than he ever knew existed. Don saw that the brothers and sisters at the Ranch weren't glassy-eyed zombies repeating a preprogrammed message. He felt their sincerity as they told about meaningless lives that had suddenly been transformed by God. Their stories touched a longing deep in his heart to be free of fear, guilt, anger and loneliness and to have real peace. He discovered that not only was he running from the police, he had been running from God.

That night Don Copeland accepted Christ as his Lord and Savior and became a follower of Jesus.

He slept in a bunk in the brother's dorm, one of several buildings at the Ranch that used to house a Coast Guard lighthouse station. The lighthouse guided ships to the entrance of Humboldt Bay, and no more fitting place could be found to offer a safe harbor for the youth of the 1970s.

Destroyed Foundations

In the 1960s and '70s, America experienced seismic upheavals that affected every level of society. It was as if the continental plates had lifted fifty feet. All of the sudden, it seemed everything was off balance. The youth of the country, rich kids, poor kids, black, white—and everyone in between—lost faith in the institutions that had supported the greatest, freest country the world had ever seen. Their parents were proud of a nation that pulled itself out of the Great Depression and then led the free world in defeating fascism. The US was a bulwark against the spread of communism and a force for what was good, right and democratic.

We had the freest country, the strongest military and the best schools. We protected the world, rehabilitated and then made friends of our enemies and helped the poor. Heck, we were going to put a man on the moon by the end of the decade!

So why did John Kennedy have to get shot? Everyone alive then knows where they were when they heard the news. The young, handsome president who gave us all hope and optimism was dead, shot by an assassin. Then, in the middle of a live TV broadcast, his killer, Lee Harvey Oswald was himself murdered before a shocked nation.

The country and the youth may have been able to handle all that by itself. But a few years later, another crusader who dedicated his life to freedom was gunned down. Martin Luther King was killed at a Memphis motel. The country's mourning for him was tempered as race riots rocked the country from one coast to another. Two months later, John Kennedy's brother, Bobby, was shot after a political event in Los Angeles. In May of 1970, National Guardsmen carrying live ammunition fired on students demonstrating against the Vietnam War at Kent State, Ohio, leaving four dead. We thought, *My God, now they're killing students!*

What was happening? Was the world going crazy? People who devoted their lives to making this a better place were being murdered. Maybe things weren't so great after all. Maybe our society had deeper problems than even our elders knew about.

It had all gone too far. The only reaction that made sense was to reject what we had been taught about truth, freedom and morality. The movie *The Graduate* seemed to hit the nail on the head. Dustin Hoffman's character, Ben, had just graduated from college. A lot of us were either in school, just out, or at least the same age. Everything offered him as the path to the American dream, from business and money, to Mrs. Robinson herself, could be had as long as he would drop the idea of becoming his own person. Simon and Garfunkel summed up the choice for Mrs. Robinson, Ben and us. Any way you looked at it, you lost.

American society was confused and disoriented. No one was sure where the country was heading. Psalms 11:3 (KJV) asks, "If the foundations be destroyed, what can the righteous do?" Assassinations, racial tensions, and riots, the Vietnam War, the draft, and the nuclear arms race had replaced confidence in God, country, and family, the values of the 1950s.

California became a magnet for many who wanted to break free from the chains of a society they no longer believed in. The Haight-Ashbury district in San Francisco was a focal point of drugs, free love, and free living. It became the Mecca for many young people whose "foundations had been destroyed."

If they were going to find a life that had meaning and fulfillment, then the old had to go, minds had to be opened, new experiences needed to be experienced. The youth of America set out on untraveled paths, discovering new rules and realities that were foreign to their parents. They began to search for a truth that transcended the turmoil of their world and could give them peace.

This meant change. The ways of their parents no longer attracted them. With a self-absorbed focus, they turned their backs on a generation that had battled and overcome much adversity and set out on their own journeys. Whether it was smoking dope and "loving the one you're with" at the college dorm, hitchhiking up and down the coasts, across the country, or living in communes, many adopted a lifestyle which became identified as counter-culture; and for some becoming "hippies."

All You Need is Love

So—let's party! In 1969, in upstate New York, 400,000 people showed up on Max Yasgur's farm to listen to the likes of Creedence Clearwater Revival; Jimi Hendrix; Crosby, Stills, Nash and Young; Janis Joplin and many more. Enduring periodic rain, not enough toilets, food or water, the three day festival turned out to be a remarkable experience of what the promoters called a gathering of "peace and love." Woodstock was the granddaddy of them all and shared the spotlight with other rock festivals and local venues like the Cow Palace and the Fillmore in San Francisco, Chicago's Kinetic Playground, the Hollywood Bowl, the Anaheim Convention Center, the Electric Factory in Philadelphia and so on.

The music era of the '60s and '70s was remarkable for its strength and diversity. The Beatles and the Stones led the "British invasion." Motown gave the world Smokey Robinson, Ray Charles, the Supremes and the Temptations. The West Coast produced the Beach Boys, Jefferson Airplane, the Grateful Dead, Jimi Hendrix and Janis Joplin. The heartland gave us Bob Dylan; Joan Baez and Simon and Garfunkel came from the East Coast, and the Allman Brothers introduced us to Southern Rock. In addition, there were many more fantastic bands and groups.

Just like cables and wires of an electric grid cover the land and reach into every home, the music of that era connected with American youth. It touched everyone and became a common language. The messages expressed what we thought and hoped and feared: Barry McGuire sang of the "Eve of Destruction" and we knew that if things didn't change, we would witness it. Jim Morrison and the Doors sang about the "Ship of Fools." That seemed to be the human condition and if it depressed you too much, you could share a cynical laugh with Firesign Theater's, "I Think We're All Bozos on This Bus." The Animals and other groups urgently warned us to escape when they sang, "We Gotta Get Out of This Place."

We were doomed to a dull, soul-killing lifetime in the local mill, factory or office unless we found a way out.

We had solutions. The Beatles declared, "All You Need is Love," and the Mamas and the Papas told us where to find it with "California Dreamin." Scott McKenzie put a pin on the map with "Are You Going to San Francisco?" Led Zepplin sang of a "Stairway to Heaven" and the title touched a deep, indistinct desire that we didn't understand.

It all sounded right, but as time went on, the "good vibrations" that we shared from the music faded. The hopes that the music promised weren't realized. The Moody Blues produced beautiful, thoughtful lyrics and music. Finally, they too quit searching for the answer when they sang "I'm Just a Singer in a Rock and Roll Band."

We were still the same. We still didn't know how to change society or get out of the hole we found ourselves in.

The anti-draft and Vietnam War movements served as rallying points for many. The stories of returning soldiers—the same age as those who crowded the concert halls—told of a brutal conflict where the lines between good and bad and right and wrong had become blurred. There seemed no end to a conflict where our friends, brothers and cousins fought and died to liberate a people who apparently didn't care. While our fathers and uncles had clashed with uniformed enemies in Europe and the Pacific, young American boys in Vietnam had to be careful that some mama-san with a baby on her back didn't carry a grenade in her bag. At the end of WW II, our fathers came back as proud liberators, heroes to both the liberated and a grateful nation at home. As soldiers returned from Nam, they were insulted and called "baby killers." No one wanted to hear what they had been through, and before too long, they didn't want to tell.

We thought we knew what was wrong with everything; we just couldn't find the answers. More importantly, we began to suspect that we weren't solving our own problems either. As a matter of fact, in spite of putting up a good front, we were nowhere close

CHAPTER TWO

Beginnings

JIM DURKIN WAS a Chicago native, now living in Eureka, California and running his own real estate office, The Sequoia Realty. Heavy set and well into middle age, his life had pretty much drifted into a comfortable routine. After a brief stint with the U.S. Navy during WW II, he remained on the West Coast. Both his parents and grandparents had died within two years of each other when he was young, and he had no reason to return to the Midwest.

The navy had sent Jim to the University of Washington in Seattle and when the war ended, he was mustered out there. The nation was flooded with young men returning to civilian life from the military and work was hard to find. A year went by and a friend told him about a job with the Forest Service in the Northern California mountains near a town called Hoopa. Jim and his friend hitchhiked down there and were soon working in the woods and living in a Forest Service camp.

While Jim considered himself an atheist, he had a couple friends who were committed Christians, and they had many discussions about Jesus and the Bible.

One weekend his boss came to him with a request. "Jim, all the other men want to go home to their families for the weekend. Can you stay behind and watch the camp?"

That was fine with him and that weekend he had the whole place to himself. Except that the Lord planned something more for him. One night as he lay in his bunk in the dark tent, he suddenly became aware of a presence, accompanied by a sensation of peace and good will. He didn't hear a voice, and he couldn't see anyone, but he knew who it was.

It was Jesus.

Jim told the Lord about his life, all the things he had done wrong and asked for help. That night Jim Durkin got saved.

He joined the local Assembly of God church in Hoopa and not too long after that, met his future wife, Dacie. After a courtship, they were married. Feeling a call to the ministry, Jim became an Assembly of God pastor. In the ensuing years, he pastored churches in Blue Lake, near Eureka and in Fairfield, California. John, James and Joy were all added to the family during that time.

At first, Jim's ministry in the church had average success, his ministry at home less so. The need to succeed or at least appear to succeed weighed heavier and heavier on him. He had a fence business that did poorly and the result was bankruptcy. That was an overwhelming, almost crippling blow for him. Like many children of the Depression, the specter of poverty seemed to always lurk outside the front door. To be caught in its clutches meant he was a failure. The stress on his life and relationships now became unbearable and after thirteen years of marriage, Jim walked away from his ministry and his family. He divorced Dacie.

Separated from those closest to him and bankrupt, you might say that the Lord had Jim right where he wanted him. He now had plenty of time to look at his life and the results of his labor, intelligence and motivations. He recognized that his life—with his family, with the church and other Christians, and his business dealings, all bore the deep imprint of—Jim Durkin. God wanted to change that. He wanted the testimony of Jim's life to bear *his* imprint, so when people saw Jim, they saw the life of God's Son, Jesus.

The first step: *Go back to the wife of your youth and reestablish covenant.*

After three years estrangement, Jim and Dacie remarried.

The next step: *Build your business according to the Word of God.*

A friend told Jim the book of Proverbs contained all the business wisdom that anyone could need. He began to study Proverbs and apply the truths to his real estate business. Starting in 1963, by 1970 Jim could tell Dacie, "We now have enough that we never have to work again."

With his marriage and finances restored, Jim also began ministering in a church in Eureka. He told of a time of prayer when the Lord told him, *Jim, when you preach from the Word, you lay out scriptural truth, and then add, "but we know." Then you dilute my Word with your human understanding and experience. Stop doing that. Believe what the Word says. Put it into practice in your life. Then, when you are ready, I will give you understanding.*

So on the wooden sign in front the church in Eureka that Jim now pastored he added the motto, "We practice the Word of God."

They Say They're Christians?

Jim was in his real estate office one day in early 1971 when some visitors crowded in. They were bona fide hippies with long hair, beards, wearing crosses and an odd assortment of clothing—which only matched if you used your imagination or were high on something. *Man alive,* he thought, *what in the world do these guys want and how quickly can I get them out of here?* Jim smiled. "Good morning, what can I do for you?"

Their answer wasn't what he expected. Speaking in King James English, the leader, David Leon, explained to Jim they were looking for an apartment to rent and also wanted to start a Christian coffee shop. And oh, by the way, three other landlords had already turned them down.

This was pretty unsettling to Jim. *Who and what are these guys? They're hippies and say they're Christians too. Is this a front? Are they some weird cult that's into drugs and sex?*

Despite his questions, Jim didn't send them away without offering them at least a crumb. "Let me look and see what I have, and I'll get back to you."

Jim was tempted to play a joke on an older, more conservative realtor he knew and send the hippies to him. But before that thought was fully developed, another entered his mind. "Whoever has this world's goods, and sees his brother in need, and shuts up his heart from him, how does the love of God abide in him?" (1 John 3:17 NKJV). He knew that voice. It was the Lord speaking to him and telling him to help these people.

Jim had no way of knowing it, but the first half of his life had just ended. Unnoticed, the Holy Spirit created a small spring of water in front of him. A trickle rose to the surface and began to trace its course through Jim's life and the thousands of people his life would touch.

He called the hippies back in. Yes, he had a vacant property, all the utilities were working, and he would let them stay there for a time for no rent. It was an old, two-story building faced with weathered brown boards that seemed to lean wearily into the street. It offered its new occupants a storefront on the ground floor and apartments in the back and on the second floor. It sat on the corner of Clark and "B" streets.

The "Jesus Freaks" (that's what the world called them) set up in the rooms that Jim gave them. He was still a little nervous though. These guys looked more like hippies than the Christians he knew, and everyone knew what kind of life hippies lived.

Finally, after a couple weeks of worry and second thoughts, he could stand it no longer. One morning at two o'clock he woke Dacie. "Dacie, do you want to go for a ride?"

Of course not, but they went anyway. After dressing, they sleepily fell into the car, headed to Clark and B, stopped in front and got out. The lights were on; they heard music, and could see people through the windows.

Oh no! An orgy of drugs and sex! I knew it!

Jim knocked on the door and when one of the young men opened it he said, "Hi, we were just driving by and thought we'd stop in. You guys are still up?"

Inside, people were talking, praying, playing guitars and singing worship songs. Not what Jim expected at all. A serious young man informed him, "Brother, the children of the night are up in the night and if we want to speak to them, we have to be up in the night too."

Oh, Jim thought, *that sounds reasonable.* He and Dacie drove home, much relieved, and went back to bed.

"Durkin"

Deliverance Temple was a classic, one-hundred-year-old, white, small-town church on the corner of Cedar and California Streets in Eureka. It had one large meeting room filled with rows of wooden pews and a baptismal tank in the middle of the stage. The rest of it was divided up into smaller rooms for nurseries, offices and Sunday school classes.

It was called the Soul's Harbor Revival Center in the 1960s, and it had a reputation. It defined "holy roller" to the neighborhood with loud, demonstrative services and "Jericho marches" that scared off more people than they attracted. The church would elect pastors, keep them for a while, and then shove them out the door when they found someone who was more "anointed."

Jim served a couple of stints there and was sent on his way just like the others.

Then, in 1966, an evangelist came to town and was invited to stay for a time as pastor. One Sunday he came to church telling of a vision the Lord had given him. It was a name, really, and he wrote it on a chalkboard and asked the people if they knew what it meant. He had written "Durkin."

The folks told him about Jim, and that he had served as pastor at the church. Certain that God had now made his own choice, they asked Jim to take over again. He agreed on one condition: he would only do so if the church voted unanimously for him. After this, there were to be no more elections for pastor—this would be the last one. And so with the agreement of all, it was settled and Jim Durkin became the pastor. One last item of business: the name of the church was changed to Deliverance Temple.

With their energetic and knowledgeable pastor, the church members spread throughout Eureka, going door to door, inviting families to attend. They assured the public that things had changed. Deliverance Temple was now a place where the Word of God was preached faithfully and the fellowship was sincere and friendly.

The congregation included what could be considered spiritual "heavy artillery." Seven older women assumed the duties of intercessors. They supported Jim in his ministry and teaching and covered him and the church with a blanket of prayer.

An Extraordinary Vision

"An extraordinary vision," is what she called it. While praying, one of the women saw a picture of Deliverance Temple. It was overflowing with young people who were all saved and filled with the joy of the Lord. She blinked and the picture changed. The room was still full, but the original group of young people was gone. Now there were new people there. She blinked once more, and again new people filled the meeting room. She asked, "Where did all those people go?" By way of answer, a large map showing North and South America, Europe, Asia, Africa and the Pacific was lowered into the middle of the room.

They went into all the world.

A little later, the Christian hippies at Clark and B asked Jim if they could come to his church.

Jim wasn't sure how well this would go over. The youth of America looked and acted so radically different from anything he and his generation had experienced. He was starting to like them, but he didn't know how the congregation would feel about it. Jim was surprised and happy with the result. Many of the families reached out to the young people and encouraged and supported them.

And besides, there was a move afoot. The spring created by the Holy Spirit was growing into a channel that flowed through Eureka and Jim's life. It would become a strong, steady, stream of youth whose lives would be transformed, and as the vision of the map showed, would take what they learned and experienced into all the world.

At about the same time, the people at Clark and B began associating with another group of hippie Christians who were staying out at a one-time Coast Guard lighthouse station. It was located south of Eureka, next to the Pacific Ocean, on a piece of land called Table Bluff. Its original purpose was to show ships the entrance to Humboldt Bay, but with the development of more modern ship navigation and warning systems, had been abandoned by the military.

Ken Smith, a pastor from Eugene, Oregon had bought the property and moved in with a bunch of young Christians. He called it the Lighthouse Ranch. Here was a place where young converts could be removed from the stresses and temptations of the world and live in a secure atmosphere where they could learn about their new life. The people at the Ranch and Clark and B had much in common, and David Leon sent young converts like Bill Wheeler to the Ranch. They all ended up at Deliverance Temple on Sundays to hear Jim's messages.

A group headed by Ron Juncal joined them. Originally from Palos Verde, California, he became a Christian in 1966 when a man from Teen Challenge stopped him on the street and told him of God's plan for his life. Ron accepted the Lord and the Holy Spirit immediately began to use the young evangelist to spread the gospel. On his own, he convened meetings in the hills around town and shared the salvation message with as many as seventy-five young listeners at a time.

He moved up to Eureka to attend Humboldt State University but his evangelistic activities didn't slow down. Ron met David Leon and got to know his brand of street preaching in Eureka. Ron had an apartment and his dynamic teaching attracted more people than his dwelling could hold. So together with Tim Leslie and Tom Peterson, he opened a Christian coffee shop in Fortuna. When David and his group began attending Deliverance Temple, Ron and his group did the same.

Not much later, in the spring of 1971, Ken decided he'd had enough of the cold, damp winds blowing over the bluff and moved to Hawaii. He sold the lighthouse property to Jim Durkin, who then registered the name, "Gospel Outreach of Humboldt County" as the legal entity that owned the Ranch.

Jim continued his church duties at Deliverance Temple, but now made regular visits to the Ranch to give Bible studies and work with Lon Mabon who he appointed as the first coordinator (or director) of the Ranch. He also was available to offer encouragement and counsel to the young Christians living there

Jim's earlier life failures had caused him to lose everything he considered worth striving for. He landed at the bottom of a pit with no means of escape. Stripped of all he thought was important, he then saw clearly God's purpose for him and the church.

He came to see that, in this life, nothing had value unless it contributed to God's purpose. All human effort should point to Jesus, the Creator of the universe and the Author of salvation. He took our sin, guilt, and penalty upon himself and offered us eternal life. Faith in him was the only hope for mankind, and God purposed that our lives would be devoted to spreading that message.

These were the things Jim was preaching to a receptive congregation at Deliverance Temple but at the Lighthouse Ranch, something different began to happen. Young Christians like Scott and Elly Snedeker (with baby Jenny), Dave Sczepanski, Susi Schutzle, Jim Wheeler, Adrianne

Lovelady Rainwater, Bill Ireland, Gregor Chello and his soon-to-be wife Linda, Peter and Jackie DePalmo, Bob Means, Laurel Sparrow and others, had a hunger to hear the truths of Scripture and Jim's experience, that he had never seen before. They had an extraordinary desire to actually put those things into practice.

There were two reasons for this: First, they had all experienced life-changing transformations. Lives that were filled with drugs, rebellion, hopelessness, and rejection of their parents' society had resulted in one long, bad trip. When the Lord came to them, they were ready to change. It was beyond dramatic.

Terri Barrow Schrater accepted the Lord at the Ranch. When God released her from fear, guilt and sin, she cried the entire night.

Bernie Heraldson was visiting his friends Tom Kennedy and Bob Gormin when he asked Jesus to save him. "I remember waking up the next morning and thinking, *I am waking up in a different world than I went to sleep in. Something is different. This is new. Something has happened and it's profound.*"

Gary Todoroff tells of walking to the large wooden cross on the bluff that overlooked the ocean. He began to talk to the God he couldn't see and surrendered his life to him. After his prayer, Gary slowly became aware of God's touch in all the creation he could see—the stars, the sky, the ocean, the trees, and bushes around him. Not only could he see, but he could feel that it was alive and then, "I was almost literally knocked to my knees when I realized that same touch was now in me."

The second reason was they had nothing else to do. They had turned their backs on society; and even with their new-found faith, they had no desire to rejoin it. Helped by the fact that they had almost no worldly possessions, they were willing and able to sacrifice "everything" and follow the Lord. When Jim taught that Jesus wasn't interested in "ordinary" Christians but that he wanted disciples, the young Christians at the Ranch embraced it wholeheartedly.

Finally, all of the energy that had been spent on drugs, free living, anti-war movements, and so on, could be dedicated to Jesus, who had miraculously and dramatically given them new life. They were like sand in the desert. Jim's teaching, experience, and the love that he and Dacie gave them were like water that was immediately soaked up.

This changed Jim too. His son, James, saw a dramatic difference in his dad. The emotional walls that had once existed now fell in the presence of Christ's love that the brethren were so free to share with one another. This young generation also had a sense of freedom and openness that affected Jim. They were willing to accept the calling that God had on the church and them individually. He could share all he had and they would still want more.

It was time to set the world on fire.

CHAPTER THREE

Salvation

AFTER SPENDING HIS first night at the Lighthouse Ranch, Don Copeland had heard enough of this "Jesus stuff" and couldn't leave fast enough. Then, hitchhiking on Highway 101 the next morning, he was almost literally chased back to the Ranch by the California Highway Patrol. That night, he accepted the Lord and became a Christian.

That's how God did things in this revival. He orchestrated events, moved people around, revealed himself to them in unexpected ways, and sometimes scared them to death. Some came knowing that their whole life led them to that point. Others fought it up to the last minute, and some were clueless. The Lord wasn't picky where he brought them into his kingdom: on a city sidewalk, in a garden, in a baptismal pool, a Hawaiian shack, a car or in a jail, at a wedding and even at a church service.

Dave Sczepanski was the oldest of eight siblings living in Midland, Michigan. His dad worked for Dow Chemical—the same people making the napalm that Walter Cronkite and the CBS Evening News showed burning jungles, villages and people in Vietnam. That world was too crazy for him. He was afraid one day he would wake up working for Dow. So he "dropped out and turned on."

After a summer spent experimenting with the drugs that were supposed to expand his consciousness, Dave was left depressed and not knowing where his life was headed. He thought California was "the place ya otta be" and picked up the Rolling Stone, a counter-culture magazine, for ideas. Now an expensive "glossy," the Rolling Stone of that day was anything but mainstream with its focus on music and alternative lifestyles. He read of different communes in the hills and forests of Northern California, and of one couple who had completely turned their backs on society. To keep unwanted visitors away, they even refused to improve a road leading to their cabin in Mendocino County. It was Scott and Elly Snedeker, and Dave would one day meet them.

When a promised ride from Michigan to California didn't pan out, he paid the $120 for a plane ticket to San Francisco. After meeting up with contacts, he hung out in Berkeley, getting free food. Offered the use of a car, he and a couple of friends decided to drive up the California coast and check out the communal scene.

While stopped at a gas station, they were approached by a long-haired hitchhiker who asked for a ride south. When they told him they were heading north, he said, "If you make it as far as Eureka, you should stop by the Lighthouse Ranch." He said it was a cool Christian commune and then said, "By the way, you know Jesus is real!"

Dave looked at his eyes. "Are your eyes dilated because you're stoned or because of Jesus?"

He dropped his head and looked away, saying in a sad voice, "I'm not living the life I need to."

They made it up to the Ranch and as they got out of their car were greeted with a beautiful smile by Susi Schuetzle.

Next, came big, thick Peter DePalmo who ambushed them with a huge, "Praise the Lord!"

Dave was taken aback. He had never seen people who were so alive and full of joy. Dave soon learned the secret of their inner peace and joy. They shared the gospel story about God's promises and how he had changed them. One brother was talking to him but then stopped. He looked directly at Dave and said, "I can see in your eyes that you are lost."

Dave was shocked. *He can see that? I know it's true, but he can see it?*

That night, Dave was led in the "sinner's prayer" by a girl who was herself a new convert. That didn't make any difference to the Holy Spirit. After the prayer, Dave said, "I felt as if somehow light was being literally poured into me. They said I floated for two weeks!"

You throw a pebble into a pond and watch the ripples widen out to infinity. When the Holy Spirit drops into a life, what starts as one saved soul often becomes a series of saved souls.

The Alaska Trailer Miracle

Wendy V. graduated from high school in Seattle and wondered what to do with her life next. She did the "hippie thing," which included living in a teepee on a commune and finding work where she could. In 1973, she was between jobs when Kathy Finney, the sister of a friend, told her she had just been hired by a shrimp cannery up in Kodiak, Alaska. The company was going to fly her up there, give her a place to stay, food, and pay her a salary. Wendy was always ready for adventure, what could be better than Alaska? She joined Kathy and they flew up to Kodiak Island.

The cannery, with its kitchen and rooms for the employees, was located on a barge. For three weeks they picked the guts out of shrimp. But it only took them two days to decide that this wasn't the adventure they had planned on. Wendy and Kathy had made friends with Cathy Davis Wilson and Chuck Coleman who were also shrimp-gut pickers. They all decided to get out as soon as they could pay off the airline tickets and save a little money.

Chuck had a suggestion. A friend of his up in Anchorage owned a place. If the three women wanted to come, there was plenty of room for everyone. That decided it, and soon they were on their way by ferry to the mainland.

The place with "plenty of room" turned out to be a twenty-six-foot, silver Streamline trailer, already occupied by Chuck's friend, Travis, his son and his girlfriend and her son. Oh well, there was plenty of room on the sofa and floor.

But the cramped quarters weren't nearly as disturbing as Travis. Both he and Chuck were strung out on heroin and supported themselves by dealing drugs. The friend was the scariest. He was a biker and didn't want guests.

One day he spoke to the three women, "I want to show you guys something." He held up a newspaper clipping from a town in the Midwest. "I was married before and was on trial for murdering my wife. They couldn't prove anything, and ruled it a suicide." The three sat in stunned silence. He handed them the clipping and said, "I'll let you decide if I did it or not."

Some "Bible thumping" Christians were living in a house, two doors down and everyone in the trailer did their best to avoid them. Several single women lived there and a married couple, Scott and Elly Snedeker, occupied the basement. The house was a ministry house of Gospel Outreach/Anchorage.

One night, Kathi Kalmbach van der Gugten and Linda France came over from the house and began telling the trailer dwellers about Jesus.

Wendy tried to make herself invisible. Hearing about Jesus from the people they had ridiculed was the last thing she wanted. She thought, *Get me out of here!* Along with a couple others, she made for the door and escaped, leaving Travis and Chuck to their fates.

They came back later that night after the women had left. Travis was sitting in a chair and when they came in he looked at them. Something had changed; he looked very different. In what was a modern-day version of the Gadarenes demoniac deliverance, he said in a quiet, reverent voice, "You guys, Jesus is real!"

Kathi and Linda had begun to tell Chuck of the love and power of Jesus. Travis was high on drugs, and even though he was watching TV and listening to Dylan on his stereo headphones, he could still hear them talking. Chuck would toss out a terrific question—*let's see them answer that one!* Each time they would give a good, convincing reply.

Then, in spite of the music in his headphones, Travis heard the question, "Do you want to get saved?"

He thought, *Are they talking to me?* The headphones came off and he answered, "Yes!"

A moment later there was another knock at the door, and Scott entered the trailer. Travis was on his knees on the floor and the women explained to Scott that Travis was ready to accept Jesus.

Travis tells the rest: "I was on my knees, and Scott asked me if that was so. He laid his hands on me and started praying in what I thought was Hebrew (never having heard of speaking in tongues). The instant he laid hands on me a cleansing took place, from the top of my head to the soles of my feet. (I have always described it as feeling like the

Tasmanian devil rushing through my body and exiting.) I lay there engulfed in tears, sobbing uncontrollably, not understanding what was happening to me, but feeling a peace (I had always felt driven) for the first time in my life. I knew God *loved* and *accepted* me exactly as I was. It was overwhelming, and I didn't know what to say or do."

From that point on, the Holy Spirit fell on the trailer. They were all touched and couldn't talk about anything except Jesus, all the time. In frustration they would agree, "Okay, let's stop talking about this!" So they would stop. Then five minutes later, someone would ask, "But what if he *is* real?" And it would start all over again. This went on for a few days as God drew them closer and closer.

One night, Wendy and Chuck went over to the ministry house for dinner. Scott sat down across from Wendy and asked, "So, what do you think about Jesus?"

She answered, "Well, he's real."

"Do you want to pray?"

Up to this point, Wendy was determined to resist what had become a strong current of conviction. Her mind was prepared to declare, "No," but her spirit proved unexpectedly stronger. She answered, "Yes."

Scott said, "Okay, go ahead and pray."

Her prayer showed how, when the Spirit is moving, a four-point "sinner's prayer" that covers all the bases isn't always necessary. She simply said, "Jesus, I need you."

Within a few days of Travis' deliverance and salvation, all of the trailer people had prayed and turned their lives over to God.

"Do You Want to Pray?"

Mike Hier, Steve Insko and I were all in the army together, stationed in West Berlin. After leaving the army, I ended up living in a small house in Orick, north of Eureka. Mike and Steve were sharing an apartment near San Diego when Mike decided to visit me.

Before he left, an acquaintance gave him a letter for a Christian girl named Mary DeVogle. He told Mike she lived on a commune near Eureka called the Lighthouse Ranch. After he had spent a few days with me, he made good on his promise by hitching a ride down to Eureka to see if he could find this ranch. He asked around and was directed to the Donut Shop, a bakery run by the folks from the Ranch.

There he talked to Steve Bartlett who told him how to get out to the Ranch and then told him how to connect with God and receive forgiveness of his sins. Steve led Mike in the "sinner's prayer" on the sidewalk in front of the bakery and a new soul was added to the kingdom. Mike immediately moved to the Ranch and began to write letters to Steve and me about Jesus, the devil, the blood of Christ and so on.

Oh no, I thought. *I mean, Jesus is okay, but you don't want to be a fanatic!* Poor Mike had fallen off the deep end.

Mike had moved from the Ranch to the Carlotta Mansion when Steve came up for a visit. "Let's go see Mike," he said one day.

"Okay," I said. *Oh no!* I thought. Something inside me didn't want to get too close to this thing I didn't understand.

We found our way to Carlotta. Unlike Don's experience at the Lighthouse Ranch, no one "hit" me with the gospel. It was a big house full of friendly people who welcomed us in. Because my pickup truck had died on the freeway, we were invited to spend the night.

The next morning we awoke and had breakfast. There was a Bible study after that. *Fine*, I had no problem with that. Then the men met to receive that day's work assignments. Since we didn't have any other plans, Steve and I volunteered to help.

They sent me out to the garden to help Mike weed. Carlotta had a goat they kept for milk, and it was over in the corner of the garden, bleating and complaining. I have a soft spot for animals so I went over to comfort it. That wasn't what it wanted; the goat was hungry, and it was feeding time. Pretty soon one of the women, Sou Sou Knife, came out to take care of it and we began to talk.

Now when I wasn't being lazy, I did okay in school—the Lord had given me a degree of intelligence. What came next happened on an entirely different level than where I lived my life or how I understood my world.

"How do you like it here at Carlotta?" Sou Sou asked.

That confused me. I mean, if you were a guest at my home and after a couple of hours I looked you in the eye and asked, "How do you like it here?" you would wonder what I meant.

"It's okay."

Then she confused me even more. "Do you have any questions?"

What? Why in the world would I have questions? Come on! I'm just visiting!

I said, "No."

Then, to my total surprise, I *did* have a question! I didn't know where it came from. "Wait, I do have a question. What's this whole thing about Jesus, his blood and all that stuff?"

I'm sure Sou Sou did a good job of answering my question. I understood *nothing*.

Then she hit me with another question. "Do you want to pray?"

"Pray? Pray about what?"

I think she told me, but now I was totally baffled—lost so deeply in the woods of ignorance that I couldn't even see the sky.

"If you want to pray, the men working in the garden would be happy to pray with you."

I went back to weeding next to Mike, wondering what in the world had just happened.

Five minutes later, I *knew* I had to pray. I mean, Jesus is love and everything, but I felt a pressure or burden over me. I was afraid not to take the step.

"Mike, I want to pray."

He led me in the "sinner's prayer" and I spoke to God. "Lord, I know my whole life long I have lived without you and gone my own way. Forgive me for that and for the sins I've committed and come live inside of me." When I finished, the pressure disappeared. I went back to work.

We stayed that night. When I woke up the next morning, it seemed as if the world in which I lived had changed, like the air itself was different. I'd finally come home. It was as if in all my experiences in life—a good family, good friends, fun traveling, sailing and so on, something had been missing, something of elemental importance without which my life was incomplete. It was God, in Jesus.

Two weeks later, I had a visitor. Earlier, my friend, Diane Biernat Doyle had promised to visit me from her home in Gary, Indiana. She was pleasantly surprised to hear I had moved to a commune since our last conversation. But not at all happy when she discovered it was a Christian commune. Diane's visit went much better than she expected and a couple of months after Diane returned home, she turned her life over to the Lord. She moved back to Eureka, to the Lighthouse Ranch.

A short time later, Diane and I made a trip back to Gary to visit her family. In the process of looking up an old friend of Diane's, we shared the gospel with her and her roommate, Jo Ellen Anderson Stopp. Diane's friend wasn't moved by the message, but Jo Ellen was, and that night she accepted the

Lord. A few months later, she moved out to the Lighthouse and began the life of a Christian disciple.

What started as a pebble dropped in a pond—looking for adventure in Alaska, a hand-delivered letter, resulted in several generations of salvation experiences.

That was only the starting point; the waves keep rippling out.

Steve Schrater got saved after his first year of college. Like a comet that pulls a trail of shooting stars behind it, he pulled a trail of souls.

Terry Barrow Schrater, Mary DeVogle, Lisa Erbe, Leon Hampton, and Chris Pritchard all followed. Terri's sisters Nancy and Lois were next on the list, and finally, Terri's dad, Cliff, got saved. At Steve's and Terri's wedding a few months later at the Ranch, about ten more people got saved.

Mary Lou Kelly Bryan was a Philly girl who became a disciple of Jesus at the Ranch. She wrote the typical letters to her sister Susi. "Jesus is Lord! His blood has cleansed us from all sin! He has overcome!"

Susi thought she was nuts, but was intrigued. She drove out to the Ranch with Ron Pileggi and angels rejoiced over two more lost souls when they gave their lives to the Lord.

They were followed by Alberta Brack, Donna Taylor, Mary Palumbo; then Mary Lou and Susi's brother, Larry.

Paul Johnson lived in Albion, California and was friends with Scott and Elly and the people on a commune called Sabine's Land. One day, he borrowed Scott's pickup to drive to Eureka to get some wood for a fence he was building. On the way, he picked up Norman Leverett. Norman lived on Sabine's Land, and had already given his life to the Lord. Paul and Norman engaged in what Paul thought was a deep, thoughtful debate on spiritual matters.

Paul confidently expounded on his theory of "Christ consciousness" until Norman finally said, "Paul, that's just a bunch of cosmic crap." It was as if a strong searchlight flashed out of the darkness. Suddenly, Paul saw that his carefully constructed answers to life were exposed. They were laughable and shallow—a joke.

Norman was headed for the Lighthouse Ranch, so Paul took him there and also spent the night. After listening to different people share God's salvation plan, he lay in his bed that night and prayed, "God, if what I've heard is true and you're real, I want you." The next morning he awoke a new person.

It seemed as though some common threads ran through the lives of those who were saved during the Jesus People Revival. No matter how smart we thought we were, how experienced or wise, most of us were clueless about the path God had us on. Like a mindless bumper car when it hits an obstruction, we would head in one direction, hit a wall, bounce off and try another way. Little by little, the Lord guided us from the broad road that led to destruction to the narrow path that took us to salvation.

This meant that we rejected the lifestyle that we had chosen as a rejection of our parent's society. We rejected our own rejection because it wasn't working either.

John Jordan was convinced he would discover true spirituality within himself. He fled the distracting influence of civilization and drove to Zion National Park to seek a deeper truth. It didn't turn out the way he expected. He remembers hiking several days into the park. He found a ledge that overlooked red and tan sandstone cliffs that formed canyon walls and rivers bordered by greenery. He had a profound thought: *The answer lies deep within my heart. That is where I'll see the light.*

Lost in meditation, John was suddenly made aware of what was inside him. "I still can't describe the experience, but God let me look into my heart, and I saw the blackest black. It was almost like evil. I saw pure darkness when he let me look into my heart. I knew something was seriously wrong, and it freaked me out. I didn't know what to do. But I realized that the answer did not 'lie within.' I immediately packed up and hiked out that day. I was afraid the ground was going to swallow me up."

John 10:27 (KJV) says, "My sheep hear my voice." As he drew us closer to the path he had chosen, God spoke to many of us. That is one of the wonderful things about God. He began to speak to us before we were Christians. Like sheep lost in the woods, when we heard our Shepherd's voice, we began to walk in his direction until we finally saw him. Sometimes it was an actual voice with no one else around, through something someone said to us, or a quiet thought that had life-changing results.

After leaving a life of drugs and rebellion in the army, I had been close to a nervous breakdown. I knew I needed help and found it with the mother of an ex-girlfriend who I knew to be "spiritual." I poured out my tale of woe, and she gave me one piece of advice. "You need to thank God."

I thought, *What? That doesn't have anything to do with this!* But then, remembering that I was the one asking for help; I decided to do as she said.

"Thank you God," I said out loud. Nothing happened. Then a thought entered my mind: *If I'm going to do this, I need to do it with some conviction.*

"Can I say it again?"

"Sure."

"Thank you God!" This time, a blanket of peace settled over me, enveloping me in the first rest I had experienced in years. I was one step closer to the day of my salvation.

Scott Snedeker was living in a drug house in Palo Alto, California. One night he saw a terrifying vision of the end of the world. He didn't doubt its reality and knew he had to get away and figure it out. He fled to the house of a friend in the Santa Cruz Mountains. While Scott was lying in bed one night, Jesus came to him. Not visibly, but he knew it was the Lord. Scott rolled off the bed onto the floor as the Lord brought his life before him, including the time when he was twelve when the Lord had first spoken to him. His home life was a shambles but Jesus spoke to young Scott and told him that if he would follow him, everything would be okay. If he didn't, he would have a life that, well, was the life he ended up actually having.

Weeping, he asked the Lord for forgiveness and asked him to help. God's peace filled Scott, and he never returned to the drug house. His path to salvation became narrower.

Lambert Hazelaar became a Christian at the age of thirteen, but by the time he was twenty-six, he was into the Haight-Ashbury scene in San Francisco. Although he was separated from God by that mind-altering, life-destroying lifestyle, God was never far from him. He was at a dance, "not entirely in his right mind," when all the loneliness of his life suddenly overwhelmed him. He sat down right there on the floor and cried out to everybody (who couldn't hear him because of the loud music—and weren't interested anyway), "Who could love me?" Instantly, a vision appeared before him. Fifteen or twenty people in white robes stood there silently. Their faces shone with love as they beckoned him to follow. Behind them he could see a grove of trees with sunlight filtering through the branches.

Lambert left San Francisco, searching for what he thought would be a commune that provided friendship and love. After a couple of dead ends, he recommitted his life to the Lord during the Mendocino revival then moved up to the Lighthouse Ranch. There he found the place the people in the white robes had shown him.

"You're Not Getting Me!"

There was no avoiding Jesus if he set his sights on you.

Jim Wall sat in the back of a church meeting where two thousand people had come together to worship and hear Bible teaching. The preacher talked about the love of God. It all made sense to Jim, and he couldn't disagree with any of it. But he told the Lord, "You're speaking to two thousand people here. If you love me, you have to send somebody to me," and he left. He didn't plan on returning. In spite of himself, he was there the next week sitting in the back again. At the end of the meeting, during the altar call, Jim stood, ready to walk out again. He tells the story. "It was as if I was paralyzed, I couldn't move, and all I could see was one man out of a crowd of two thousand, all the way across the auditorium. It was like what you see in an advertisement—everything else was fuzzy and blurred but he was clear. And he was coming straight for me."

The man walked right up to Jim and looked directly at him. He had one simple, but profound message. "Jesus sent me to tell you that he does love you."

Sometimes the Lord's voice had to prompt those who were saved to get back on the path. Susie Kelly Burbank accepted the Lord at the Ranch and then moved back to Philadelphia. Although saved, she wasn't following the Lord. One night as she lay in bed in her apartment, she heard her name called.

Susan.

The voice was very clear, and she got up to see if someone was there but saw no one. She went back to bed, and it happened again.

Susan.

Again, she looked, but no one was there. The next morning, she knew the Lord was the one calling her to follow him. She packed her bags and headed back to California to the Lighthouse Ranch.

Irene Tower Barney had a similar experience. After giving her life to the Lord, she pretty much still lived as a non-Christian and became pregnant. One day the Lord spoke to her, "Irene, if you don't follow me, I'm going to take your child from you." She repented, and began to follow the Lord with her whole heart.

Resisting was hopeless if God had already chosen you.

Judi Wildman Jordan was a "college hippie" who had become jaded and hard. After rejecting God, she experienced the "worst four or five years of my life." But God wouldn't leave her alone, and one night she and a girlfriend read the book of Revelation. They became terrified because they knew it was true. They hit the road—for no clear reason and with no goal. After several scary experiences, the girls ended up at the Lord's Land in Mendocino. This was a different world for Judi. All the men had long hair and scraggly beards and the women wore long dresses and aprons. But everyone was nice, and they shared the good news with the two girls.

Not being one to go halfway, Judi went out into a field alone and had a showdown with God. She yelled at him and blamed him for her crummy life.

"I didn't want to hear the gospel any more, I was so mad. Out in the field I remember insisting, 'I'm not going to kneel!' Then I kneeled. Then I cried, 'I'm not going to pray!' Then I prayed. 'You're not going to get me!' Then he got me.

"I remember my knees buckling and being on my face and, I mean, I really got saved. I walked back to the big house and everyone who saw me said, 'Oh, you just got saved!' The next morning I woke up and said, 'I'm not leaving. I'm home.' I gave everything to my friend and told her to call my mom."

On the Road Again

Americans have this thing about them. Probably starting with the early Pilgrims and Jamestown settlers, we have added the travel gene to our national DNA.

In the '60s and '70s, young people by the hundreds of thousands hit the road in their hard-working Fords and Chevies, iconic VW bugs or vans, or with their thumbs stuck out.

Where were they headed?

"Just down the road, man."

"I'm thumbing to California."

"Heard about this really cool festival up in the mountains/desert/San Francisco/Colorado." Or, "I don't know! Where are you going?"

U.S. Highway 101 and California 1 were natural corridors for this moving mass of youth. Sometimes they shared the same stretch, and sometimes they split off from one another. A hitchhiker could find a ride and smoke some grass from Ventura, go north past Santa Barbara, up the coast through Big Sur and Santa Cruz, then on to Mecca itself, or, as the map showed, San Francisco.

Past San Francisco, the roads split and Cal 1 followed the rugged California coast through Fort Bragg, rejoining 101 just south of Garberville. Highway 101 left its sister and followed the Russian River, continuing north through Petaluma, Santa Rosa, and Cloverdale. Beyond Ukiah the road met the enormous, impressive redwoods and wound over hills and valleys and around the huge trees.

At countless places on their journey, travelers could find a place to "crash" and something to eat. People—mostly hippies like them—had a house, an apartment, a garage, a trailer, or even just a porch to offer their guests. If nothing was available, then a city, county, state, or national park offered at least a picnic table that could be used as a shelter or bed, depending on the weather.

The roads continued up to the Oregon border, but for many, Eureka was the last stop. Highway 101 was like a funnel, pouring wandering souls into the Lighthouse Ranch, Carlotta, Living Waters, and the Lord's Land.

This was a typical scene: A skinny, long-haired guy with a scraggly beard and carrying a backpack walks out of Pete's Market on the south side of Eureka. His clothes haven't seen soap in a while and neither has he. He stuffs his hair under a floppy hat as he stands by the side of the road and sticks out his thumb, hoping to catch a ride south on Highway 101. As the late afternoon sun descends toward the horizon, a car with four people in it—two guys and two girls, pulls over. They ask, "Where you headin'?"

"Down to San Francisco, man. How far you going?"

"Not that far but we can take you a ways. Jump in."

"Thanks, dude. Got any dope?"

"Nope, sorry. But if you need it, we've got a place where you can crash tonight."

"Far out. That'd be cool; it's getting late. No grass, huh?"

"No man. I gave that up when Jesus came into my heart. I don't need that stuff anymore. I have all the peace and joy I was looking for. Jesus gave it to me."

Now the hitchhiker realizes that he had felt something different when he got in the car. What was it? There was peace, a kind of joy, and somehow it seemed they accepted him. He was a little confused. Then it dawned on him, *These guys are Jesus Freaks.* But they didn't seem like the weirdos that everyone rolled their eyes about.

It turned out they were living on a Christian commune called the Lighthouse Ranch. He spent the night there and heard more about Jesus.

"Have You Heard About Jesus?"

Walter Burbank felt lost and knew he needed God. His family had moved around, and then his parents got divorced. He left home in Montana and hit the road for Los Angeles where his family had lived before. Rides took him over the Cascades to Seattle, then south. The weather was cold and wet, and he was happy for any lift that would get him out of the elements.

The road followed the Northern California coast through Eureka where Walter was dropped off south of town. When he stuck his thumb out, a car pulled over, and he jumped in. Jerry Lee was driving and had four college students in the car. Walter listened as Jerry told them of God's transforming power. He dropped the students off and when he left the freeway at Hookton Road, Jerry asked Walter, "Do you want to spend the night at the Ranch?"

"No, thanks."

Walter's next ride took him as far as Fortuna. The driver asked him, "Have you ever heard about Jesus?" They talked for a while and Walter knew that something was happening to him. For the first time in years, he began to feel happy. It felt like a weight was being lifted off him. The Christian driver asked Walter, "Do you want to pray and accept Jesus?"

"No, but I'll think about it."

In two rides he had heard plenty about Jesus and the gospel. He needed to spend some time thinking about it all. He stuck out his thumb again.

A VW bus pulled over with two guys and a girl in it. They were sitting in front, and Walter had to sit in the back on stacks of advertising newspapers. As James Jankowiak drove and Saundra listened, Kim van den Plas turned around and asked, "Have you heard about Jesus?"

"Well, now that you mention it, yes."

"Do you want to pray and accept the Lord?"

"Yes."

CHAPTER FOUR

"Lord, Make Me a Disciple!"

JIM DURKIN STARTED a weekly advertising newspaper in the winter of 1971 to support the work at the Lighthouse Ranch. An early issue of the *Tri-City Advertiser* showed Dan Katz in an ad, making a pitch for one of the G. O. businesses—Our Father's Carwash.

"Hi, my name is Dan. My life was like a room with a window. I tried all kinds of trips to clean the haze off the glass, but I could never see clearly. Jesus broke the window . . ." and he goes on to invite the readers to get their cars washed at Our Father's.

Really? A newspaper ad for a business and he's talking about Jesus breaking the window of his life?

You read on. Nearby, sandwiched between offers for used cars, lawn mowers, cords of wood, and free puppies, are Bible Scriptures like, "The Son of Man has come to seek and save that which was lost," or "Jesus Christ, the same yesterday, today and forever." These and other verses and exhortations aimed to introduce the shopper to the claims and promises of God.

After we're done chuckling over this kind of "advertising," something becomes apparent. The people who put this paper together were serious. They saw life in an entirely different way than the rest of the world did. They were operating in another kingdom, with a different reality, and different goals. They saw every activity as having a purpose greater than simply cleaning dirt off a car or selling used tools to whomever. Sure, they believed a clean car was good. Buying food and clothing with the money you earned and living a good life was important. But what was of immensely greater worth to these people was to introduce the world to the God of their salvation.

Their experience of God's love, grace, and forgiveness, and the fellowship of others who had received the same, was unlike anything they had ever known before—traveling the world, climbing mountains, sailing the oceans, being with your closest friends, taking drugs, rooting for a championship sports team, starting the career you always dreamed about, or growing up in a good home. No matter what their definition of happiness, peace, or success had been, it belonged to another existence that, by comparison, was colorless, lifeless, and didn't meet the deepest longing of their souls. In the same way that 1 Corinthians 2:9 (NKJV) says, "Eye has not seen, nor ear heard, nor have entered into the heart of man, the things which God has prepared for those who love Him," the experience of knowing Jesus was radically different from anything they knew or expected. There was no comparison.

Jim Durkin preached the same message that many pastors of the era shared. "Lose yourself in God. Follow Jesus with your whole heart. Know the Lord. Be a disciple." What made it different was when Jim told us to "surrender everything to the Lord," he had already done it. His teachings didn't follow a Bible school curriculum for church growth; they were based on his own life. He had lost it all: family, finances, ministry, and finally his own self-image. That was when he began to experience the truths of God's love, purpose, and calling at a level that produced a life-changing message. Jim didn't try to be powerful. The Lord took everything from him. Once he was empty, God filled him with the Holy Spirit. That's where the power of his life and teaching came from.

Having lost all, Jim knew the only worthwhile goal in life was to live for Jesus, "with all your heart, soul and strength." He wasn't talking about the type of Christianity that could be found in the neighborhood church on Sunday or even at a Bible college. He told us, "This world is going to hell. It's coming apart at the seams, governments are collapsing, the economic system has reached a limit . . . and the only hope for these hell-bound, lost people—this world is going to hell—is *not* Christians. This world is *loaded* with Christians. What God wants and needs and demands are disciples! That word means a whole-hearted follower."

The goal of his life was to change us from a bunch of lost misfits into dedicated disciples, warriors of the cross—people who could maturely and intelligently handle the Word of God with love and power and be victorious in the fight against the devil and his forces.

Jim urged us to be open to those who could teach us. He said, "Jesus said, 'If ye continue in my word, then are ye my disciples indeed.' Jesus wants disciples. He wants us to go to those with the gifts of God in their lives and say, 'Teach me the Word! Show me how to live it! Train me up in the way I should go. I want to be a soldier; I want to be a follower!'"

He told us that, ultimately, we could only bring our desires to the Lord and ask him to do the impossible in us. "But the minute you become a disciple, brother, you'll be fought, you'll be hit, you'll be slammed, but you'll have direction and you'll know how to fight back! And brother, instead of needing counsel, you'll give counsel. I've known people forty years in Christ who are still babes. They can't give up this, and they can't give up that . . . endlessly what they can't do. All of it is true but only for one reason. They never became a disciple of the Lord Jesus. But the moment you say resolutely in your heart, 'Lord, make me a disciple at all costs!' then confess your utter inability to be one, 'Lord, I know I can't do it, nothing in me can do it,' and then forsake all and follow Him—he'll help you, and he'll set you free, and he'll make you a whole new person."

Being a disciple in Gospel Outreach wasn't for everyone. The ranches weren't "wild" to gather as many occupants as possible. Jim said that we extended the invitation found in Revelation, "Whosoever will, let him come." That didn't mean that whosoever wanted to, could stay. The offer was open to all who were willing to lay aside their own plans for their lives and follow Jesus with their whole hearts.

Anything that didn't fit the teachings of the Bible was discarded. Innumerable joints, baggies of marijuana, drug paraphernalia, and packs of cigarettes were discarded as new disciples put action to their vows of commitment. Couples who came together were questioned closely.

"Are you legally married? Can you prove it?" Boyfriends and girlfriends who came together were usually sent to different ranches. Young people under the age of eighteen either got parental approval or were sent home and invited to return later.

Anyone who felt their personal theology allowed for things the Bible prohibited was asked to leave. Some newly saved and even older Christians admired the commitment, fellowship, and love for one another that we shared and wanted it too. Then they found the requirements were too steep and moved on.

Not a Simple Decision

John Jordan got saved at Living Waters and told the head elder, Tom Peterson, that he wanted to stay. Tom sat John down and told him that it wasn't a simple decision. Tom then opened his Bible and read the words of Jesus. "If anyone desires to come after me, let him deny himself, and take up his cross, and follow me" (Matt. 16:24 NKJV).

Tom asked, "What do you think of that?"

John said, "I am ready."

Then Tom read, "So likewise, whoever of you who does not forsake all that he has, he cannot be my disciple" (Luke 14:33 NKJV).

John repeated, "That's what I want."

Tom read another verse, "No one, having put his hand to the plow, and looking back, is fit for the kingdom of God" (Luke 9:62 NKJV).

Tom asked again, "What do you think of that?"

Tom kept on asking and John replied "Yes" each time.

Finally, John said, "If you only knew how much I do want to leave all that. I want to be here."

We didn't think disciples were only a phenomena of the first century. We didn't hope that someday we would become disciples.

We were disciples.

Purpose and Vision

Jim understood that God's salvation plan for a lost world had one purpose—that the person of Jesus, who had taken our sin upon himself and suffered our sentence of death, and his name be glorified in all the earth. Jesus was the lifeline God provided for the world. Through him alone can mankind be restored to the One who created and loved us. Our transformed lives, our words and our actions, together with the Holy Spirit, were to point the way. This was God's purpose. Jim called the practical manner in which this was to be done the Vision.

To fulfill the Vision, Jim taught us there were three areas to which we as individuals, and as a church, could devote ourselves.

Conformed to His Image

First, we were to become like Jesus (Eph. 4:22-24). Our personal desires, actions, and world view were to line up with the example Jesus gave and be manifested through the power of the Holy Spirit who lived in us. There was much in us (our "flesh") that was tied to the world (old habits and memories) that would try to defeat us. To help, Jim taught us to live in faith—to "believe, confess, and act." We were to believe the truth, speak it, and then act on it.

When we read in John 17:18 (NKJV) that Jesus prayed, "As You sent me into the world, I also have sent them into the world," we believed that Jesus was talking about us, individually and as Gospel Outreach. We confessed this earth-shaking truth—God Himself had sent us—to one another. Then we acted on it. We lived like people who had received a special commission to not be a part of this world, but to bring his truth to those who were still in bondage. To the best of our understanding and ability, we rejected the allure of worldly success and focused instead on introducing people to Jesus.

Jim wanted us to see ourselves the way God did. He gave us the Old Testament example of Gideon. Gideon was the youngest son of an insignificant family from a small tribe of Israel. Nothing in his background or his circumstances hinted at how God would use his life. This was a perfect analogy for us young Christians, as Israel was oppressed, God had a plan of salvation, and Gideon was part of it. When God spoke to him, Gideon had great difficulty believing he could lead his people. Nevertheless, God called this scared, timid young man a "mighty man of God." It took time for him to fully grasp the concept that, rather than being a weak nobody, and through no effort of his own, the Lord had made him a powerful warrior. He learned the needed strength would come from God, not from him. Gradually, he began to see himself as God saw him, a "mighty man of God."

Jim taught us when Gideon began to see himself as the Lord did, it transformed him, and he was able to do the things God had planned for him. Just as with Gideon, God had a plan and role for our lives. Jim told us we were "mighty men and women of God." We needed to see it, believe it, talk about it, and put it into action.

Among all the religions of the world, Christianity is unique in its view of women as shown in Proverbs 31, which shows a picture of the "virtuous woman of God." Jim and Dacie together explained that Proverbs 31 was not a standard by which to judge the wives and sisters in Gospel Outreach. It was, first of all, a completed result of salvation and then a set of attitudes to strive after. Rather than seeing them in a "worldly" manner—all the things that husbands and men could find to complain about—we were to see our women in the light of God's Word. This would help create the freedom for them to grow into the people God made them to be.

One in Christ

Next, Jim understood from Jesus' prayer in John 17:21 that he desired all believers to be "one"—that is, in unity with one another. Jesus said our unity would show the world that the Father had sent the Son. In John 13:35, Jesus tells the disciples that in a world full of "salvation" schemes of every type and persuasion, the world will know we are his disciples if we love one another. Jim taught us that our unity was more important than our opinions, and he tried to protect us from splits based on teachings or personalities.

He outlined two kinds of truth. First there is absolute truth that will never change, as in John 13:20 (NKJV)—"He who receives Me receives Him who sent Me."

Then there's what Jim called "workable truth." These were principles and practices that might be valid and fruitful for a particular time and place but never should be reasons to divide the brethren.

When Jim and Dacie moved out to the Ranch, Dacie still wore the traditional Pentecostal headscarf, a practice common in some churches. Jim recognized it as a usage that had no application at the Ranch. The sacrifice of Jesus, the truths of the Bible, and the Holy Spirit in us were of vastly greater importance than any traditional or cultural customs could be.

Not only were we to share this love and unity with one another, but with all other Christians as well. While we had a strong loyalty to our brothers and sisters in Gospel Outreach, we knew Jesus loved all believers and required the same of us.

When we went to different cities and countries, one of our first priorities was making contact with established Christian churches and groups. We expressed our support for their labors and assured them that our vision was to share the gospel with non-believers—not take people from their churches.

One of the tree planting teams—actually a tree thinning crew—worked outside of the town of Pierce, Idaho. Jim's son, James Durkin, "pastored" the team. He was there to give teaching, counsel, and spiritual direction. James reached out to the various churches in the area, and before the job was done, we were all fellowshipping together and even had an all-church event in Pierce. The older Christians from Pierce admired our zeal and love for the Lord, and we appreciated their maturity and friendship toward us.

Preach the Gospel

Jesus' final instructions on earth were, "Go into all the world and preach the gospel . . ." (Mark 16:15 NKJV). As each individual believer is being changed into the image of Christ and joined together with his brothers and sisters to become the body of Christ, the message of God's plan of salvation is then taken to all the world.

Jim repeatedly charged us, "You young people are God's hope! Commit your lives to him! Prepare yourselves for the work you have to do. God needs you *now*! I pray even if you don't know what your ministry is, that you know this for sure—you will have a part of preaching this gospel in all the earth, then shall the end come."

We Added the Zeal

The population of the Lighthouse Ranch went from about twenty in the spring of 1971 to over two hundred by winter. There were so many people getting saved at the ranches, that there was nowhere to put them. That fact, together with the Great Commission Jim constantly held before us, added urgency to the sending out of teams to start new churches.

That was Jim's example and those were his teachings. To that we added youthful energy and zeal. A lot of zeal.

No hitchhiker on Highway 101, or anywhere near us, was exempt from hearing the gospel. It was understood: you see a hitchhiker, you pick him up. Usually, it was the newest converts among us who had the most success in bringing in lost souls. Their salvation experiences were still fresh and the Holy Spirit used that to win over those whom God was calling.

We shared the good news with hitchhikers and when we hitchhiked, we shared it with the people who gave us rides. We told the people in line at the grocery store, and then we told the cashiers. We told the drunks or the junkies lying next to the fountain, and we told people on the street that we handed tracts to. When we gathered on the streets or in the parks to sing songs, we preached it to the assembled crowd. We shared it with the person sitting next to us on the bus and on the plane. We told the people we handed the *Tri-City Advertiser* to, and then we printed it in the newspapers and other Radiance publications like the *Gospel Paper*. We told it to the Donut Shop and car wash customers; we told it to tree inspectors. We told the guy at the gas station. We especially told it to our parents and siblings. We told our old high school friends. We told everyone.

Young Man's Syndrome

That same zeal affected our relationships with each other—mostly for the good, sometimes for the not so good. Our love for each other was real and unfeigned. Jim's preaching, the Word, and the Holy Spirit revealed areas in our lives that needed to change, and we were determined to let that happen. Sometimes, when we saw the same areas that needed changing in others, we could be just as determined that they change too. Having more zeal than maturity or experience, we occasionally put pressure on each other to become more "holy" or more "committed." Ron Juncal had a term for it that applied especially to the brothers: "YMS," short for "Young Man's Syndrome."

Once Jim left Eureka with Dave Sczepanski and traveled back to New York to visit the churches there. While he was gone, the Eureka elders examined the G. O. in-town Eureka houses and the people who lived in them. After some deliberation and looking at the different gifts, abilities, and jobs the brethren had, they decided it made perfect sense to reshuffle them all, putting them with others who were like-gifted. It seemed as if Wisdom herself approved and they began the process of moving everyone to a house where they would fit in better. A brother would return home after work and get the news, "You don't live here anymore. We moved you over to the Williams Street house."

Jim returned, erupted, and read them the riot act. Essentially telling them, "You can't treat people's lives like a deck of cards," he stopped the whole thing in its tracks. Dave shared Jim's outrage and was quietly thankful he wasn't in Eureka to take part in this stroke of genius. This was Young Man's Syndrome in action!

Training Your Soul

An important principle that Jim taught us was "training your soul." David in the Psalms would speak to himself, "Why art thou cast down, O my soul? . . . hope thou in God" (Ps. 42:5 KJV). By doing so he would influence both his feelings and actions to do God's will.

Jim told us we could do the same. When we felt like complaining about the food, the work, the rain, the trials, a brother or sister, the elders, or whatever, we could actually change our attitude, and maybe even the situation, by "confessing" the truth about it. In a more positive vein, that confession or training could help us to become the people God had made us to be. So, we were—in spite of our feelings or the circumstances—"blessed by God's love, thankful in tribulations, able to do all things through Christ who strengthens me," and so on. A good thing when we applied it to ourselves. But, whenever a brother or sister tried to "train" someone else's soul, then they were taking the place of the Holy Spirit and usually got it wrong.

We understood "Not my will but thine" was to be the dominant attitude in everything we did. So if an elder or house head came to a brother or sister and said, "Brother, we need your help digging the hole for the septic tank," or, "A tree planting crew needs another sister—you're going," we were expected to say, "Amen!" and cheerfully go about doing something we maybe dreaded or hated. It was best not to show any negative attitude because it was commonly believed the elders would then purposely give you a job you didn't like. It would be a good opportunity to "train your soul."

Susan Jensen Insko remembers, "The sisters wouldn't admit that they didn't want to go tree planting—because they were afraid that then they would have to go. I wanted to, and they thought I was crazy."

During the Jesus People revival, it seemed as if new Christians were being born into the kingdom every minute. All the ranches and houses in Gospel Outreach experienced rapid growth. A young man or woman—who was maybe twenty-two years old, but who was "three months old in the Lord," might be considered an "older" brother or sister.

And because in the three months since he or she had gotten saved, perhaps another twenty or thirty new converts joined the ranch, they were older, relatively speaking. If they showed some talent for study, teaching, or leadership they were used to provide those things to the rest of the group.

The absence of truly experienced, mature leadership was understandable and not really the fault of anyone. Most established churches were a little leery of close association with a bunch of Christian hippies. Those men and women who were capable of the leadership that the G. O. ranches needed were already doing that for their own congregations. It took divine intervention from God to move Jim Durkin to assist in this harvest of young people.

So we worked with what we had. While the results were at best spotty—because we're talking about young, untrained, untested, and still maturing leadership—what remains is the work that God did in us and through us. If anything, it revealed the great need we had for the Holy Spirit to help us, to be our comforter, and teacher—which is exactly what the Lord wanted us to learn.

A lot of youthful enthusiasm, but somehow God was able to keep us going in the right direction and bring about the changes he promised. We worked earnestly to be the people God wanted us to be as we grew in faith and in grace. This produced a group of people who earned the respect of other ministries who knew us. Gospel Outreach was considered the "Green Berets" or "Special Forces" of the Jesus People movement because we didn't adapt the gospel to our life situation—we gave our entire life to the gospel.

Several G. O.ers visited other ministries. They came back with the impression that, while the brethren loved the Lord, were serving Him and had some outstanding individuals, they weren't filled with the same level of understanding and commitment to God's purposes that were considered normal in Gospel Outreach.

Scott Snedeker said, "I met an assistant pastor from a New York Vineyard Church once. He asked with a voice of awe, 'You're from Gospel Outreach?' He stopped and got this look on his face and said, 'You guys are incredible! *What happened to you guys?* You're like, off the charts. We have five or six couples from G. O. in our church, and they are off the charts. You serve and you're warriors.' He was serious. He asked me, 'What made you guys like you are?'"

Scott said, "I've heard that so many times."

CHAPTER FIVE

A New Song

A FEW YEARS AGO, many years after Gospel Outreach ceased to exist as a worldwide group, there was a gathering of a hundred or so G. O.ers near Seattle, Washington. It was three days of worship and fellowship with no formal teaching planned. Friday night was the first meeting and as we greeted each other in the main meeting room, the four or five musicians tuned up and got ready to lead us in song. What happened next was a familiar experience to us all but not one that we had had often in the past few years. As the musicians began playing, we began to worship and *immediately* every one of us was caught up in the presence of God's Spirit. Faces shone with joy and love as we found that familiar place of adoration for the One who so freely shared his life and love with us.

This was the worship of Gospel Outreach.

There was a lot of good preaching in G. O. Jim Durkin, Ron Juncal, Tom Kennedy, LeRoy Nidiver, and others, clearly and powerfully laid out God's plans for our lives. We were thrilled and amazed at the wisdom of the Father.

While the truths and principles they taught are timeless and have become a part of us, I can only remember a few specific sermons. However, I will never forget and still sing the songs of worship that our worship leaders and musicians shared with us.

The music of the 1960s and '70s became a big part of the youth culture of that time. It was our expression of how we saw the world around us and what we hoped for it and ourselves. So when the Beatles sang, "All You Need is Love," it was more than good lyrics put to good music. It was our souls' desire being bared to the world. We all heard it, agreed with it, sang along and were bound together by it.

When we came together at the Lighthouse, the Lord's Land, and the other ranches, we discovered a new kind of song. With the radical transformation we had experienced—every one of us would have said, "From death to life, from darkness into the light of Jesus," we left behind the music that had promised so much and delivered so little. The lyrics and music that had exposed the emptiness of the world and proclaimed our lofty ideals was itself revealed to be bankrupt. Countless record collections and sound systems worth hundreds (today, thousands) of dollars were given or thrown away without regret.

Now, our worship of God showed us, and the world, what had happened to us. Rebecca beautifully sang Psalm 98, "Oh, sing unto the Lord a new song," and that's what we did. A great many of the songs we sang were Psalms or other Scripture put to music. Unlike the songs of our previous existence, these were powered by lives that were daily being sacrificed to God and his purposes. The trials of being converted from the habits, personal hang-ups, and the self-will of lost souls to become disciples of Jesus, produced deep, sincere worship and thanksgiving to the One who loved us and saved us.

Praise and worship were important elements in everyday life. Usually one or two songs were sung before a meal. Standing in a circle, holding hands, or with arms draped around the shoulders of their neighbors, people closed their eyes and worshipped. There was no formula for this. Bill Ireland remembers that regardless of musical ability, anyone could start a song. The amazing thing was that—even in the humble setting of saying grace for the meal—we worshipped and experienced the presence of God. This was true whether there were a dozen tree planters gathered together, thirty people at Carlotta, two hundred at the Lighthouse Ranch or even a carload of brothers and sisters delivering the *Tri-City Advertiser.* You didn't need a musician or guitar to worship. People would sing to the Lord as they washed dishes alone, worked in the garden, or rode together in a car heading to church, another city, or going tree planting. It was the language we spoke and the result was a constant awareness of the presence of God in and about us.

The singing was heartfelt. Distractions or wandering thoughts weren't a problem. If we sang of God's mercies being renewed every morning, we knew that applied to each of us right then, that very morning. When the words of the song declared, "I've got a river of life flowing out of me," we knew that meant the Holy Spirit, and we expected to witness his works all around us. No one had to be "encouraged" or scolded to participate. We sang with conviction, gusto, and joy. We had experienced the miracle of God's salvation, were thankful and wanted to declare it to all creation. We knew who Scripture was talking about when we sang Isaiah 55:12 (NKJV): "For you shall go out with joy, and be led forth with peace; the mountains and the hills shall break forth into singing before you, and all the trees of the field shall clap their hands." It was talking about us and all creation would worship the Creator and rejoice with us, as we took the gospel to the far corners of the earth.

Before Bible studies and prayer meetings, a brother or sister with a guitar often led us in songs. The music did what music is supposed to do—filled our souls with the knowledge of God's love, truth, and presence and penetrated to our spirits.

Being a disciple wasn't easy. The charge to give up our lives to God required daily sacrifice and while the benefits were many, the experience could be painful. Worship helped to release the stress and keep us focused on God's love and his promises.

Tree planting was discipleship on steroids with plenty of physical and spiritual challenges. Many a tree planter testified that, after planting all day in the rain, mud, and wind, the worship before dinner was the deepest and most fulfilling they ever experienced.

We learned Scripture from songs taken directly from the Bible.

"Rejoice in the Lord always, and again I say rejoice" was a simple chorus from Philippians 4:4 that repeated just those ten words. The repetition could drive you crazy, but the verse was deeply and lastingly imprinted on our minds. It reminded us that, whatever the circumstances, God encouraged us to rejoice.

"If any man come after me, let him deny himself . . ." the words of Jesus recorded in Matthew 16:24 (KJV), became a statement of who we were—disciples of Jesus. We sang it with our whole hearts, determined that, if Jesus had given all of himself to us, we would do the same for him. Each time we sang we made a fresh, new confession of faith and our desire to follow him.

The words and messages from these Scripture songs and many others stayed with us throughout the day. This allowed the Holy Spirit to continue ministering life-changing truths to our souls as we advanced in discipleship.

Church meetings at Deliverance Temple and the Veteran's Hall in Eureka were always occasions of joy. There brethren saw friends from the other ranches, the in-town houses, or maybe a tree-planting team just back from the slopes. Vet's Hall, with a seating capacity for several hundred, had a wooden floor. Probably more than a handful of floorboards were loosened as hundreds of feet clad in boots (considered suitable wear for both men and women) enthusiastically stomped percussion to different songs. Whenever the song adopted by the tree planters as their own as the "Tree Planters' Song" ("I will sing unto the Lord for he has triumphed gloriously…") was sung, the whole neighborhood knew that G. O. was holding a service there.

Not a Performance–a Celebration

Gary Todoroff headed Radiance, the media arm of Gospel Outreach. As he pursued the recording, editing, and cataloging of Jim's teachings, he began to notice something—there were a lot of very talented musicians in G. O.

Musically, they were all very capable, but there was an added element that put them on a level with other beloved Christian musicians like Keith Green and Phil Keaggy. When they sang, they worshipped. Quality production was always important, but worshipping God and glorifying Jesus were even more important and their songs showed it. Instead of meeting a producer's deadline, or coming up with a new song because "it's been awhile," their music flowed out of lives that were daily surrendered to God. It wasn't meant to entertain or be a performance. It was meant to celebrate the love and grace of God and the salvation he had freely given us.

Paul Johnson lists many of them: Bill Ireland, Karl and Sarah Richey, Rebecca Wilmarth Muller, Rense Miller, Dan Katz, Joel and Nancy Severson, Paul Johnson himself, Christine Schimke, Fred Simmons, Gene Fowler, David Wilmarth, Sam Griffith, Diane Helbert Belman, Layne Fish, and others. Among the group was the lead singer in the San Francisco production of "Hair" and one of the originators of Surf Music, before they got saved.

Bill Ireland says, "Everyone was unique; no one was a carbon copy of another."

Rense Miller elaborates. "I would say that there were three different types of gifts or styles among the musicians. I played a lot with Rebecca and I saw her develop a 'voice of the Spirit.'"

When she played it was almost prophetic; the brothers and sisters knew God was speaking to them personally. Bill Ireland and Fred Simmons shared that same gift. Bill's choice of songs, often accompanied by Sandra Filler and Tim Leslie, expressed a quiet, unpretentious and reverent heart that looked to God as the goal of its seeking. When he sang, you felt like he was expressing the deepest part of your heart. We always thought of Fred Simmons as being our version of Bob Dylan because of his music style and similar appearance. His love and devotion to Jesus were "out front" for everyone to see. So great was his joy in knowing the Lord, that his words and music could barely keep up with what his heart wanted to express. Together with Joe Esposito, he wrote, "Be So Glad When I Get Back Home," and sang it for the brethren the night before he died in a tree planting vehicle accident.

Rense sees his gift as "echoing God's Word." What set him and the other musicians apart is rather than finding and using songs that the Christian church had been singing for years (we did that too—at Deliverance Temple we used, and loved, the old Pentecostal white songbook), Rense and others would find meaningful Bible verses and write music for them. This was an invaluable service to the brethren because it helped us to memorize the Word.

Bruce Porter, Sam Griffith, and Craig Kent sang songs that in Rense's words were, "people oriented—they made singing God's Word fun."

Paul says that Joel and Nancy Severson's singing style was like that of the Carter Family (or the Chuck Wagon Gang). Not many of us knew who the Carter Family was, but we all loved it when Joel, Paul, and Nancy got together and sang. Because they were a part of us, even when they pulled out dusty old revival songs like "Must Jesus Bear the Cross Alone?" we could wholeheartedly join in and worship the Lord. "A Soul Winner for Jesus" was a popular fast-paced song that was easy and fun to sing and declared our desire to reach the lost for Christ.

Lambert Hazelaar was the head elder of the G. O. group up in Alaska. His wife Marnie played the violin so beautifully during church services that people actually got saved when they heard her music.

Our musicians didn't achieve the fame or exposure of better-known artists and musicians, probably because that wasn't their goal. What could be better or more fulfilling than worshipping in the presence of God with your brothers and sisters? It's hard to imagine any other audience that could love and appreciate them more than we did. In our eyes, there were none better at entering into the heart of God and opening the door to his presence. Besides, we were family.

Worship and teaching were combined in a series of Christian music festivals that Gospel Outreach organized called the Festival of the Son. Ron Juncal got them going and the first festivals were held at the Lighthouse Ranch then at Living Waters. Others took place in the Santa Cruz area. Hundreds attended the first ones, and then thousands came to worship and hear the messages of Jim Durkin, Ron, and others.

Both Gary and Paul had experience in the world of music production and media recording. Gary worked at the local Eureka TV station as a production engineer. Paul was an originator of "surf music" in the early sixties when he formed a band in San Pedro, California that had a devoted following of surfers. They told him, "Your music makes us feel like we're sitting on our boards, waiting for a wave. It's surf music." He also had a promising career as a studio guitarist, playing with many of the famous bands of the era, including Sonny and Cher. Both Gary and Paul recognized the unique gifts of the G. O. musicians and saw the value of recording their music and making it available to everyone.

Paul moved up to Eureka from Mendocino in 1973 and took over the production of the recordings and cassette music tapes. Joined by Johnny Ruffle (our resident English disciple), Sam Griffith, Rense and Mary Miller, Mike Hier, and his future wife Kathy, they set up a makeshift studio in the nursery in the back of Deliverance Temple. This was a step up from the previous studio, which was in the garage of Jim and Dacie's house on Humboldt Hill in Eureka.

At first only "modest" tools were available. Slowly they assembled good quality, and in some cases, state-of-the-art recording and duplicating equipment. With a team of people that was devoted to both excellent work and to one another, they preserved for us the music and worship that meant so much to us. Several cassettes were produced for the individual artists, but the jacket for *Refiner's Gold* best sums up the guiding theme: "As crude ore is subjected to the refiner's fire to bring forth pure gold, so are our lives in the care of the Lord. In like manner, the tapes recorded by

Radiance Music Ministry . . . were carefully listened to and refined until those selections that represent the pure gold of this ministry's music now shine forth!"

Radiance Media Ministry

Radiance was launched by Gary and had humble beginnings just like everything else in Gospel Outreach. When a ranch visitor left three cassette players and a switch box, Gary saw these could be used to record sermons and teachings for the teams that were being sent out to different cities. The vision for a media ministry began to grow.

Gary recalls, "My job at Channel 3 (TV) set the standard for broadcast quality. The job taught me, and we stretched our equipment to the very limit. When we had gone as far as we could, the Lord provided us with the next level of equipment. Someone would contribute, or it would be budgeted."

While living at the Ranch, Gary contributed 90 percent of his income to Ranch operations. As Radiance began to grow, that money was used for the developing ministry. He recalls, "We were able to get equipment that helped us produce sound quality of the spoken word that was as good as anyone else."

Assisted by the musicians and others mentioned above, Gary was joined by Bob Doerr, Craig Kent, Peter and Linda Morgan, Steve Insko, Mary Jane Phillips, Steve Tipton, and others who brought with them recording, photographic, organizing skills, or just willing hearts and hands.

At first, it wasn't easy to keep the help. People who Gary trained regularly left to join church-planting teams. Finally Gary explained to his co-workers, "You don't need to leave here to preach the gospel. We're heading out into the world every day!" And indeed they were. Radiance publications and cassette tapes were covering the globe, reaching places where G. O. brothers and sisters may never have shown up.

Susan Insko remembers her early Christian experience at home in Iowa was profoundly affected by listening to Jim Durkin's sermons on Radiance tapes. Nowhere else could she find teaching that so clearly explained God's purpose for her life, and she moved out to the Ranch to become a disciple.

Rense experienced the same thing. He got saved in Mendocino when Jim and some of the leaders from the Ranch came down for revival meetings. Rense and his wife, Mary, didn't join G. O. right away but fellowshipped with the local Christians in the Fort Bragg area. Listening to Jim's messages on Radiance tapes convinced them that God had a higher calling on their lives, and they moved to the Ranch.

In addition to the cassette tape service, Radiance developed a publication arm. With Dave Sczepanski and Joseph Anfuso serving as editors, Radiance published the *Radiance Monthly*, a collection of teachings from Jim and other G. O. leaders, as well as testimonies and reports from the various G. O. churches; the *Twilight Times*, which printed essays from noted Christian thinkers and writers like C. S. Lewis, R. E. McMaster and Billy Graham; *Leadership Resources*, a newsletter-style sheet that addressed leadership issues in the church; *The Gospel Paper*, which was a witnessing tool aimed at non-believers; and the *G. O. Report*, a "family letter," which reported the goings-on with the different G. O. groups.

In the time before computers and the Internet, the Radiance publications and cassette tapes were an important source of teaching for the teams sent out. In Germany we were able to follow the development of the principles that Jim Durkin had laid out and see how they were shared and received in different places in the world. We were also able to keep up with the rest of the G. O. family. The brothers and sisters with whom we lived at the Lighthouse Ranch, Carlotta, Living Waters, the Land, or in Alaska had also gone on teams to different cities and parts of the world. We were always glad to hear how they were doing.

Thank-you notes came in from all over. M. Daniel from Anakapalle, India wrote, "Thank you very much for your little booklets, plus cassette # JD 130 *Spirit, Soul and Body.* I am using such tapes in Bible classes and on special occasions." An American missionary from Almeria, Spain thanked the brethren at Radiance. "We so much appreciate your tape library service, the reason being that we are serving the Lord out here in the 'boondocks'!" R. O. from Penang, Malaysia said, "Thank you for the tapes. They are being used in house groups, Bible studies, etc. We are thankful for your assistance. The Lord is moving here. People are getting saved."

What stands out in all the letters is the gratitude they express—Jim's particular message of God's purpose and vision, together with discipleship, was hard to find anywhere else. Wherever the reader or listener happened to be—India, Nigeria, Taiwan, Anchor Point, Alaska, Phoenix, Atlanta, or even Eureka—Gary and the people at Radiance made it available to everyone.

The development of the Radiance Media Ministry is striking picture of what happened to the group of young people whose lives were dramatically changed by God's saving grace. Before landing at the Lighthouse Ranch, Carlotta, or the other ranches, they lived self-focused, pointless lives with few achievements of which they could be proud. Now, by the miracle of God's power, they were taking the gospel into all the world, both physically and with all the intelligence and resources they could lay their hands on.

Gospel Outreach was shifting into high gear.

CHAPTER SIX

The Lighthouse Ranch

A FEW YEARS AGO, I was visiting the Smithsonian Museum of History in Washington D. C. After a full day of looking at objects and exhibits that told the American story, I was ready to leave when I looked across the hall and was surprised to see the maritime section. I have always loved boats, ships, and the sea so I hurried over to see at least a couple of displays.

In a small room, in a glass case on a pedestal, was a work of art—a lighthouse lens, made by craftsmen in France in the late 1800s. Up close I could see the diamond-like facets of the lens that could reflect a warning beacon to the horizon. As I read the history of this particular lens, I found it was used on the East Coast of the U.S. for many years and then was placed in San Francisco for a time. Before it was retired in 1974 and brought to the Smithsonian, it was used in the lighthouse on Table Bluff, in Humboldt County, California.

This was the lens from the Lighthouse Ranch! I was stunned! It was like meeting up with a beloved friend of long ago. I felt like grabbing other museum visitors, pointing to the lens, then pointing to myself and saying, "See this? See me? I was there! You wouldn't believe what powerful things took place there!"

The lighthouse, which of course gave the Lighthouse Ranch its name, was still showing ships the entrance to Humboldt Bay when the first Christians arrived. Bob Doerr and Debbie Long remember the dark nights at the Ranch when there was still limited electricity. No outside lighting meant walking between buildings in the dark could be a scary experience. The powerful lighthouse beam would sweep around the property, alternately illuminating the buildings, then flashing on the row of cypress trees that surrounded the place. Shadows were tossed everywhere, jumping back and forth with the light. In the imagination of a lone brother or sister walking between buildings, it was a perfect set up for demons to pounce. They had to be brave, keep ready their shield of faith and sword of the Spirit and walk fast.

Set on about eight acres of land, the lighthouse was made operational in 1892. Later, radio and compass transmitters were added and different buildings were raised then razed as the need dictated. The military automated the lighthouse in 1953 and then moved all the personnel out.

When Ken Smith bought the property in late 1969, there were seven dilapidated buildings, the water tower, and plenty of space for gardens and parking lots. The first thing visitors noticed when arriving at the Ranch were the cypress trees with their dark green leaves. These provided a welcome windbreak from the winds blowing in from the ocean. As they turned left off the road that continued down to the beach, a small sign with a big message greeted them: "Whosoever Will, May Come."

To the right was the water tower that held water pumped up the hillside from a well at the bottom of the cliffs. The water supply was mostly reliable but was overtaxed when the Ranch population grew past one hundred. Next to the tower was the garage where the assortment of personal vehicles and big blue Zion, the ranch bus, were maintained.

Immediately in front of that was a large two-story structure. Built of brick and stucco, it had the same weathered coat of white paint as the other wooden buildings. Attached to it, left of the entrance was another two-story affair. With its slightly different floor height, it looked like it might have been added later.

A dark brown wooden porch with a large door that was never locked led into the dining room. This was the main building—the center of all the activities on the Ranch. On the ground floor were an office, the kitchen, and the large dining hall, full of wooden tables and benches and a big wood-burning heating stove next to the wall. Because it was the largest room at the Ranch, the hall was also used for Bible studies, church services, impromptu times of worship, and an after-hours place of fellowship and prayer.

The second floor of the main building started out as the brothers' dorm. When the dorm was moved into a separate building, it was divided into five to six apartments for married couples and single sisters.

On the right side of the main building, was a long, narrow, one-story house for the coordinator or coordinators of the Ranch. This was divided up into two apartments with just a thin sheetrock wall to separate them.

Between the coordinator's house and the bluff was the two-story duplex that housed single mothers and their children. It had a basement and stairs that led up to the raised porch and first floor. The Ranch laundry and the Free Store were in the basement. To its right was the one-story building that was the single sister's dorm that could house up to twenty-four women.

The lighthouse itself was originally located on the spit at the bottom of the bluffs. The Coast Guard decided it could better serve ships looking for Humboldt Bay if it was on top of the bluffs, so it was moved. Set on a concrete pad, the thirty-foot high structure could now send its beams much further out to sea. That took care of this world's physical dangers. To that, the ranchers added another symbol of safety and hope. Between the lighthouse and the edge of the bluff, they placed a large cross.

All of those buildings were built as living quarters for the Coast Guardsmen and their families. The young Christians managed to pack a lot more people in them, but when the river of God's Spirit began to flow through Table Bluff, more room had to be found or created.

A *Really* Big Piece of Furniture

There was a building that the military had used for its signals house for foghorn, radios, etc. It was closer to the bluff, just a stone's throw from the Lighthouse itself. When Ken Smith moved in, the empty building was converted into a prayer chapel. Later, with all the new believers on the land, it was decided to turn the signals house/chapel into a new brothers' dorm. That's when it could have earned a place in "Ripley's Believe it or Not!"

The chapel was a one-and-a-half-story building without a second floor. Essentially, it was just one room with a very high ceiling. Since it would serve as a dorm, it made sense to build an extra floor, making it a true two-story building. But there was a problem. The county required architects and contractors to design and build the new addition according to code. The *Tri-City Advertiser*, Our Father's Car Wash and the Donut Brothers weren't making enough money to provide for all that.

What to do? Obviously, it would only be subject to the code if a new floor was built, and that floor was bolted to the walls, as then it would be part of the building. What if a new floor were built, but not secured to the walls? It wouldn't be part of the building because it would be free standing. It would be, well, a really big piece of furniture.

So that's what they did. They built the world's largest piece of furniture, divided it up into 4' x 8' cubicles and filled it full of brothers. With every space having its own lamp or light bulb—and with electrical wires running all over the place, it looked like a bowl of exploded spaghetti. Someone complained to the fire inspector and he came out to see for himself. He must have "understood the times" because, after examining the dorm, and all the young men who were in the process of straightening their lives out, his only comment was, "Looks a bit crowded in there." He left and never came back. As the home of up to sixty single brothers, it was a mess, but for them, it was heaven on earth.

People kept getting saved and the Ranch got more and more crowded. Soon, the chickens were evicted and their shed was turned into a brother's coop. It wasn't too bad, actually a step up from the wall-to-wall brothers in the dorm. Breck Wilson called it our "beach condo."

The pottery barn surrendered its mission of turning out Maranatha Pottery, which moved to a building in Eureka, and a bunch of brothers moved in there.

Life on the Ranch

In the single women's house, an alarm went off at 6:00 in the morning, and the sisters who had breakfast duty that day got up, dressed, and headed for the kitchen. The layered look was in vogue. Some sisters worked hard at making Free Store handouts harmonize into attractive outfits. Most were happy to have approximately the same pattern and color on different layers of dresses, skirts, shirts, blouses, sweaters, and headscarves. In the dark, damp, cold winter mornings, a coat helped even for the short walk to the main building.

Dodging any tardy demons still playing in the beams of the lighthouse, the sisters collected in the kitchen and formed a circle. Holding hands they would sing a song and then pray, thanking God for their salvation and each other and asked him to bless the work of their hands. They prayed for the rest of the brothers and sisters at the Ranch, that God would protect them and help them to grow in his love and grace.

Enormous military-sized pots were brought out and filled with water that was then brought to a boil on the huge gas stoves left over from the Coast Guard days. One sister made the oatmeal that, together with nine-grain cereal, was almost the only breakfast served at the ranches. Himalayan blackberries were collected from the bushes that grew in big patches all over Table Bluff and added to the hot cereal. Cream came from the Ranch cow and yogurt was set aside for pregnant and nursing mothers. Leftover cooked oatmeal was often baked into loaves of bread which, with a little honey or molasses, tasted pretty good.

A sister made tea while another set the table. Nobody worried about matching the tableware. Every plate, fork, spoon, glass, and cup was an orphan from the Salvation Army or someone's donated collection. The lack of design harmony was more than compensated for by the different colors and patterns. The modern oranges, yellows and blues of the '60s and '70s were well represented in the colorful plates and cups.

Wake up time for the rest of the Ranch was usually at 6:30 a.m. Cade Newell, who was the brothers' dorm steward, made sure of that. One of the few African Americans at the

Ranch, part of his job was waking up the Ranchers every morning. Carrying a large bell, he would walk around the property, ringing it loudly and calling on the young disciples to "Arise and shine, for the light has come and the glory of the Lord has risen upon thee!"

By 7:00, everyone was assembled in the dining room. As with every meal, they either stood in a large circle with arms draped over each other's shoulders or sat at the tables. Usually worship before a meal was spontaneous and a capella. If someone felt a particular song "on their heart" and was bold enough, he or she would lead the rest. Then the praying began. It didn't stop until everyone who felt "led by the Spirit," and who could overcome nervousness, got their prayers off their chests. This could take a while and often, by the time they were done, the oatmeal had cooled.

On the big chalkboard on the wall were messages and prayer requests, including a plea to pray for the Beatle, George Harrison. Then everyone would grab a plate or bowl from a table and carry it over to the pots of food set on tables next to the kitchen where the sisters would serve.

On more than one occasion the kitchen sisters said another "miracle of the loaves and fishes" took place when pots of food fed more mouths than the head count or recipe had planned for.

Carolyn Sprague Smith remembers kneeling on the floor with other sisters when food was scarce and praying the Lord would make up for the lack. He did, and it always worked out.

Everyone on the Ranch either knew or was told of the apostle Paul's injunction to the Thessalonians, "If a man won't work, he shouldn't eat." To that was added, "If you don't make it to the meal on time, you won't eat."

Dinners were mostly vegetarian with the all-time most despised meal being "fava bean casserole." Everyone hated it and it earned its own nickname as "train your soul casserole."

Lunches were usually a repeat of the previous night's dinner with a twist. Carolyn said dinner leftovers were *always* made into a soup—even the "train-your-soul casserole"—and served with biscuits.

While the commitment to serve the Lord was high, the amount of nutritious, stomach-filling food was low. Hungry brothers had to be barred from the kitchen, especially the area around the refrigerator. That meant that only sisters could raid it when no one was looking, then repent later for their moment of weakness. The scene in the dining room could be chaotic as hungry brothers would vacuum their plates in minutes, hoping to improve their chances for a second helping.

Irene Barney recalled that life at the Lighthouse Ranch was always fast paced. "If you wanted to slow down, you went to Living Waters."

After breakfast, time was spent on personal hygiene, getting living spaces picked up, and spending some personal time reading the Bible and praying. From 9:00 to 10:30, a Bible study was held in the dining room, together with worship.

After that, chores were assigned. The sisters took care of the laundry. Terri Schrater remembers there were only three wringer-washers when she came to the ranch. They were old, but were electrically powered. If the laundry sister had long hair and got distracted, she could end up losing a handful of hair in the wringer. Terri thinks that that happened once or twice. Susan Insko used to write encouraging Bible verses on scraps of paper and put them in the clothes bags.

The women were in charge of cooking, the laundry, cleaning up the dorms and community buildings like the dining room, chapel, prayer cabin, and watching the young children. Single sisters carried the biggest load, while less was required of single and married mothers. Susie Burbank's chores started after breakfast. She prepared twenty lunches for the brethren who worked "in-town" in Eureka ("the peanut butter/banana/granola sandwiches were the best!"). Then she helped serve lunch. At the same time, she was nursing her son, Luke, and was totally worn out after that.

Ranch Children

For a population that could number more than two hundred, children were the least represented age group. Which is not surprising, considering the average age of the disciples was about twenty-two. Irene remembers there being fifteen or twenty little ones—all of them under school age.

Parents were expected to watch and care for their own children, except during Bible studies when the kids would have a babysitter in an adjoining room. Discipline was administered as the parent or parents saw fit. It seemed like the only instruction the Bible gave was summed up in, "Spare the rod, spoil the child." So the rod wasn't spared, and the child didn't get spoiled. Sometimes this happened to excess.

Susie remembers any adult could spank a child for some infraction. That meant that someone who didn't really know the kid, and maybe grew up in a bad home situation, could administer "correction." Young adults, newly saved, and just learning for themselves the lessons of commitment and submission to authority, would sometimes demand the same from small children. When the little ones didn't seem to get in line, severe spankings were sometimes dealt out.

Fortunately, this wasn't widespread, but it happened enough that it remains a painful memory for some.

Not yet old enough for school, the little ones who were both sure-footed and curious had a huge playground to spend their days in. There were cows, pigs, and goats to watch, old vehicles to climb around on, mechanics and gardeners to help, rocks to throw, and dirt to dig. If you were lucky, like little Jamie Barney, you got to watch the chickens get their heads cut off. After this world-changing experience, while eating chicken at dinner with Irene, Jamie excitedly shared how the headless chickens "kept running around squirting blood everywhere!"

Salvation and joining G. O. almost always had a beneficial result for the children whose parents got saved. In the hippie years, a well-known song encouraged us to, "Express Yourself!" Some young parents thought a child's name was an opportunity to express themselves and have a little fun—at the expense of the kid. So, Charles and Donna Chambers named their son Space. Leslie Dixon remembers a little boy named Gentle Thunder who played with her son. Good thing he was Gentle. Terry and Fran Furnald's son's name was Blue. Steve Fish remembers a guest visiting the G. O. church in Silverton, Oregon who commented on the unusual names of some of the kids. She met Sweet Pea and Redwood Bye, the children of Dave and Harmony Bye and was really intrigued by Steve's son, Jelly Fish. It turns out little Joel Fish had introduced himself and was still working on the pronunciation of his first name. Fortunately, like Saul, many were renamed, reflecting their new lives. Except for Joel who eventually learned how to say his name.

Life at the Ranch for the young mothers-to-be was exciting and fulfilling in many ways. Still, it was a world away from how they had been raised. Taking special care of nursing and pregnant mothers was a priority that received added impetus from a recognized authority. Dr. Crane, a general practitioner who lived in nearby Ferndale, told the Ranch leadership he would deliver babies for free—as long as pregnant and nursing mothers got good, nutritious food. And they did. Being cared for by Dr. Crane was comforting to the mothers, and he is fondly remembered. His services weren't limited to delivering babies. He also took care of minor surgery and other problems. Dr. Jon Omey was a Eureka dentist who did much to help brethren with dental problems. Both of the men, brothers in the faith, served willingly and either for free or at a much-reduced cost.

"Eeew! Mom Ate Road Kill!"

The rancher's food came from everywhere, but it seemed actually paying for it was the least used means of procuring it.

A dairy in Fortuna regularly gave the Ranch ten-gallon cans of fresh, unpasteurized, whole milk. This was ladled out into quart Mason jars and given to the moms and pregnant women. Susie Burbank remembers, "It was the best milk ever! I have never tasted milk as good as that from the Fortuna dairy." The mothers also got the daily egg collection, which they could prepare in their own rooms—usually within smelling distance of the other brethren.

Another nearby dairy contributed yogurt and a neighbor allowed the ranchers to glean his potato fields. Berries from the area were collected by the bucketful in season and added to oatmeal and biscuits. Chickens were raised and contributed both eggs and meat.

Jim Durkin was fond of telling of self-assured young men coming to him and volunteering to join the Ranch as leaders—they wanted to be in charge. Jim told them, "I'm sure you have impressive abilities, and we're glad to have you." Then he told them, "Your first job will be to clean out the chicken coop."

The brethren weren't above dumpster diving, and the local Safeway store was a reliable source for some of the five essential food groups. Once, during a Gospel Outreach wedding up in Alaska, the family of the groom and bride commented on how tasty the wedding meal was, especially the chicken. A young sister excitedly agreed, pointing out that not only did it taste good, but just the day before they had pulled it from a store dumpster!

The large garden supplied an abundance of chard, squashes, zucchini, the hated fava beans, and other vegetables. Many ex-Ranchers feel they ate their life's quota of chard and zucchini in the relatively short time they were at the Ranch, and never wanted to see those vegetables again.

The garden also produced enough carrots to feed everyone, including a Table Bluff native. Tim Nabakowski was the garden steward for a while and noticed carrots and other crops were disappearing and it didn't appear to be the work of a hungry brother. Tim finally discovered the culprit. He had a couple of cats that did a good job keeping varmints away. One day they cornered a big fat squirrel near the woodpile. Tim grabbed a stick and wacked the critter with it, which ended the ravages in the garden. Paul Demeire skinned it, rewarded the cats with the head, then turned the dressed animal over to the kitchen, which, I guess you can say, finally benefited from all those devoured carrots.

This was only a small step up from another source of animal protein—road kill. All the ranches would get calls from the local sheriff letting us know that deer steak or roast was ours for the taking as the result of an unfortunate meeting between a deer and a vehicle. All we'd have to do is "go down to milepost four," or wherever, and pick it up. There was usually someone on the land who could skin and dress the carcass. That day at least, everyone had animal protein. Chris Noonan Funnell says her adult children still tease her with, "Eeew! Mom ate road kill!"

Frank Lagielski tells of an interesting offer for a supply of chickens. One day a flatbed truck pulled up to the Ranch in front of the main building. The back was full of chickens in cages. A couple of bearded, scraggly characters got out with a business proposition that would potentially help relieve the tight food situation in two ways—they wanted to trade chickens for sisters. No deal was made and they left disappointed but with all their chickens.

Trips down to San Francisco were made on a regular basis to purchase (here's where the money comes in) flour, oatmeal, barley, beans, rice, oil, sugar, and other essentials that couldn't be grown, gleaned, or gathered. In the early years, before money from tree planting began to come in, there wasn't much cash to go around. The amount spent at the ranches bordered on the ridiculous. A few dollars a week was usually thought sufficient—and it turned out it was. Carolyn remembers that later, when she was the "shopping sister," she took three dollars per person per week and an armful of store coupons and went shopping in Eureka.

Working Men

Many of the men worked in town in the various businesses such as Our Father's Car Wash, the *Tri-City Advertiser*, the Donut Shop, or Radiance Media. Gary Todoroff, with more professional training and life experience than most ranchers, worked at the local TV station. In the early years, his income contributed substantially to the Ranch's finances. The other brothers were assigned jobs on the land, in the garden, in the pottery barn, or working on vehicles in the garage. That was a never-ending job.

Most of our vehicles were dubbed "faithmobiles" because equal amounts of mechanical knowledge and faith were needed to keep them running. A couple of times, the Lighthouse Ranch got contracts cleaning up spills from derailed trains. Part of the pay was to keep whatever could be removed from the scene. The workers were able to bring back building equipment, food, and other valuable items to the Ranch.

There were additional work projects on the land too. The different gardens and livestock needed manpower; the old electrical wiring was in sad shape, and then there was the "hole that people forgot."

Frank tells the story, "With more people living on the property than it was originally designed for, the septic tank had a hard time keeping up. At times, the Ranch population approached three hundred. So the idea was adopted to dig a large hole outside of the kitchen to catch the dish and laundry water runoff. This would relieve some of the burden on the septic system. The brothers got busy digging a thirty-foot-wide hole, fifteen feet deep. They were going to fill it with rocks and then the job would be done. The work dragged on, and by the time it was done digging, everyone who knew what the hole was for was gone and it was just used as a trash pit. It was the hole that people forgot."

Boy Meets Girl

Of course, with all those single men and women living in close proximity to one another, something had to give. And boy did it ever. To the ranchers, it seemed like there were "weddings every weekend, sometimes two!" Many of the unions were founded on the typical formula of, "boy meets girl, girl meets boy." But unlike the relationships we experienced before becoming Christians, a real effort was made to be holy and virtuous. Above all, we wanted to please God and do things his way. Situations where our virtue could be compromised were (mostly) avoided. This didn't keep the occasional brother from approaching a pretty sister and declaring, "God told me we're supposed to get married." This actually worked a few times—but the resulting marriages usually didn't last.

Weddings were special to us because our relationships before we got saved were so wrong. Most of them were plagued by a shallow commitment to each other that was influenced more by personal desires than truly serving and loving the other person. The devotion to your mate usually went as deep as a popular song of the time that preached, "Love the one you (happen to be) with." We thought we knew what love was, but were never quite able to pull it off.

Now that our lives lined up with the lives God always intended for us, we could celebrate and enjoy a relationship with the opposite sex that was holy and life giving.

Each wedding was a family event—not just for the wedding couple's immediate family, but for everyone else on the Ranch, including the brother or sister who had just gotten saved the day before.

Couples could get married at Deliverance Temple, at Vet's Hall, in front of the cross at the Ranch, in the garden at Carlotta, at one of the parks in Eureka, or down at Living Waters or the Lord's Land. The weddings in the buildings invariably followed a formal pattern, but the ones held out-of-doors were more relaxed. Vows were often exchanged under a tree, chairs were provided for the bride and groom's families and everyone else stood, sat, or lounged around on the grass. Flowers almost never came from a florist's shop, rather nearby fields and roadsides supplied them. The couple and the reason for the occasion would be announced, followed by shouts of "Hallelujah!" "Praise the Lord!" and "Thank you, Jesus!" Then two or three musicians would play guitars and violins and sing spiritual wedding songs and other praise or worship choruses. This wasn't a performance for the wedding party—for them and the musicians and the assembled brethren, it was worship. They closed their eyes, raised their hands, and sang with all their hearts. The parents watched—some wondering what this was all about—but others were impressed with the Christian enthusiasm the young people showed.

Even in wedding ceremonies our zeal for sharing the gospel couldn't be held back and the salvation message was often a part of the ceremony. After all, unsaved family and friends were present. The only thing lacking was an altar call. The result? People got saved at weddings. Tim and Anne Nabakowski specifically requested it, and Anne tells that three people received the Lord the day of their wedding. Terri Schrater remembers that around ten people became Christians the weekend she and Steve got married. At a wedding at Living Waters, Tom Petersen included God's offer of salvation with the marriage message: John Jordan and David Monroe both got saved.

Many non-Christians who watched the people and the festivities at ranch weddings were touched in ways that surprised them. Diane Doyle felt only revulsion towards the brethren at Carlotta when she first visited. She wanted nothing to do with people she couldn't understand and didn't want to be around. The next day was Tim and Anne's wedding in the garden. When she saw the love, joy, and peace of the brothers and sisters who came to celebrate, all of her earlier loathing disappeared and she told me with a voice of wonderment, "Marc, these people—their eyes shine!"

Rebecca Wilmarth Muller's father attended her wedding. Afterwards, he wrote a letter that had to give her as much joy as anything else. He said, "God bless you! We saw the wonderful work of God being done in your beautiful wedding . . . I felt the love—and I got saved! Give our love to Jim and all the blessed brothers and sisters at the Ranch!"

A Christian Boot Camp

By the time Jim Durkin got the Ranch from Ken Smith, he and Dacie had been Christians for many years. They had served their churches faithfully and endured many of life's hardest trials. Jim saw that the group of young believers Ken had assembled was zealous, but in spite of their love for Jesus, they were clueless about how to follow God.

When I became a Christian and joined G. O. in the summer of 1973, there were still stories going around of the pre-Durkin days of "zeal without knowledge." Brothers and sisters were supposedly delivered from the demon of chocolate and demons were cast out of doorknobs.

So, at the age of forty-six, in a move—which to us when we finally reached the same age and station in life seemed incredible—Jim and Dacie dropped everything and moved out to the Ranch, to live communally with a bunch of Jesus Freaks.

Debbie Long says, "Jim and Dacie's presence brought stability and direction to the young believers. It really helped the Ranch to begin to focus on God. Things began moving."

Shortly after they set up housekeeping, a meeting was held that everyone was required to attend. Some decisions needed to be made about the direction and character of this group of young, eager, and untrained Christians who lived on Table Bluff.

The discussion addressed what the Ranch would *not* be, what would be allowed, and what would be prohibited.

Radios? Television? Newspapers, record players, smoking cigarettes, or drinking alcohol?

It was decided only cassette players would be permitted. That would allow sermons and worship music to be heard. The brethren wanted the Ranch to be clean of worldly influences. They wanted to be undistracted in their pursuit of the knowledge of God and his ways. They set for themselves a high standard of conduct and devotion to God that would mark the Ranch as a place of serious discipleship. This would not be a Christian retreat center, instead it would be a kind of Christian boot camp—just like the military—that would produce men and women of God who would walk in the same level of commitment as the early church in the book of Acts.

The young disciples determined to get rid of the "idols" that had been important parts of their lives. They collected these articles and marched down to the beach at the bottom of the bluff and started a big bonfire. There they threw in their old rock and roll records and cassettes, leftover cigarettes or marijuana joints, books on eastern religions, meditation, books from Baba Ram Das and Carlos Castaneda, the occasional *Encyclopedia Britannica* and—we're talking about being free from vanity, you know—a set of hair rollers. Of course, later there was regret about getting rid of some of those things, but for this period in their lives, nothing mattered as much as knowing Jesus. Anything that hindered had to go.

"Are We All Going to Die?"

Terri Schrater's dad was concerned. After graduating from high school, his daughter had gone to a family cabin near Garberville to try to sort out her life and get a handle on her future. The next thing he knew, she was up near

81

Eureka at some Christian commune. He called the Eureka Police Department and asked, "Who are these people? What did my daughter get herself into?"

What he heard from the authorities reassured him. The people at the Lighthouse Ranch were law abiding. In fact, where once many of them had done drugs, some had stolen stuff, and been in trouble with the law and society, it seemed they had all changed and were now eager to obey the law.

In Terri's case, she was still only seventeen, and not legally able to move onto the Ranch without her parents' written permission. She was sent home but returned three weeks later with their blessing.

A good relationship with law enforcement was essential, given the problems that some visitors brought with them.

Irene Barney and Susan Insko remember one day when a nice sedan pulled up to the main building. As Susan watched out a kitchen window, she thought it wasn't the usual "faithmobile" that she saw around the Ranch. Men wearing suits climbed out. Not the usual Ranch attire. They opened up the trunk of their car and pulled out shotguns and rifles and the thought occurred to her, *Are we all going to die?*

The men disappeared and returned shortly with a fugitive, a murderer who had been hiding out at the Ranch with his girlfriend. The FBI had gotten a tip, and together with the police, they coordinated the bust with the Lighthouse leaders.

But more serious events also took place. One Tuesday evening in May of 1973, the ranchers returned from a service at Deliverance Temple. It was dark and some of them were strolling along the side road next to the garden before turning in for the night. There they came upon the lifeless body of Dave Peterson, a brother who had remained on the property as part of the Ranch watch team. Church attendance was mandatory for everyone at the Ranch. Dave had tried to get visitor Carl Lewis to join the churchgoers on the blue bus, "Zion." He proved to be stubborn and finally told Dave he would drive in his own car. No one knows exactly what happened after that, but when he left the Ranch, Dave was dead, run over by Lewis' car. Lewis was later apprehended by the police in Redding, was tried and convicted, and went to prison.

Making the News

The Lighthouse Ranch attracted both national and worldwide attention. The *Mother Earth News*, a "back-to-the-land" magazine that preached an early form of environmentalism and self-sufficiency told its readers about the Ranch—describing it as a commune that really worked. In 1972, the Corporation for Public Broadcasting aired, "Lighthouse at Loleta" a television documentary about the Ranch that did a good job of portraying the Ranch's atmosphere of devotion to God.

Wendy, a member of the G. O. church in Munich, West Germany had just installed a TV set in her apartment in early 1982. She plugged it in, turned it on, and there was a German broadcast about Gospel Outreach, the Lighthouse Ranch and Rios Montt, the G. O. Guatemala church member who had been made president of his country. Of course, it was all in German. Her surprise turned into the jaw-dropping, eye-popping kind when she saw her friend John Jordan being interviewed. He had been one of the Munich church leaders before returning to Eureka.

Young people traveling in Europe, the Middle East or Southeast Asia showed up having heard from the grapevine about "some commune up in Northern California. I think it's Christian."

When pimps in San Francisco got wind of the Ranch, they began to send their prostitutes up to get off drugs and get some rest. They told the women, "Just say 'Praise the Lord' and 'Please pass the potatoes.'" We found out about that when some of them got saved and were delivered from that life.

With a policy of "whosoever will, may come" the big nets that were the ranches pulled in all kinds of fish. Some were a bit weird. Frank (who wasn't weird, in spite of giving up on verbal communication and showing up with a beard down to his belt and hair just as long) says, "Weirdos? It was full of weirdos!" Larry and Claudia Jamison remember one character who dressed entirely in white. He would stand on top of a table and strike a silent, heroic pose. Then he would suddenly jump under the table and declare, "I was almost raptured!"

Bill Ireland remembers one fellow named John. "He was a skinny little guy who showed up at the ranch totally psychotic. He used to stand outside the brothers' dorm, facing the wall, babbling nonsense into the air. Once, one of the married sisters opened her closet and found John standing there—wearing no clothes. Then one day I saw him again, and he was totally normal—'clothed and in his right mind.' He was actually quite intelligent and sweet. Don't know what happened to him. But, thank God."

When local church leaders once criticized the Ranch about the kind of people who lived there and called themselves Christians, Jim told them of the good qualities and positive direction of the Ranch, saying, "Salvation is beautiful, but conversion is messy."

It was unlike anything these young Christians had expected. Most felt (and still feel) it was the closest thing to heaven on earth they would ever know. The wonderful times of worship with Rebecca, Dave Wilmarth, Fred

Simmons, Sam Griffith, Karl Richey, Gene Fowler, Sarah, Bill Ireland and others, when it seemed as if everyone sang with one voice and knew God was right there with them; the Holy Spirit anointed teaching of Jim, Ron Juncal, Tommy Kennedy, and others, that left them awestruck at the wisdom of God; the effect all these things had on everyone, so if it were possible, their love for the Lord continued to grow, so they *had* to tell the world about Jesus—they didn't see how this could ever end. But Jim had told them to be prepared because Jesus had commissioned them to "go into all the world and make disciples."

Debbie Long remembers, "Jim told us, 'You're not going to like this, but the nucleus [of leadership] we are developing is going to expand out. You're not going to like the changes, but they're coming and you need to get ready.'"

With the Ranch population closing in on two hundred by the end of the 1971, it was time. That winter, Jim signed the lease for an old deserted house about fifteen miles from the Ranch in a town called Carlotta.

CHAPTER SEVEN

The Carlotta Mansion

"Could There Ever Be a Better Life?"

THE LARGE, VICTORIAN-STYLE home called the
Carlotta Mansion was ornately trimmed but had seen
better days. Built entirely of redwood lumber in the late
1800s by John Vance, a lumber/railroad baron, it was surrounded by fields and enormous redwood trees. The garden
was framed by white trellises filled with flowers and bushes
imported from Europe. Being far from the coast, it enjoyed
more sunny days than the Lighthouse Ranch or Eureka, and
on those days, no one wanted to be anywhere else.

Bernie Haraldson once spent an afternoon at the Carlotta
Mansion with a group of Lighthouse Ranchers. As Bernie
relaxed with the brothers and sisters, he looked around
at the blue skies, the forest, the hills and fields, and the
white-trimmed, yellow house encircled by tall redwoods.
Filled with wonder he asked himself, *What kind of life is
this we have? Could there ever be a better life?"*

Most of the brothers and sisters who lived at Carlotta would agree with Bernie—there was none better.

The two-story house was painted a coat of sunny yellow paint, and the window frames were trimmed in white in the summer of 1973. The colors blended in perfectly with the green and red of the trees and the blue skies. Not much could be done for the inside. There was a big living room and next to that a piano room with a winter garden attached to it. In the living room, a dusty rug covered most of the floor. The king of the room was a long, ancient sofa pushed up against the common wall with the dining room. It lorded over a realm where no two pieces of furniture matched. A wood stove that was the main source of heat for the whole house completed the picture.

Off the living room was the dining room filled with several long tables with benches big enough to accommodate a house full of people. Adjoining that was the kitchen, a hallway, and a bedroom.

Stairs led up to the second floor, which had five or six bedrooms occupied either by married couples, or served as sisters' dorms stacked with wooden bunks. No earthly paradise can match the perfection of the heavenly, and this one had its flaw too. The house only had one bathroom, one toilet. The line in front of the bathroom door was less an opportunity for fellowship than for desperate prayer. Woe the pregnant mother whose bladder demanded immediate attention in a house whose population could range from fifteen to forty-five. Tony and Jane Tuck were the house heads for a while. Jane joked that, with so many people, each person was assigned a day of the week when he or she could use the bathroom.

Narrow stairs led up to the attic, which served as the brothers' dorm. The bunks and beds were lined up in two rows—not unlike an orphanage—and the one window faced the front of the house. A prayer room was built across from the window, on the opposite wall.

Places like the prayer room at Carlotta, the Lighthouse Ranch, Living Waters, or Mendocino were secluded from the noise and bustle of the day. Small groups of brothers or sisters studied the Scriptures, prayed together, or just talked about this new life they had received from God.

Ron Juncal was the one who discovered Carlotta. His pre-G. O. ministry, the Maranatha Coffee House in Fortuna, was looking for a communal house for new converts. Through Gale Willy, a Fortuna, guitar-playing "cowboy-Christian" (what was he doing with all these Jesus Freaks?), Ron, Tim Leslie, and others, learned about the "haunted mansion." Long deserted and needing much repair, they looked at it and thought, *Perfect!*

At about the same time, Ron brought his group into association with Jim Durkin and Gospel Outreach. In late 1971, Jim, working together with Gale, sealed the deal for a five-year lease.

In May of 1972, work was begun to clear the house of the wisteria plants growing through the windows, weeds, poison oak, junk and bats. The bats didn't want to leave the attic. Several things were tried, including smoking them out. Steve Schrater finally convinced them to go with a BB gun, and the brothers could move into their new dorm. That helped for a while, but too many generations of bats remembered the attic, and they would occasionally stop by for a day's rest.

The house was tired. The plumbing was tired; the electrical circuits were tired. Terri Schrater, Laurie Zeff Baca, and Rose Kiewit remember rusty water coming out of the pipes. You knew the clothes had been washed because there was a slightly orange tint to them. Kay Dragon tells of dark, gummy stuff popping out of the kitchen faucet, and says she was sick most of the time.

Kerosene lanterns supplied lighting needs until the first group of pioneers could get the electricity hooked up. Terri said that no electricity in the house meant no vacuum cleaner. Without a vacuum to clean the rug, she would greet the brothers coming in covered in wood chips from work at the mill they started. She would sweep them off with a broom before they could come in.

The town of Carlotta (named after John Vance's daughter) had only one store, a post office, and a lumber mill, so offered no job prospects. Gale helped the brethren set up a small mill that turned 2 x 4 boards into 2 x 2 grape stakes which were then sold to vineyards down near Ukiah. They called the mill "Split Stuff." The equipment was old and worn out, including a 1949 forklift that did the heavy lifting. Henry Zeff says when a load of wood was wet, the forklift would tip forward and a couple of guys were needed to climb on the back to level it out again. Like a lame dancer, it did fine turning right but had trouble going to the left. The 2 x 4 boards were fed into a large table saw by a brother on one end, and the cut 2 x 2 boards were then caught by the another man—the "tailer"—at the other end. Sometimes it seemed as if the saw blade resented the hard work because, every now and then, it would hold the boards for just a second, then shoot them out like arrows. The tailer had to be ready. The 2 x 2 boards were sharpened on other saws, thrown into a pile, stacked, bundled, and loaded onto the next semi truck headed south.

As with many of the Gospel Outreach businesses or "work projects," Split Stuff fulfilled two goals. The first, of course, was to make money to support the house. Second, it was an ideal training ground for new Christians. Each day was started with prayer, reading the Word and maybe a short Bible study. We learned what God had done when he saved us, and how we were now in the process of being "converted." This was an important phase of our lives if we were to actually experience the promises of God and begin to live the life to which he had called us.

The hard physical work and the tensions that sometimes arose between brothers supplied opportunities to react in "newness of spirit" rather than in the habits of our former lives. As we were being converted, we experienced more and more of the freedom that God had for us. When we laid aside the old habits and fears, they were replaced with the joy of the Lord and love for the brethren. Rather than something to be dreaded, conversion was embraced as the road to joy. We also began to experience something that, in our former "worldly-wise" opinion we thought impossible for Christians—we had a lot of fun.

Tim Nabakowski was land steward at Carlotta. One morning at about 7:00 a.m., he was up in the brothers' dorm in the attic and looked out the window. He saw a group of brothers walking down the road to the mill. As they walked, they were praising the Lord and dancing. Tim thought, *This is just like a musical—except that it's real. This is real life and they really* are *joyful!*

Maybe because we all lived under one roof (though there were a couple of small houses in the back for married couples), the brothers and sisters at Carlotta had a sense of family not experienced by the other ranches. We worked at Split Stuff together, cooked, cleaned, and washed dishes together, tended the garden, and painted the house together. We prayed, worshipped, and studied the Bible as a family.

Sometimes, the elders from the Ranch or Eureka would send out a new convert who needed the more relaxed, accepting atmosphere of Carlotta. There they could heal from a wrecked past and begin their journey into the new life.

Rob Anderson remembers, "Carlotta Mansion was a beautiful experience; it was almost a Christian fairy tale except it was real, and full of the Holy Spirit. It was healing, and nurturing . . . it was what I needed."

Linda's life was falling apart when the Lord saved her in Lemoore, California. Through a "typical" series of miracles, the Lord brought this young woman who would become my future wife up to Eureka to the Lighthouse Ranch. After spending her first night with Augie and Anita Lueras in their home, she drove out to the Ranch. There, the brethren greeted her warmly, but she still felt uncomfortable in what was obviously a discipleship center. They then sent her over to Carlotta. There, after the stresses and trials of the previous couple of years and the drive up to an unknown future, she could finally relax. At Carlotta, Linda experienced safety and love. This would be her home for the next period of her life.

James, Jim Durkin's son, was made the house elder, following a stint by Jim DeGolyer. James felt Jim's leadership and teaching would be a hard act to follow but promised the Lord to do his best to continue it. Instead, the Lord showed him that Carlotta was a family—that was all that was required. That would meet the needs of the people whom God brought out to the house in the redwoods.

Everyone received an allowance of three dollars a week—not much, but you could keep yourself supplied with candy bars for a while. These could be bought from the store located at the foot of the driveway leading up to the house. New converts had to be warned against enthusiastically sharing their new faith with the long-suffering store owners. They had heard it a hundred times and were ready to throw the next witnessing Christian out the door.

For all its idyllic setting and family atmosphere, things could get pretty exciting at Carlotta. Once, when Gary and Jeannie Crouthamel were the leaders, the house got taken over by some men with evil intentions. This happened in the summer of 1974 while I was at Carlotta.

The Hijacking of Carlotta Mansion

It all started with a knock at the door. Gary was sitting in the living room, reading a magazine. *That's strange,* he thought, *why would someone be knocking at the door?*

At Carlotta, most visitors just came through the unlocked door and it was usually open anyway. They never knocked.

Gary himself had drifted in. His life had once consisted of living from one drug-induced high to the next. His encounter with Christianity had put an end to that and now, several years later, he was helping those in need. Gary's humility, uncomplicated spirituality, and care for others resulted in him being appointed head of the Carlotta Mansion.

Theresa was a sixteen-year-old runaway who avoided school and ran with a much older crowd. Not knowing what to do with her, county authorities turned to the Carlotta Mansion for help. Gary and his wife Jeannie agreed to become guardians of the trouble-prone girl.

It wasn't easy; Theresa didn't want help. She was hard to manage and continued to hang out with her older friends. Things came to a head one afternoon when four of them drove up the long driveway to the house. They wanted to pick up Theresa and go somewhere.

Gary met them outside. "I'm sorry, but she can't go with you. As a matter of fact, I don't even want her running around with you." He studied their hard faces. They weren't used to being told, "No," and clearly didn't like it. As Gary watched their car disappear down the driveway, he cautioned himself, *Be careful. Keep Theresa away from them, but try not to provoke a confrontation.*

That night, like every other Tuesday night, we piled into our faithful, battered vehicles and drove into Eureka for the midweek church service. Gary thought this would be a good opportunity to talk to Theresa, so he and Jeannie stayed home with the girl and two others from the house who were assigned to "house watch."

That's when there came a knock on the door.

When Gary opened the door he saw that the afternoon's visitors had returned with a new guy. Now there were five of them, and it looked like they'd done some serious drinking.

"What do you want?" he asked.

Crowding the doorway they announced loudly, "We're taking this house over!"

They pushed their way past Gary into the living room demanding, "Where's Theresa?"

Gary hedged, "I'm not sure, everyone went to church tonight."

Two of them immediately raced through the house searching for the girl.

The other three stayed downstairs. One of them, Theresa's boyfriend, stared angrily at Gary. He swore, "I can't stand you, you _____!" and with that, let fly a punch that knocked Gary to the floor.

The new guy, the reinforcement, turned just as Gary struggled to his feet. "What happened?" he demanded.

"I punched him!" growled the boyfriend.

Victor, the new guy, swatted the boyfriend with the back of his hand. "Don't do that!" he ordered.

The search party returned, pushing Jeannie, the house-watch pair, and Theresa in front of them. They were all shoved onto the long couch next to the dining room door. Now the hijackers were together with their captives. The men began to curse, throwing out threats of what they might do to their prisoners.

Gary and Jeannie, more than the others, knew what could happen. Their pre-Christian past had included drug dealing and turf battles. They had experience with people like these and knew things could quickly get bad.

Gary began praying and at the same time searched for a little bit of hope. He had to keep these evil men from doing something really bad. He looked at Victor who seemed to be different from the others. Maybe there was something there.

"You're not like these guys," Gary said.

Scarcely had he uttered those words when Victor fired him a withering look. "Shut your mouth before I shove a pillow down your throat."

The other four were working on a plan. It didn't look good. With each passing minute, the tension in the room mounted. The drunken hijackers seemed to be working themselves up to something.

I have to confuse their plan, Gary thought. *Maybe I can drive a wedge between Victor and them.*

He looked at Victor again "You don't seem like these guys," he repeated.

The man's angry reply was drowned out by the raucous laughter of the other four. The boyfriend looked at the women on the couch and laughed, "Alright! This is going to be fun!"

Lord Jesus, Gary prayed urgently, *we need your help now!*

At that moment, and for the second time that day (or year for that matter), there was a knock at the door.

Victor motioned to one of the others. "Open it."

He opened the door. There, in full uniform and seeming to fill the whole doorway, stood the biggest policeman Gary had ever seen.

His appearance was met with shocked silence. Wordlessly, the policeman looked at the people on the couch. Then his gaze shifted over to the boyfriend and his buddies. Then he looked at Victor. He spoke. "Victor, what's going on here?"

The boyfriend, not understanding why a cop would be on first-name terms with the gang's new friend, repeated the question with a little more passion. "Victor? What's going on?"

Rather than answer, Victor thrust his hand into his jacket pocket and stepped quickly back into the dining room doorway. "Don't anybody move!" he shouted, "I've got a gun!" Everyone froze in astonishment. Then he motioned to the four would-be hijackers, "You! Get down on the floor; this place is surrounded!"

Victor spent a few minutes with the officers, then after the four hijackers were cuffed and taken away, came over to Gary and the others, visibly shaken, even close to tears. "I'm so sorry this had to happen," he said. "You folks did so well. Theresa's boyfriend was involved in a killing. He was in Vietnam and came back all screwed up. In fact, he went to Nam all screwed up. We've been watching him worried he might try something else. I was afraid this was it. But you guys handled it beautifully."

Gary looked at Victor. "You weren't one of them. I was right!"

"Yeah," he said. "You almost blew it for me. I'm a detective with the Fortuna police and I was—well, I wasn't supposed to—but I was in a tavern in town this afternoon having a beer. Those four guys came in and sat down at the table next to mine. They didn't know I was a cop, but I recognized them. Every cop around here knows the boyfriend. They started ranting and raving about you people out here. The more they drank, the more they talked about coming back out here and doing some serious damage. I decided to play it cool and acted as if I agreed with them. When it looked as though they would really do something, I said I wanted in on the action. Three of them jumped in their car and one rode with me. My car is unmarked, but it's got a police radio and a shotgun in it. The idiot never noticed! We parked at the bottom of the hill and walked up the driveway. Part way up I told them I had to go back to the car and get something. I really did—I had to get help! I radioed for backup then hurried up the hill to the others. I didn't know what these guys were going to do—they're really capable of anything."

As the police really couldn't pin any more on them than causing a severe fright, they were released with a warning. Theresa never did settle down and ended up running away. Gary and Jeannie kept helping young people straighten out their lives and then eventually moved to New York with the G. O. team that started a church in Brooklyn.

In 1975, Split Stuff was shut down. Wood grape stakes were being replaced by metal and besides, the brothers who worked there could make more money for the house by planting trees.

In 1976, the five-year lease for the mansion expired and preparations were made to leave it. With many brothers and sisters leaving on teams heading for distant cities or shores, the house was no longer needed. The coup d' grace was supplied by a couple who claimed they were Christian, but at the first opportunity, took off with all of Carlotta's money as well as other valuables.

Like the other ranches, the Carlotta Mansion and all the people who lived there provided a resting place for those who had given up on the world and sought a new life in Christ. The beautiful setting and the atmosphere of God's love and grace turned many an upside-down life right-side up. Living under one roof and growing together in the things of God was a special experience for everyone who lived at Carlotta.

A little further south, another Gospel Outreach family came together in a town with a funny name.

CHAPTER EIGHT

Living Waters Ranch

W HERE'S GOPHERVILLE YOU ask? Well, of course, it's just down the road from Whitethorn, about half way between Garberville on Highway 101 and the Pacific Ocean. In the minds of its original inhabitants, it qualified as a mill town because, in addition to the lumber mill and a collection of houses, it had a saloon. By the late 1960s its heyday was past, and it sat alone in the forest. All that remained was a big, rusty, cone-shaped incinerator like hundreds of others that littered abandoned mill sites in the western U.S. There was a scattering of dusty, cobweb-filled cabins occupied by a few squatters. A thick blanket of moss covered the cedar shake roofs. Banks of Himalaya berry bushes concealed rusty abandoned cars. The Matole River (a stream really) ran down the middle of the land.

Tony Tuck bought the property in 1968 as part of his search for utopia. Clean the place up a bit; invite some counter-culture types to settle in, and you could end up with everyone's dream: a community where one and all had everything in common and shared friendship and respect;

a place where children and everyone else could live free of the rotting influences of a society that only cared about money and status. The kind of commune where a person could get back to the land and enjoy life the way it was meant to be.

It was one more step in Tony's search for meaning in life that had him making the obligatory pilgrimage to India. Everyone knew that Western society had no answers and India was where you could connect with your inner self and find peace and fulfillment. He got as far as a small mountain town on the Pacific island of Bali when his direction was unexpectedly changed. He was meditating outside the inn where he stayed. "It was during this sitting that I felt an almost foreign question arise within me. *What would you really like to do?* To this day I believe God was asking that question, even to me, who gave Him no place." A strong impression came quickly. *I would like to live together with my close friends somewhere in remote redwood country.* "This thought would not leave me."

Tony cut short his India trip in Singapore and headed home to San Francisco. Driving his VW bus, he roamed Mendocino and Humboldt Counties north of the Bay Area, until he came upon an eighty-acre piece of property near the settlement of Whitethorn, known by the locals as "Gopherville." With his father's help, he bought it.

Tony, his high school friend Jim Bettin, and others, spent a good deal of time cleaning the place up, getting rid of squatters (who didn't want to leave) and moving in.

He had become friends with Jane a few years earlier in San Francisco. In spite of each going their separate ways, they stayed in touch. When Tony got the Gopherville commune up and running, she would come from the city and visit. Eventually, Tony invited her to make a permanent move to live there.

At first, everything worked they way they thought it should.

Tony had the vision for the commune and decided who could live on the property. He didn't want any slackers. Instead, he looked for people who were talented, motivated, and willing to contribute to the "family." There was much to do. All the buildings needed renovation to one degree or another, water tanks needed to be built, and the refuse from the mill and rusty car wrecks had to be removed. Gardens were planted, tended and harvested. There was a blacksmith shop. Animals and kids were born and raised. They cleared the land and the whole place began to look like the garden of Eden. Books were written, art was produced, and some of the parties were legendary. Jane remembers there were usually about eight families on the land and a few kids. One guy had two wives.

Jane says, "We all had this idealized vision that we could live together in harmony and love and could do things differently from anyone else in the world. We were 'checking out' from society—except that we were living off government Food Stamps—big time. I told the welfare department I had eight kids! That's how it was for about two and a half years."

It took that long for everyone to reach the limits of their "self-realized," inner beings. From that point, their friendships and quality of life didn't get any higher, deeper, or better. Instead, Tony said, "We began to admit that this new world was filled with ourselves."

Life in the typical commune of the 1960s and '70s was like riding a shiny new bicycle that has no chain. You gave it a good shove, hopped on, and started pedaling. The initial push moved the bike for a short distance while you pedaled for all you were worth. In spite of your efforts, the bike slowed and lost balance. Instead of reaching the destination, you and the bike ended up on the ground, in the dirt.

Things started going downhill at Gopherville. People began stealing from each other. Some almost died from the drugs. Children who were raised to be "free" and unrestrained were unrestrained and running wild with no one supervising them. This wasn't the utopia it was supposed to be.

Tony figured that somewhere, someone had to be doing it right. He and Jim hit the road and planned to hitchhike through the Southwest, looking for successful communes. The only lasting impression they got from their travels was a severe case of the flu. They returned to Gopherville with nothing to report and no new ideas.

Then the Lord began to move.

Tony said, "There was a buzz going around about Jesus. Of course, when we heard this familiar name, we knew that surely wasn't the way. Nevertheless 'something' was happening, but we didn't know what it was."

Tony remembered three distinct occurrences as God began to draw them to his kingdom.

He was in his cabin when there was a knock on the door. He opened it and there stood a stranger who explained to them that he was a fisherman and had just had a miracle catch; he wanted to share it with them. Tony looked behind the visitor for a cooler of fish, but instead, the man told them of meeting Jesus. Tony said, "He looked just like us, but had more light. He was a very real sort of guy, and we listened."

Then there was the day everyone was working on different parts of the land when each person heard a strange noise that no one could identify. The forest around the commune was usually pretty quiet. A bird, the wind in the trees, someone hammering, or chopping wood in the distance, or the voices of kids playing were what they usually heard.

There was something of a harmony in the woods. Sounds didn't compete with each other like on a city street; they complemented each other. This sound was very unusual, and didn't seem to belong. They had to find out what it was and each of them dropped what he was doing to find the source. The sound led everyone to the road where there was a pile of logs.

Sitting on the logs were three men they had never seen before. They were singing—loudly—right there in the middle of the forest. The Gopherville residents didn't recognize the songs—because they were singing hymns. Everyone stood around just listening and watching. Tony said, "What a scene! It was nothing seeing a crowd of people playing drums by the swimming hole, but smiling men singing was the first of many new sights we would see. The church had come to us."

Then Tony told of visiting a friend in San Francisco who was a poet. Bruce wrote Zen poetry and had already published his first book. What he told Tony turned his world upside down. He said he was now a born-again Christian and he had burned all his books. Tony was shocked. "It was like hearing him speak Egyptian." They talked and argued late into the night. Tony just couldn't come to terms with what Bruce told him.

As he headed up to his bed, Bruce's wife suggested, "Why don't you ask Jesus the things you've been asking Bruce?"

As Tony lay in bed, he felt uneasy. Nothing made sense. He hadn't found peace in his own life yet, but at least he had a good idea of where it *couldn't* be found. Now he wasn't so sure.

"Before going to sleep that night I recalled how I had always said I really wanted the truth. I noticed how I could not ask this Jesus the question like she suggested. I felt like a hypocrite because if He really was the truth then I'd have to be a Christian. That thought was unacceptable; this forced a question on me, 'did I really want the truth?' I was stunned by my duplicity. I felt ashamed of my inner response and forced out a meager prayer: something along the lines of: 'If you're real, show me.' Then I went to sleep."

On the drive back to Gopherville the next day, Tony was aware of a profound change. "I knew something very real had taken place. My mind was having thoughts such as I had never had before. Something had happened! God, the real God, was knocking on my door! It was very new. The feeling, thoughts, and the sense of new things didn't end, but grew."

Everyone noticed, especially Jane. "I was furious!" Raised Catholic, she'd heard enough about God and Jesus and had no use for them or those who called themselves believers.

Things became strained between Tony and Jane and they had a huge falling out while down in San Francisco. Jane was devastated and felt as if it was the end of their relationship. At 2:00 a.m. one morning, she went out to Golden Gate Park and sat alone under one of the big trees. She cried and cried until she felt like her insides were about to come out. Slowly she became aware of the presence of Jesus. He showed her that knowing him was not like the popular spiritual movements of the time. Those gave the appearance of searching for truth but never produced real results. Knowing Jesus meant having a relationship with someone who was alive. She tearfully accepted his offer and sat there under the tree, now surrounded by the love of God.

Jane was changed—she was a new person, filled with the life of Christ. Her friendship with Tony was history; she had a different focus for her life—knowing Jesus. She didn't return to Gopherville but stayed in San Francisco learning about her new life. She lived with an assortment of new Christian friends ("sofa surfing"), including Holy Hubert in Berkeley.

One day she got a letter from Tony. "Please consider coming back. We are now a Christian commune with brothers' and sisters' houses. I really miss you." She didn't think twice and headed right back to Gopherville.

Tony had returned to the land from San Francisco a changed person; his whole outlook on life was different. Around the same time, his friend Jim also made the step and became a Christian. A few more people accepted Christ, and before very long, the one-time hippie communal family split into two groups. It started to get awkward. At the meal they all shared together—usually dinner—the Christians would pray, and the others would chant "Ohm," or something similar, to create their version of spiritual unity with the universe and the food they were about to eat.

It became obvious to Tony that God had a plan for Gopherville. Maybe that's why he was given those thoughts that had so surprised him on Bali. Maybe it was supposed to be a Christian, not a hippie commune—one that would actually experience the love and community that the worldly communes always strived for but could never attain. Tony remembers, "It was a tough year. We tried to continue to all flow together, but it didn't work."

He made a decision. The name Gopherville would be changed to Living Waters; it would be a Christian commune; and whoever wanted to stay could, but everyone would live in obedience to the Word and Spirit of God and His will. All others had to leave.

This was very difficult for some. A few of the people had spent considerable time and money renovating or even building their homes. They thought they would be there forever. Tony's decision and pronouncement left some bitter; but they had no choice—they left.

Tony and Jim had heard about the Lighthouse Ranch and had already made contact with Jim Durkin and the Christians up there. The relationship began to grow but the new believers at Living Waters didn't wait. They started holding church services down by the Matole River. Jane remembers, "It was amazing how the Holy Spirit was our guide and teacher. Sometimes people would show up and say that they were older, spiritual Christians and would teach us. But their message would be, maybe, one-tenth off and the Holy Spirit would show us."

They got to know an Assembly of God congregation in Garberville whose building had a neon sign that declared, "Jesus Loves You." These brothers and sisters, whose denomination was born during a revival, showed love and understanding for the young Christians who were the fruit of a new move of God's Spirit. Larry Jamison tells how they brought eggs, bacon, and sausage to Living Waters, and would cook for everyone.

They were also on hand for a baptism at the river of a married couple whose baptismal robes were their birthday suits. Jane says, "I clearly remember all the women from the Assembly stood along the river bank and simply closed their eyes, turned their faces heavenward, raised their hands and sang 'Praise the Lord, thank you Jesus, Hallelujah' over and over again until the bodies were wrapped in towels. For me, it was a gracious act that softened my heart toward the established church. They were splendid!"

Before long, the relationship with Jim Durkin and Gospel Outreach was solidified and leaders from the Lighthouse came down regularly to fellowship and teach the young Christians who, as the baptismal example showed, needed some good teaching.

When I talk to brothers and sisters who lived at Living Waters and ask them what made it special and different from the other ranches, they respond, "Tony."

In the early years of Gospel Outreach many of us saw Jim Durkin as our example of a Christian leader. He had a strong personality, could hold congregations in awe with his sermons and presented a clear vision of taking the gospel into the world. He was the leader who rallied us around the flag and led us into battle.

Tony was different. He was quiet and contemplative. His character was such that people immediately respected him, wanted to hear what he thought, and accepted his leadership. While he could get as angry as anyone else, he was kind, and didn't hold people up to a standard before accepting them as his brother or sister. He had everyone's confidence. They knew they could honestly share their dreams and trials with him. Tony would encourage them to reach for their goals, or to examine their thoughts and actions in light of God's Word. He was convinced that the relationships we had with one another were a bona fide experience of God's kingdom.

Tony wasn't in a hurry, but he was always doing something.

Jim Wall remembers his first impression of Tony. Jim and Sue had just moved down to Living Waters because there was no room at the Lighthouse Ranch. He saw Tony doing something in the dirt on a hillside and walked up to introduce himself. Next to Tony was a bunch of raspberry starters, a trowel, and a bucket of chicken manure. Jim sat down, they began to talk and he offered to help Tony plant the raspberries. Sure, but Tony didn't trust him to dig the hole—he might dig it too deep or too shallow. He also wouldn't let him put the bushes in the ground—he might not do that right either. Jim's job was to put one scoop of chicken manure around the plant when Tony was done. Jim laughed as he recalled the experience. He says, "After three or four hours, I had a friend for life, someone with whom I never would have connected in the world." Jim says, "The greatest, fondest memory I have of Living Waters was the day my spirit and soul connected with Tony."

Everyone who lived at Living Waters valued the experience. There was a real sense of family—the goal that every commune in America strove to achieve, but only those whose father was God attained. The isolation of Living Waters helped. They felt they were far removed from everything and therefore needed to rely on each other more. And, of course, there was the influence of Tony's personality.

Living Waters tried different ideas for raising money. When Jim Durkin sent Peter and Jackie DePalmo down from the Lighthouse Ranch to provide leadership, Peter started a leather shop, making belts, Bible covers, and purses. At one point, they had a pillow factory (in the middle of the forest)! Someone thought raising worms would be a moneymaker too. What made that a good idea was the big chicken coop. The worms were put in trays below the coop, which caught the chicken poop. The worms devoured it, grew fat, and everyone was happy. And then someone would leave the door open and ducks would come in and eat up all the worms. Ducks could be seen waddling away from the coop with worms dangling out of their mouths like spaghetti.

When the *Tri-City Advertiser* got started, the ranches would earn income from their members who helped deliver it. Brothers and sisters from Living Waters would make the drive to Eureka and help distribute the paper. Then they would have dinner at the Lighthouse Ranch and head home.

The Gospel Outreach tree-planting teams got their start at Living Waters. The unceasing search for an income-producing occupation had not found a solid solution until

Jim Lane, one of the members, made a suggestion. "Why not plant trees?" He had done it before, it was hard, but the money was good. The timber and paper companies and the Forest Service had thousands of acres of clear-cut land that needed to be reforested. Jim said they should check it out. So they did, and unknowingly, created a new chapter in the experience of the Gospel Outreach.

The area around Whitethorn was known for skunks. One day a critter was found in the office next to the pantry. No one wanted to risk getting sprayed, until a brother named Hal stepped forward and assured everyone, "It's okay; I'm an expert on handling skunks." He explained, "If you can get them by the tail, they can't spray you."

He was wrong. He got sprayed, the office got sprayed, and even the pantry was blanketed with the odor. Hal spent the next few days out in the forest. No one would sit next to the brethren from Living Waters at church and the oatmeal from the pantry had a new and very distinctive flavor.

Peeps' Jeep

Most of us were young; many of us were ex-hippies and had little money and few of this world's goods. The book of Acts in the New Testament tells how the early disciples shared their possessions with one another and "no one lacked anything." We wanted to be like that too with what little we had. It was understood that when we turned our lives over to the Lord, it meant not only our spirits/souls/ bodies but also all of our possessions. Everything was presented to the Lord to be used by him as he saw fit. So, it was something to rejoice about when someone showed up with a vehicle that both ran and was in good shape.

Larry and Claudia Jameson visited the Lighthouse, the Lord's Land, and Living Waters and decided Living Waters was where they wanted to start their new lives as disciples. Larry offered Tony the keys to their van and his money and they moved into a cabin on the other side of the river. It was all to be used for the good of the brethren and ranch.

Sue Wall remembers driving up to Eureka with Nancy Lane in the car a sister had brought to the ranch. It ran fine, but the ignition key didn't work. That wasn't a big problem, because a screwdriver did the trick. So everyone was happy when a brother by the name of Ray Peeps showed up with a new Jeep. It was clean, it was reliable, and it wasn't a faithmobile.

Being in the middle of the forest, occasionally a tree needed to be cut down to make room for a new building or just for firewood. In the parlance of the woods, if you're just cutting down one or two, it's called "dropping" a tree. Larry Jameson had a chainsaw out and was dropping a tree close to a couple of buildings with vehicles near them. He cut a wedge out of one side of the tree so it would fall in the desired direction—away from everybody and everything. But when he made the back cut the tree didn't fall where it was supposed to. Larry watched horrified as it twisted to one side and fell directly on Peeps' Jeep, crushing the cab.

He was aghast and went looking for Peeps. He didn't know how to break the news to him. "Brother, have you given your car to the Lord?" he asked.

"Yes, I have."

"Well," Larry replied, "he just took it!"

Life at Living Waters

The brothers and sisters loved being with each other and had a lot of fun (except maybe Peeps that day), but there was a real spiritual dimension to life at Living Waters.

Jane remembers, "It was very structured. There were meetings in the mornings, and on Monday, Wednesday and Friday nights. These were regular church services with singing, clapping, dancing, prayer, and teaching. Sunday, we would hold church services in the dome or down by the river." Until they got an old school bus, trips to Eureka to attend services at Deliverance Temple or Vets Hall were limited by the lack of vehicles.

After the 7:00 a.m. breakfast and the morning meeting, everyone would begin their stewardships. At 9:00 a.m. a big bronze bell would sound throughout Living Waters. Everyone would drop what they were doing and spend the next hour in prayer and reading the Word.

Kristine van Dooren remembers that, in addition to the regular prayer times, the brethren occasionally fasted and would hold all-night prayer vigils.

Every visitor saw the big cross at the entrance with the welcoming words, "Whosoever Will, May Come" painted on it. Kristine says, "This cross was nothing like the typical 'pretty' crosses that I had seen in church. It looked more like the cross that Jesus actually hung on, which was impressive in itself." For many lost and lonely individuals, that message touched a deep place in their hearts and they knew, "I'm home."

Because it was twenty miles west of Highway 101, Living Waters didn't get the flood of hitchhikers or visitors that the Lighthouse or Carlotta did. The occasional traveler did wander in, but also the overflow from the Eureka area ranches reached the one-time mill town. When Larry and Claudia arrived in the summer of 1972, there were thirty people on the property and by winter, there were a hundred.

A Weird Neighborhood

Larry was once walking along the river—crossing a neighbor's property—when the guy came out of his cabin wearing no clothes and carrying a rifle. Larry assumed he must have been one of the local nudists because, "His whole body was tan." He glared at Larry and ordered him to "Stay off my land!" Larry agreed that would be a good idea and turned around.

Living among the characters who inhabited the country around Whitethorn in the hills of Mendocino and Humboldt Counties put to rest any notions of peace-loving hippies who only sought a deeper communion with Mother Earth. There were reasons they had dropped out of society, and some of them could get violent. They stole chickens, pigs and burned the bus that was used to take everyone to the Sunday church services in Eureka. Once the brethren discovered a guy with a slit throat lying on the ground by the cross. Someone had dumped him there figuring if he were to get any help, the Christians at Living Waters would give it to him. They got him to a doctor who patched him up.

Claudia says, compared to the other ranches, "We lived in a weirder neighborhood." But for the brothers and sisters at Living Waters, none of these were earthshaking or even especially disturbing experiences. This was life on the land, and it was there God put them to learn to be disciples and spread the gospel message.

The brethren weren't shy about sharing what they had discovered. They told the counter-culture types living in the hills and communes around them that they had once lived the same futile lives, but Jesus had shown them what real life was.

Not everyone was welcoming. Peter DePalmo remembered a fellow who rode up on a horse with an unslung

Winchester rifle and threatened to start shooting. Pointing the rifle at Peter, he ordered him and the others to stay away from the people on his neighboring commune. "Stop telling them about Jesus, sin, and God's plan for their salvation!" Peter, whose character and appearance resemble an immovable piece of granite—didn't move. The guy rode off with a warning, "Leave my group alone."

Peter met him again years later. At a Festival of the Son, the father of one of the boys in the DePalmo's youth group came and introduced himself to Peter. It was the same man who threatened him from horseback at Living Waters. He was almost weeping as he thanked Peter for the strong stand he made for the gospel, and as it turned out, for the sake of his salvation.

Whenever there is a Gospel Outreach reunion, it doesn't take long for the one-time Living Waters brethren to find each other. They share a common link to a special place in God's heart that was the result of him moving powerfully in their lives and the character and gift that was Tony Tuck. At Living Waters, they experienced a genuine foretaste of the fellowship we'll all have when we come together again in God's presence.

Tony is already there. He passed away in his home in February of 2012 while standing next to Jane. She says, "When Tony died, he fell down in the kitchen like a falling tree, but his eyes were open. They were sparkly, seeing something so glorious! It reminded me of the first day I met him. They seemed so blue to me. Light coming out of his eyes with great joy—dazzling light. I'm so happy I witnessed that."

CHAPTER NINE

Sabine and the Lord's Land

"The Most Foolish Story You've Ever Heard"

JIM DURKIN LOOKED out at the fifty or sixty people who crowded the pews at the small Albion Chapel, just south of Ft. Bragg, California. They were all Mendocino County types: men with shoulder-length hair and beards, women with long dresses, wearing colorful bead necklaces and bracelets. All dressed in the rough, outdoor, back-to-the-land style that showed it had been some time since society had shaped their fashion and living choices. Elly Snedeker, who with Scott once lived in those same hills said, "Everyone lived a life that was 'out there.' LSD, tarot, brown rice, Jesus, it all meant the same."

Scott was a part of the team that came from the Lighthouse Ranch with Jim to minister. He watched as Jim began his message. "I'm going to tell you the most foolish story you've ever heard. I'm going to tell you about a man named Jesus who died on a cross for your sins."

The room was dead quiet, all eyes fixed on Jim. He told the unadorned story of God sending his Son to take the sin and guilt of every man, woman, and child who ever lived or will live. This was the "fairy tale" that so many of them had ridiculed as they acquired new "wisdom" from their drugs and meditations. He didn't appeal to their reason, he didn't ask them to "give Jesus a chance," and he didn't apologize for the simplicity of God's offer of salvation.

Jim finished. Each person sat in expectation and wondered what was next.

"If anybody here believes this foolishness, I want you to raise your hand."

Scott was amazed at the response. "Every one of those hard-core, mystical, cosmic sinners raised their hands. Every one."

The Holy Spirit was moving in Mendocino.

It seemed as if there were communes on every hilltop and every ridge in Mendocino County, north of San Francisco. On Navarro Ridge, just east of Albion, was a commune called Sabine's Land. Like all the others, it offered a retreat from a world that seemed to have gone crazy. From the beginning, there was a difference.

Most of the area's communes were populated by the youth of the sixties and seventies who because of "philosophical" reasons separated themselves from society. Too young to really know much about real life, theirs was more a "torment of the soul."

By the time Sabine purchased her 140 acres, she had experienced more life and tragedy than any of her neighbors were likely to ever see.

Born in Germany in 1925, she experienced fear, loss, sadness, and death as a young woman during World War II. She saw cities reduced to rubble by American and British bombing raids then experienced the helpless terror of foreign armies marching across German fields and through cities. In one of the last, most devastating, and controversial bombings of the war, the city of Dresden was leveled by waves of Allied bombers. Up to 25,000 people were killed in the bombing and resultant firestorm. Sabine was there and survived it with her younger brother.

When the war ended in 1945, an aunt who lived in the U.S. offered to sponsor Sabine to come to New York, and in 1949, she made the move. There she supported herself with housekeeping jobs during the day and at night studied hospitality management.

With a degree in hand, she secured a job as hostess at a yacht club restaurant in Miami, Florida. Being sociable, intelligent, and a hard worker, Sabine soon rose to the position of manager.

Everything seemed to be working out. The unceasing worries and horrors of the war were now just a memory. Living in America, she avoided the privations a defeated Germany was suffering. Among her customers she counted the Shah of Iran (with whom she danced) and Richard Nixon (with whom she didn't dance). The only thing missing was a well-established, rich husband—and she got that too. In 1953, she married the millionaire Clifford Ball, and later, two sons were added to their family.

Once Sabine had obtained all the ingredients of what seemed a successful life—husband and children, wealth, travel around the world—everything began to fall apart. The marriage drifted into shoal waters as her husband became an alcoholic, then it finally hit the rocks. After ten years, they divorced, and Sabine took her two sons and moved to the West Coast.

As the 1960s developed, she witnessed young people being drawn by the thousands to San Francisco and Haight-Ashbury. She saw them leave the security of a life their parents had built and wander into the depths of an ocean whose bottom they couldn't touch. Drugs and an uninhibited lifestyle left them adrift and lost. Sabine was moved with compassion and looked for a way to help. The back-to-the-land movement was picking up steam, and more and more communes were being planted in the forests and hills north of San Francisco. She bought 140 acres near Albion, south of Fort Bragg, and set up her own commune. She had seen a generation destroyed by world war and wanted to have a place where young people could find shelter and have a chance to restore sanity to their own lives. Her property was called "Sabine's Land."

People who lived on or visited the Land all describe it in terms of wonder: "An enchanted place," "hobbit land," and "mysterious." Much of the acreage was forested, but the top of the ridge was about twenty acres of cleared land where most of the people lived.

Scattered around the hilltop were huge, old-growth redwood stumps. In the early years of logging on the Mendocino coast, loggers cut notches four or five feet above the ground and inserted "spring boards" to stand on. From that height they could make their falling cuts above the thick part at the base of the redwoods. This left tree stumps eight feet in height and as much as fifteen feet in diameter. Over time, ivy and other bushes made their homes on top of the stumps and they began to look like enormous mushrooms (something the hippies thought was "far out!") The enchantment factor shot way up when a thick coast fog would roll in, shrouding the whole area with a mystical, fairy-tale feeling.

Davy and Harriet Bye describe Sabine's Land when they arrived in 1971 before revival hit. "There would be around two hundred people living there in the summertime, most

116

of them camping out. In the winter, that number would fall to one hundred."

Utopia Wasn't Working

Sabine wanted to make it a place where young people could contribute their gifts to the community, learn to live with one another, and get their lives back in order. But, like most other communes, it didn't turn out that way and bickering among the back-to-the-landers broke out. Harriet (who was known as Harmony back then) remembers, "It began falling apart and people could only get along when they were stoned."

It was plain for all to see utopia wasn't working. Everyone felt there had to be real peace and love *somewhere*; they just had to find it. Sabine took off for India because everyone knew those people had the inside track on self-enlightenment.

For others, the peace and love they sought found them. They felt being "spiritual" was a good thing; doing the *I Ching*, reading the *Tibetan Book of the Dead* was good; meditating, having a guru, smoking dope or dropping acid, all fit in with an acceptable search for the truth. While Jesus was okay—everyone knew he was an enlightened teacher—the Christian religion was something those in power used to subdue the masses. It wasn't for deep thinkers or those who really wanted the truth.

In spite of this attitude, the Holy Spirit was already spreading seeds over the hills.

Linda and Jon Bilderbach lived on Sabine's Land. Unlike everyone else—they were believers and Linda held Bible studies in their cabin. Scott and Elly used to visit them, and Linda would pray over Scott and speak in tongues. They freely shared their faith with whoever would listen.

Norman Leverat lived on the Land too. Without attracting attention, he became a Christian. A short time later, Paul Johnson drove up to Eureka and gave Norman a lift. After what seemed to Paul a deep theological discussion where he expounded on his "Christ consciousness" approach to life, Norman did him the favor of shooting it down. "Paul, that's just a bunch of cosmic crap!" A deflated Paul took Norman to his destination, the Lighthouse Ranch, and decided to spend the night there. Paul gave his life to the Lord that evening and the next morning, woke up a new man.

Something was beginning to happen. The hills of Mendocino County, that haven of young misfits, was beginning to experience what was thought impossible—a Holy Spirit revival.

They started getting saved. Tomas Dertner, Jim Buchanan, Jim (the flute) Degolyer, Dave and Pamela Brown, Joel and Nancy Severson, Leroy and Cindy Metzger, Michael and Doreen Goodman, Sara Crystal, and so many more were amazed to find that Jesus and life in him was what they had always been searching for. All of the sudden it made sense. None of the other philosophies or movements ever delivered what they promised. It was all empty talk. Jesus was real and the transforming power of his salvation and the Holy Spirit really did change lives.

Sabine returned from India, no wiser than when she left, except perhaps having learned that India held no answers for her. Together with Harriet Bye, Elly Snedeker and others, she drove up to Eureka to see Katherine Kuhlman, a noted evangelist and "faith-healer" of the 1950s and '60s, who was holding meetings at the Municipal Auditorium.

The men weren't interested, so the women dropped them off and went to the meeting hall. To these hippie women, it had to be a strange experience. Katherine always dressed in long flowing white dresses, wore lots of make-up, and was very flamboyant in her presentation of the gospel and prayer for people. She seemed the stereotype of the society they had rejected.

But this was a revival and God used anyone who was willing. They were all touched by the Holy Spirit and began to feel his tug on their spirits. After sharing about God's love and power to heal both spirit and soul, Katherine invited people up for prayer. Elly went forward and joined the group on the stage. Katherine prayed for one person after another, some of whom fell, "slain in the Spirit." When she got to Elly, a poor little Jewish girl who had never come close to this kind of experience, Katherine asked her, "Honey, you don't really understand what's going on here do you?" A weeping and confused Elly mumbled, "No, I don't." Katherine answered, "Well, I'm just going to pray for you that Jesus will bless you."

When the choir sang "He Touched Me," Harriet was deeply moved—God was beginning to make himself known to her. After the meeting, they rejoined the men who had gathered at a friend's house to smoke some pot. When the women came in and told of the amazing things they experienced, the men laughed and ridiculed them. Harriet says, "For the first time, I felt the presence of evil."

During the meeting, they had noticed a bunch of hippies sitting behind them. They looked like the group from Sabine's Land, but they were praising the Lord and shouting "Hallelujah" as Katherine spoke and prayed. They invited the women to stay at their place that night, instead of making the long drive back down to Mendocino. Their place was the Lighthouse Ranch. Elly got saved that evening. A few days later, Harriet turned her life over to the Lord.

Sabine was unconvinced. She told Harriet, "I've been all over the world and have met godly men." This just didn't look the same; she couldn't understand how it could be so easy.

"Sabine, You're a Sinner!"

Meanwhile, the connection of the new Mendocino believers with the Lighthouse Ranch continued to grow and trips were made north to get teaching and encouragement. Everyone on Sabine's Land knew their commune was coming apart at the seams. Unlike Tony at Gopherville, Sabine held the reins of the Land loosely. Everyone could pretty much do as they wished. The growing group of young believers knew they needed more than an occasional visit. They asked Jim to send down one of his elders to begin to shepherd them and hopefully bring some order to the place. This move was actually endorsed by the non-Christians on the commune too. They realized something had to be done; some sort of leadership was needed.

Jim sent Tommy Kennedy who was accompanied by his wife, Randi and one and a half kids (she was pregnant) and they moved into a small cabin. Tommy set about clearing the land of people who tended to bring more disharmony than unity, including one guy who insisted on working in the garden naked. He left and others joined him when they received compensation for the improvements they had done on their cabins. This included buying a teepee for one Land resident.

Tommy is a gifted teacher and he began giving Bible studies. More and more people attended and started getting saved. He also made occasional visits to Sabine's cabin to share the message of salvation with her.

Sabine was pretty sure she didn't need it. Tommy says, "She thought of herself as a righteous person." She could look around at all the young people who were obviously in need of a spiritual foundation. That wasn't her. She led a good life, had been through a lot, and helped people.

Tommy was getting nowhere with her and each talk left him frustrated. She didn't see how Jesus could be the only way—how could God label all other religions as liars and charlatans? She got angry, "God is intolerant!" Finally, one day he was sitting in her cabin along with a young Christian named Jeremiah when he told her, "You know, Sabine, we're all sinners—you're a sinner. You know that, don't you?"

Tommy remembers, "She was shocked! She looked at me and said, '*You call me a sinner?* Look in my eyes and say that to me again!'" He looked her in the eyes and told her the same thing again. This time, Sabine surrendered. Like so many others, she resisted as long as she could the growing conviction that Jesus really was the way. Yielding to God produced all the changes she had sought in her life and more.

Jim's evangelization continued, and Davy Bye and others got saved. Lambert Hazelaar was there. As Jim spoke, the Holy Spirit's presence was so strong that Lambert, who had first encountered Jesus when he was young, was reduced to tears. "When Jim began talking, I started crying. I had a handkerchief, one of those big red bandanas we used to have. When the meeting was finished, it was so wet I think I just left it on the floor."

After the final meeting, a solid core of believers remained, most of them living on Sabine's Land. For them, everything was dramatically different. They were now alive, full of God's Spirit and changed in ways they had never imagined possible. Sabine renamed her property, the "Lord's Land." It would still have the same goal of rebuilding lives, but now the work would be done by the Spirit of God and the teaching and encouragement of his Word.

Lambert, who as a young boy had given his life to the Lord, rededicated it, and together with Gus and Jenny Acosta, moved up to the Lighthouse Ranch. More new Christians from the Lord's Land followed.

The revival continued. Rense Miller became a Christian at Albion Chapel. Alex Elsaesser had an experience that shows when God is moving, he can use even the most mundane situation to produce amazing results.

Alex and his wife, Renie, were caretakers on a two-thousand-acre ranch in Plumas County, California. They had the ideal set up. They took care of the animals, were left alone and could smoke all the dope they wanted without being bothered. When Renie was back East visiting family, she attended a Billy Graham Crusade and got saved. She returned, and around the same time, other friends of theirs got saved and moved to the Lord's Land. Alex and Renie went to visit, and far as Alex was concerned, heard more of the gospel than he was prepared for. Still, he was moved and prayed. He asked the Lord to show him if he was real. God's response according to Alex? "Nothing."

The next day, they went with the brethren to a small Foursquare church in Casper, near Ft. Bragg. Alex remembers, "I was sitting there when this guy named Herman gets up. His appearance was what you might expect from someone with that name—a Marine haircut, a total redneck. He looked around and said, 'I see some new faces here. Why don't we all stand and greet each other with the song, "Smile Awhile."'" (This was an old ice-breaker song in some churches—very, very corny!)

Alex cynically rolled his eyes as everyone began to sing: "Smile awhile and give your face a rest/lift your hands to the one you love the best/then shake hands with someone new . . ." As the song continued, to Alex's surprise, and with no effort on his part, his hands were suddenly raised in the air.

Before he knew what was happening, he began to be filled with the Holy Spirit. "After that moment, I was changed, and I never smoked cigarettes, took drugs, or swore again. It was a sign from the Lord that he was real."

Quaint, Primitive or a Trial?

"Quaint" was the word some used when describing the Lord's Land, while others called it "primitive." That left a third group who called it a "trial."

Most of the houses on the Land had no electricity and only some had cold running water. Everyone decided that a good water pump with a pond next to it would solve a couple of problems. The pump could fill the pond—which they would then stock with fish—and supply water to the rest of the cabins. They got busy digging. A lot of sweat and many shovelfuls later, they had a respectably-sized pond that could hold a good school of fish. Then they sank a pump into the ground. Nothing. The well was dry; no water. It was then they understood the principle of getting a well working before digging a huge hole for a pond.

Bathroom facilities were old-fashioned outhouses parked over holes next to the houses. They all had wood stoves for heat—with a pile of firewood, a chopping block, and an ax next to the door. Bathing was done up in the sauna.

All the Gospel Outreach ranches were blessed by older Christians who welcomed the work of God in the lost youth they saw wandering around. The Lord's Land had Brother Webb, a Foursquare pastor who ministered at the Casper church where the brethren often attended Sunday services. He contributed two clothes washers and dryers to the new saints.

Laurie Eaton's experience was typical. "I had just gotten married in San Clemente and a week later we arrived in what was to me, a foreign land. Kaja (our daughter) was almost two years old and struggling to adjust. I was miserable and wanted to go home. I had been a full time waitress and part-time college student with my own apartment. We moved into the A-frame house after two weeks of sleeping on Cindy and Leroy Metzger's living room floor. It was the rainiest season Mendocino County had experienced in ten years. I chopped wood every day just to keep our tiny little home warm. Each chilly and rainy morning Kaja and I would trudge up to the Big House in our rubber boots, through the muddy roads."

Craftsmen with Imagination

The tall redwoods, rugged hills, and the enormous mushroom-shaped tree stumps inspired the hippie craftsmen who combined the beauty of the outdoors with uninhibited imagination. Windows supplied unending palettes for these artisans. Stained glass panels were created with intricate and unusual patterns that no Catholic or Episcopalian church would recognize, but were colorful and beautiful in their own way. Some houses had what could only be described as a crazy patchwork of windows with: different shapes, sizes, and spacing on each side. The homeowners wanted to be able to see the night sky too, so it was a common practice to put windows in the roof. Builders took what they saw in their minds then translated them into glass, lead, and wood creations. Workshops, playhouses, and outhouses all became works of art while still serving the needs for which they were created.

Redwood was the most available building material and it was used for everything. Walls, doors, roofs, fence rails, furniture, carvings, and even totem poles were crafted out of the beautiful wood. In the absence of electricity, kerosene or Coleman lanterns supplied lighting and cooking was done over old wood-fired kitchen ranges.

The diet was as primitive as the accommodations. Laurie says, "I was assigned to cook with the very limited ingredients of flour, salt, and baking soda. Thumbing through *The Joy of Cooking* (a wedding gift), I came upon a recipe for crackers. I never was a good cook but this was something I could try out, hopefully without burning it. As I rolled out the gooey dough someone suggested I add sweet chopped onions, sesame seeds, and fresh pressed garlic. I popped the dough into the oven and to my great surprise they came out delicious, chewy, and edible. They were a great success! I was relieved. From that point on I was asked to bake crackers every time I went to the Big House . . . something I have yet to repeat forty-one years later! I eventually made many precious friends and adjusted for the short three months we were there!"

Chris Funnell remembers, "One of my first memories was walking into the Big House, and on the table was some road kill—a deer. There were flies everywhere, and I got really grossed out and thought, 'Eeew! We're going to eat this?' Little did I know that was a delicacy! Real meat! Give me a month, and I wouldn't have any problem with that. We didn't get much meat on the Land."

All the women got stewardship assignments—making sprouts, making yogurt, cooking the meals, and watching over the little kids while the Moms went about their chores. The men mostly tended the garden that supplied vegetables, had jobs locally, or planted trees with the Gospel Outreach crews.

The Land, whether quaint or a trial, left an impression on everyone who lived there, and so did Sabine. Becoming a Christian finally freed her to work together with the Holy Spirit in spreading God's love and grace to everyone she met.

Everyone agrees with Chris who says, "She was a people person, a mother type."

When Chris first arrived at the Land to visit her friend Janet Anastasia Mason, Sabine invited her to her cottage for coffee. "She made me a cup of strong, good tasting coffee, and we all sat around on the floor because she didn't have a table. I was enchanted by her little cottage and the hobbit-like environment. She really focused on me and found out if I knew the Lord. She told me that God had to be in my life, and it was no accident that He brought me here." Sabine smiled as she spoke, and Chris says, "She was beaming all this love and told me a little about herself and her background. She never put pressure on someone but spoke very directly, honestly, and sincerely."

Rense Miller remembers hitchhiking together with Peter Morgan before they became Christians. Rense was AWOL from the Air Force and they were carrying some "illegal substance" with them to celebrate Rense's birthday. While trying to catch a ride in Fort Bragg, a highway patrolman stopped to check them out. Before he could ask more than a couple of questions, a small, yellow station wagon pulled up behind them. It was Sabine. She told the patrolman, "Officer, these boys are my friends, and I was going to give them a ride home." Rense completes the story, "Needless to say, my first experience with this wonderful woman was very special and life changing."

Of course, Sabine had never met the two before, but with the extraordinary heart God gave her, she saw two lost young men who needed the Lord. A short time later both Rense and Peter got saved.

Alex said she, "personified the love of God. She showed God's love to everyone."

Closing it Down

Sabine's Land, reborn as the Lord's Land, saw many lives pulled from the pits of sin and death—but not much could be done for the land itself. It was much more primitive than quaint and couldn't sustain a healthy community. In 1974, Bob Means was sent from Eureka to be the director. Seeing the inadequacy of it all, he determined to shut it down. He was "encouraged" by Mary Miller's mom who, appalled at the unhealthy living conditions, threatened to call the county health department. According to Rense, Bob's response was, "Yes! Please help us get out!"

Living on the Lord's Land with the brothers and sisters and learning together the ways of their new life was a precious experience for those God saved. When the decision was made to close it down, it seemed as if the Lord and the Land collaborated to give the brethren one last gift.

There was a pottery business that helped to support the ranch and finished wares were sold in San Francisco and Los Angeles. Alex remembers when it was decided to stop using the Land for Gospel Outreach, the business was to be packed up and sent to Eureka, where it would continue as Maranatha Pottery. Before they closed the doors for a final time, they had one last firing of pots. The fire got out of hand and the entire building burned down. To the controlled fire in the kiln, was added the heat from the wooden structure being turned to cinders. A few hours later, everything had cooled down to the point where they could pull the remaining pots out of the kiln. They were amazed to find the most beautiful pottery they had ever made.

Jim Durkin, mid-1970s. No one could share vision like Jim Durkin.
(Photo courtesy of Radiance.)

Jim and Dacie Durkin (Radiance).

Deliverance Temple. A prayer warrior saw a vision of Deliverance Temple "overflowing with young people who were all saved and filled with the joy of the Lord" (Radiance).

The Lighthouse Ranch (Courtesy of Chuck Coleman).

(Chuck Coleman)

Some of the G. O. family after a Sunday service at
Vet's Hall, 1975 (Chuck Coleman).

David Leon (photo courtesy of Gary Todoroff).

The Donut Brothers walked the neighborhoods of Eureka and Arcata, selling their wares and sharing the gospel (Radiance).

Our Father's Car Wash (Radiance).

Lighthouse Ranch Tri-City crew getting
ready to board Zion (Gary Todoroff).

The saints at Carlotta (Unknown).

Living Waters brothers and sisters (Gary Todoroff).

Tony Tuck (Gary Todoroff).

Lynn Jankowiak and Jane Tuck with children (Gary Todoroff).

Jackie DePalmo and Pam Lagielski on kitchen
duty at the Lighthouse Ranch (Gary Todoroff).

Elder's conferences were held yearly in Santa Cruz (Radiance).

Sabine and her cabin on the Lord's Land, Mendocino (Gary Todoroff).

Sabine and Jane Tuck (Gary Todoroff).

Tree planters praying before the start of work (Radiance).

Lawrence Taylor planting trees at the edge
of a snowfield (Radiance).

The Germany Team's last job. "We took a picture, threw our boots away
and packed for Germany" (Photo courtesy of Greg Hogue).

Alex and Renie Elsaesser (l), Harry and Sandy Hewet (r) (Radiance).

Left to right, Nancy Fulson, John Jacqua, Jim Wall and
Ron Juncal at the L.A. Invasion, 1974 (Radiance).

Hitchhiking took us all across the country. All you needed was patience and a thumb (Chuck Coleman).

The team to France. Mark and Mary Richards, Jim and Diane Boutcher (photo courtesy of Diane Boutcher).

CHAPTER TEN

Go Into All the World . . . and Work!

A S THE LOCAL Gospel Outreach groups at the Lighthouse, Carlotta, the Lord's Land, Living Waters, and in Eureka began to grow, a decision had to be made how they were going to be financially supported. Humboldt County in northern California was always a poor logging and fishing area. It was claimed that when the Great Depression hit, no one noticed.

As the Holy Spirit swept through the land, the ranches were flooded with hundreds of new, young and mostly unskilled converts. While the need was obvious, the solution wasn't, at least to many of the new converts. When the subject of work came up, young theologians quoted Scripture: "We're saved by grace, brother, not works." Pastor Jim Durkin had to spend some time teaching that work was God's plan for providing for the saints and everyone else. The verse "If anyone will not work, neither shall he eat" helped to put an end to most arguments. Jim also said we had to get off welfare. "You can't live on welfare, and more importantly, you can't give when you're on welfare."

In Eureka, a few different moneymaking ideas were tried, all with two goals. The first—to make income to cover food, gas, vehicle, medical, housing costs, and so on. The second was to spread the gospel with the people we came in contact with. An added benefit soon became apparent. The self-discipline, experience, and faith required to operate the businesses were the same qualities needed when we took teams to the far corners of the earth.

According to Frank Lagielski who oversaw many of the early businesses, they were more successful at spreading the gospel than making money. One of the first ideas was a home remodeling business that kept Steve Schrater, Frank, and Bernie Heraldson busy. That was dropped after it was discovered that the remodelers damaged as much as they fixed. They learned this when a customer's kitchen, full of solvent fumes from a newly applied counter surface, blew up.

One house-painting project turned into a gospel advertisement for the unsuspecting homeowner and neighborhood. While waiting for the off-white exterior house paint to arrive, one of the brothers used a dark blue color to paint a gospel message on the side of the house. "Jesus Loves You!" was spelled out in bold, exuberant letters. It would only be there a few hours and the real color would cover it up. The ordered paint arrived, the job was finished, and the painters/evangelists returned to the Ranch, having done that day's duty to fulfill the Great Commission.

The next day, slowly, a faint image in blue began to appear on the side of the house facing the street. Jesus loved everyone—the neighbors, pedestrians, people driving by, and especially the homeowner! The homeowner called the Lighthouse crew back to remove it. They tried painting over it a couple more times, but the message that had stood the test of centuries, wasn't going to be that easy to get rid of.

They finally had to sand all the coats of paint off and repaint the side of the house.

That effort was followed by Maranatha Pottery, Ephrata Leather Works, Our Father's Car Wash, and the Donut Shop.

The Donut Shop was a storefront bakery located at 426 B Street in Eureka. But what made it different than any other bakery in Eureka, or probably the entire West Coast, were the "Donut Brothers." Charles Chambers was the first, followed by Chris Prichard, Michael Dalton, Larry Thomas, Dick Fulsom, Justin Perlstein, Chris Herz, Doug Henshaw, Robbie McKee, Roger Dusatko, Roger Reinhart, Howard Bowers, and Mike Doyle. Dressed in clean white shirts and slacks, they pushed around white wooden carts with big crosses on the sides, full of donuts, bread, and other pastries. The Donut Brothers crisscrossed Eureka and nearby towns and areas, selling their products to homes and businesses. Whenever the opportunity presented itself, they shared the gospel and prayed for customers' needs.

Once, Chris Prichard dropped Michael Dalton and his cart off at the top of a street and was supposed to pick him up again at the bottom. When he arrived, Michael was nowhere to be seen. Chris waited a few minutes and when he still didn't show up, parked the van and went looking for the Donut Brother. He saw his cart on the sidewalk in front of a house and walked up the porch to find the front door open. Michael was inside praying for the customer. He had rung the doorbell, offered his donuts, and ended up in a conversation with the lady of the house. She revealed she was suffering so much from rheumatism that she couldn't lift her arms above her waist. Even prayer was no help.

Michael asked, "Have you prayed in the name of Jesus?" She answered, "No."

Michael began to pray for her—in the name of Jesus—and when Chris came in, she was crying for joy. The pain had left and her arms were raised above her head!

The brothers at Carlotta were kept busy at the grape stake mill called "Split Stuff." There, 2 x 4s were cut into 2 x 2 boards, sharpened, and sold to grape vineyards near Ukiah.

The *Tri-City Advertiser* was a moneymaker that employed brethren in sales, set-up, and distribution. Since no one had ever published any kind of newspaper before, it was a case of "learn as you go." Starting in August of 1971, it had a circulation of 15,000 in Humboldt County with a staff of five. By November of that year, the circulation had grown to 23,500 with a staff of eleven.

While delivery of the *Tri-City* was free, the advertising wasn't. Actually, compared to today's prices, it was almost free. The November 10, 1971 issue informed would-be advertisers that an ad required a one dollar deposit (refundable if the item didn't sell within a month) and a *voluntary* payment of between two to seven dollars if the item did sell. By scanning the personal ad section, readers could find a 1969 Malibu Super Sport (sorry, automatic) in excellent condition for only $1995. Bill had a 66 Dodge Sports Van with camper—phone number provided but no price. You could find most of what you needed or thought you needed: puppies, kittens, boats, luggage, music instruments, and so on.

Business advertising brought in most of the money. Local businesses like Bucksport Sporting Goods and Campton Heights Market shared advertising space with G. O. businesses like the Donut Shop ("Warm, fresh donuts delivered to your home, office, meeting place—$.95 picked up; $1 delivered"), or Ephratha Leather Works run by Peter DePalmo on Fifth Street.

Our Father's Car Wash advertised too, and thought that a little honest, personal testimony would help bring in the customers. Wearing a yellow rain slicker and hat, soaping up the back window of a Cadillac, Peter is pictured telling us: "About one month ago, the Lord impressed upon our hearts to become more involved in . . . Our Father's Car Wash. The reason why he has me working at the car wash is not completely known to me, but it is becoming more and more evident every day. To be a servant of the Lord Jesus."

Well, what can you say? I would let him wash my car.

There was plenty of space for Bible verses and religious or general interest articles. Lon Mabon, the first Ranch coordinator, wrote about "Putting on Christ." Dave Sczepanski grabbed readers with "Interesting Things about Humboldt County." Bob Gormin told about Ulysses S. Grant's lonely sojourn in cold, damp Eureka.

Every Tuesday, teams of people would come into Eureka from the Lighthouse, Carlotta and Living Waters to pick up stacks of the free weekly. Wearing newspaper bags full of the *Tri-City*, we would walk the streets of Eureka, Arcata, McKinleyville, Fortuna, Ferndale, and the areas between, flipping papers on porches while avoiding dogs, especially in McKinleyville. (The men were better at this than the women—they just wanted it to be over with!)

Alaska had a ServiceMaster franchise and got its own Donut Shop when Frank Loosli and the brothers took a disassembled bakery oven and reassembled it without the benefit of instructions.

Vinyl and leather repair began when Jim Durkin read an article about it in a magazine and then saw someone doing it in the local Denny's. He had Peter Steimle get training in Eureka, and Peter trained others. The cost of equipment and supplies was not great, and the brothers who did it only had to supply initiative and hard work. This they did. Wherever G. O. teams took the business, it did well and helped cover their financial needs. Almost all of the vinyl and leather businesses were named "New Life" (for vinyl and leather furniture . . . and for people too). Both Chicago and New York grew large businesses employed from ten to fifteen brothers (that's big in the world of vinyl repair).

Driven by the research and encouragement of the businesses in Chicago and New York (George Leys and Gary Crouthamel and others) these businesses proved to be tools of the gospel. They provided income, a training platform for young converts, and time flexibility so the work of the ministry could be done. In addition, the business concept opened up doors of ministry, including residence visas and work permits, for team members in Germany and France. The business in Germany produced new businesses and opportunities for Christians in several other countries.

Living Waters came up with something that appealed to those who, as hippies, had sought deeper communion with nature. It was called "tree planting." Making Living Waters work financially was even more of a challenge than for Eureka or the Humboldt County ranches. It was near the town of Garberville, which was the center of . . . nothing. (Now it's the center of pot growing on the North Coast.) So one of the members there, Jim Lane, reached back on his experience and proposed they get a contract planting trees for one of the lumber companies. He had done it before. He warned them, "It will be the hardest work you have ever done, but the pay is good."

He knew what was needed and soon, a team with equipment was headed for the mountain forests and the first job. Jim had schooled the brothers on the finer points of finding good ground for the two-year-old seedlings, proper spacing, how to swing the hoe-dads, no J-roots, and how to do it fast. If you didn't work fast, you wouldn't make money, and you might lose the contract. So, off they went to the races.

After a morning of work, they stopped for lunch. No one spoke; they were exhausted and something had become obvious. There was more to tree planting than just putting trees in the ground and making money. They worked on steep mountain slopes carrying thirty-pound tree bags. The ground was covered with logging debris and rocks, and, as Jim had promised, the work was extremely hard. After the first five minutes, as previously unknown and unused muscles checked into brain central to signal "overload," they were ready to quit.

The brothers discovered they were going to have to develop new resources of strength to do the job. They found those through worship, the encouragement of the Word and Spirit, and each other. They saw that tree planting would be a school that taught them how to deny their flesh and walk in the Spirit in spite of obstacles or weakness. Soon, teams were heading up to the slopes from all the ranches and no one had issues with the concept of "work" anymore, at least not for long. It can probably be said that part of the strength of commitment and identity as disciples in G. O. can be traced to the tree-planting experience.

Church Planting Teams

Jim Durkin never wanted to build a "mega-church" in Eureka. His vision was to "preach the gospel to the ends of the earth," and he continually ministered that to us. As a result, church planting teams were formed and sent out. Starting with Coquille, Oregon, teams were sent to Alaska, Los Angeles, New York, and all over the U.S., then to Germany, Guatemala, and other countries. The businesses we took with us enabled us to do what we considered our real job: sharing the gospel.

In 1981, after I received training from the G. O. leather-repair businesses in Chicago and New York, I took my new leather repair knowledge with me back to Munich, Germany. After a couple of months in the business, I was lying in bed one night when a vision began to form in my mind. It seemed to take on a life of its own and grew until I saw a picture of how the Lord wanted to use this skill in Europe. He showed me it would become the largest of its kind in Germany, open up doors of ministry to Eastern Europe and be a tool of the gospel. Within a year, we began expanding in Germany, trained Christians in Communist Yugoslavia, and brethren in the G. O. church in Florence.

The France team couldn't enter the country as missionaries, but could as businessmen. We were there to supply the products when they set up their own leather-repair business. I also trained members of a Swedish church in preparation for a church plant in Vienna, Austria.

Glass Flowers

The G. O. church in Munich looked for a business that could employ the marginally skilled and still earn money to support outreach to the community. Wendy V. had joined the church after traveling with Scott and Elly Snedeker. With Elly, she had begun collecting flowers, drying and pressing them, then putting them between glass plates framed with lead. Wendy had the needed supplies with her to do this.

She showed Thomas van Dooren, the head elder, and he thought it was a great idea.

And so, The Glass Flower—"Die Glasblume" in German—was born. It became many things to the church in Munich and was perhaps representative of many of the G. O. businesses. It accomplished several goals: income for the communal houses, training for young Christian converts, and friendship and fellowship for everyone. I worked for a time in the business before returning to the U.S. (when I got my leather repair training).

First, the flowers had to be collected from one of two sources. The flower wholesale market was a reliable supplier of the large, garden-style flowers that provided the frame for smaller flowers. I would usually arrive at the big hall full of tables and boxes of flowers and plants at 7:00 a.m. By that time, the farmers and store owners were already done with their business and were enjoying a typical Bavarian breakfast of white sausage, fresh rolls with jam, and wheat beer (*Weisswurst* and *Weissbier*). In Bavaria, there is no such thing as "too early" for a *Bier* and, as they say, "The *Wasser* will kill you."

We collected the smaller flowers from the foothills of the Alps. A group of us would pack lunches and our flower presses, load up our VW bus or maybe our little, two-cylinder Citroen cars—affectionately called "ducks" because they were so ugly, they were cute—and head south to the mountains. There we would find a flower-covered hillside and get to work plucking the brightly colored yellow, blue, red, white, or purple flowers. On the way home we would stop for cake and coffee at some village café overlooking a beautiful alpine valley. Tough work, but somebody had to do it.

We had to find the kind of customers who would want to buy the Glasblume and saw there were two possibilities—gift shops and flower shops. The very first trade show where we tried to sell our Glasblume was the Florist's Show in Nurnberg, a two-day weekend affair. Peter van der Gugten and I loaded up boxes with a few hundred pieces and made the drive north from Munich. We arrived early on Saturday, found the space we had been assigned and hung our Glasblume on the walls of our booth. That day there were a lot of visitors to our stand, but we only sold seven pieces. We were crushed. It looked like the trip was a waste and trade shows weren't going to work for us.

The next day we sold every piece. We didn't have time for lunch as a steady stream of store owners came by and snapped up Glasblume by the box full. The day before, everyone had seen them, talked about them, and finished up their trade show by buying them. We were stunned and grateful.

Before the Work Began

Usually, a workday started with prayer, worship, encouragement, and exhortation. We understood that God intended that we "be transformed by the renewing of our minds." Rather than receiving an intellectual understanding of the Bible in a school setting, much of our understanding came from taking the Scripture we learned and applying it to every part of our lives. We knew that every situation was a God-ordained opportunity to change how we saw ourselves and our circumstances. We weren't supposed to react to life the way we had before we got saved. His plan was to change us into his image because he had a job for us to do in this world. Only people changed through obedience and surrender to the Word and the Spirit could do this job effectively. It wasn't easy and wasn't always fun. But the experience of shared commitment, trials, and love for one another produced a group of people who had a good understanding of what God was doing in their lives and in the world. It is a remarkable testimony to our Father's desire that the brothers and sisters of Gospel Outreach will always have a special place in their hearts for one another.

For the first several teams of G. O.ers who went "into all the world," work often meant a communal work project that included creating finances, and just as importantly, creating disciples of those who labored in them. We had learned through our experiences delivering *Tri-City*, pushing donut carts, creating pottery, picking apples, making grape stakes, creating Glasblume, or planting trees, that when the truths and principles of the Word of God were applied to a work situation, lives were changed. Young (and old) converts became disciples who were ready to take the gospel "into all the world."

CHAPTER ELEVEN

Tree Planting

MY FINGERS WERE freezing, my toes were freezing, and my tree bag full of two-year old Douglas fir seedlings was leaking cold water down my pant legs. We were planting trees on a mile-high butte in Colorado and it looked like we could touch the snow-heavy clouds that seemed close enough to smother us. At lunch, sitting in our truck, we had the usual debate about wearing rain gear. You could wear it and get wet from sweat, or not wear it and get rained or snowed on. We didn't take it. John Jordan was my barometer—he was so thin that he picked up the slightest change in the weather.

We would smack our hoe-dads in the ground, open up the hole, flip the roots into the bottom of the hole and, with the same step, stomp on the ground next to the tree and launch ourselves ten feet to the next spot.

A few snowflakes drifted down around us and John started to get cold. Then more. We decided to reverse direction and start planting back toward the truck to get our rain gear. Pretty soon, it was snowing. Then just like that, a full-scale blizzard was blowing the white stuff in our faces, and we couldn't see ten feet in front of us.

We abandoned planting and ran laughing past the other brothers on the team. Fifteen feet from our crew cab pickup, we tossed our hoe-dads and tree bags in the air toward the truck bed. They landed at the same moment we tore open the doors and piled in. We were followed by the sound of other tree bags and hoe-dads banging in the back and doors being opened as the others fled the storm. We couldn't stop laughing at the sudden, dramatic weather change.

We were the remainder of the Germany team, finishing our last planting job and getting ready to leave the U.S. for Germany. We earned the money for the move by planting trees.

Sometimes I liked planting, many times I didn't. But nothing could replace being with the brothers and sisters out there, or the work that God did in my life through it all. I was right where the Lord wanted me to be.

The G. O. tree planters worked all over the Northwest—Northern California, Oregon, Washington, Idaho, and even Colorado. The money we earned went toward financing teams, supplying the needs of the ranches where we lived, and helping make the teaching and training possible. Larry Jamison took over the management of the tree planting business, named Living Waters Restoration after the death of Jim Lane. He bid on the jobs, organized the crews and the resources that kept us out on the slopes. Later, Kim van den Plas was made manager.

In the beginning the equipment was primitive. Our first jobs used surplus army tents and we drove whatever vehicles we could find. When a sudden snow blizzard forced us to pull out of the first Roseburg, Oregon job, the only vehicle that could get through the drifts and break trail for the pickups was a '63 Ford Fairlane. As the money started coming in, we upgraded to four-wheel-drive Dodge Crew Cabs. These could seat seven people up front and hold all our equipment in the back. The four-wheel drive feature didn't keep us out of trouble. We found it only meant that when your pickup got stuck somewhere, you were further away from help. The only piece of equipment that didn't change was the hoe-dad.

Our accommodations consisted of whatever was cheap and handy. The work was usually up in the mountain forests, far from civilization, so we often set up camp near a stream that was close to where we were planting.

The army tents didn't last long. They were huge, difficult to secure properly, and would blow down with the first big wind. They were also hard to heat. Everyone was expected to bring his own sleeping bag or blankets and air mattress. In Roseburg, my mattress was a seven-foot piece of tree bark in which I laid out my sleeping bag. Fit like a glove.

Then we got small, white canvas tents that two or three people could share, more or less comfortably. The tents had a hole in the roof for a stovepipe and were warmed with tin stoves that, as long as the wood was dry, heated quickly. If the wood was wet then the effort expended at keeping the fire going would warm you more than the cold stove. At night, we'd load them with wood, turn down the damper and flue, and curl up nice and cozy on our cots in our bags. The next morning we froze. There was always a debate as to whether one of us should get up, quickly start the fire, then jump back into the sack and wait for the tent to get warm. The alternative was to grit our teeth, jump out of bed, pull on our ice-cold clothes and boots as fast as we could and race to the kitchen tent, which the sisters had already heated up. Most tents had holes in the roofs from sparks flying out of the stovepipes. Some brothers would build a roaring fire that turned the stove and stove pipes cherry red.

Then a bunch of sparks would fly out and occasionally a tent would burn down.

Out in the woods or in the mountains, bathroom facilities were non-existent. If we were in or near a campground, we could use theirs; otherwise, we had to create our own. In eastern Oregon, planting in the Umatilla National Forest, we were a long way from everything. The only bathing opportunity was a freezing mountain stream. At the beginning of the job, a brave soul could take a couple of quick ten-second dips to soap up and rinse off. By the end of the job we were tougher. We could last twenty seconds.

A couple of teams found abandoned fire hoses and fifty-five gallon drums. They rigged these up to make camp showers that mostly worked well. The hose would be connected to a water source uphill or upstream, with the remaining length rolled down to a drum where it would be coiled inside. The rest of the hose that didn't fit in the drum was led to a shower stall where a nozzle was set up, maybe made out of an empty coffee can. The drum itself was filled with water and a fire was built under it. The hot water in the drum heated the water flowing through the coiled hose, which supplied warm water to the shower. It never got too hot because the water moved through the drum too quickly. But it was better than a freezing mountain stream.

If we were near civilization, we occasionally found more substantial lodging in motels—not very often—too expensive—and churches. In Cottage Grove, Oregon, a rented house served several teams for a few months. We were still freezing and working hard on the slopes, but coming back to a house was almost luxury.

The food reflected the tight budget. We ate a lot of carbohydrates from pasta, rice, beans and bread, but the meals were a little skimpy on the protein. John Jordan remembers this changed when the Germany team was planting and invited a tree inspector to dinner. He was horrified at our diet and made his view known. "When men are working as hard as these guys are, they need protein!" Our fare improved.

The work wasn't limited to planting trees. We also sprayed deer repellant on newly planted seedlings. Deer liked to eat the soft tops of the young trees, and the repellant was smelly and offensive to them—and us. Steve Tipton remembers climbing trees to harvest pinecones. We also thinned miles of young forests and helped fight a forest fire in Idaho.

Sisters on the Team

None of this could have happened without the sacrificial, hard work of the sisters who served us. Most of our jobs were done in the short days of winter. The sisters would have to wake early in the morning, anytime between 2:30 to 5:00, depending on the job. They started the fires to begin making breakfast and to heat up the kitchen tent and themselves. It was dark and cold, and not uncommon to hear cougars or coyotes in the woods. More than one team had to reckon with the presence of bears in the neighborhood.

Their duties included driving down the mountainsides on logging roads to shop and do laundry in town, making the breakfasts and dinners, and preparing lunches for us. They prayed for us too. The women's presence was an important addition to the experience. Planting and thinning trees was hard physically, and surprisingly, mentally also. We had to deal with negative, complaining thoughts, and learn to focus on the positive. The sisters were always a source of joy and encouragement that helped us to deal with the challenges. At the time we looked at them simply as co-workers who endured the hardships like we did. Now we look back, and see them as special women who did something many would have avoided at all costs.

The always-uncertain finances of the ranches benefited much from the scores of brethren sent out to plant trees. This income meant that food improved, repairs could be made, and leaders who traveled around ministering to the scattered churches could be supported.

Jim was a little concerned that the tree planters might be spending too much time out on the mountain slopes and not getting the Bible teaching that was part of preparing us to take the gospel to the world. So he started a tree planter's school, which was organized by Leroy Nidiver. In theory, we were supposed to spend one month planting, then one month back in Eureka. Classes were held in Deliverance Temple with teaching from Leroy, Tony Tuck, Jim, and others. This worked for a while, but with brethren being sent out to different cities and countries, no one remembers it lasting for more than three or four months.

No matter what the living arrangements were, once we got out on the slopes we left comfort behind, and it was best not to think about it. I remember one job when on two separate mornings as I slept, I was having a pleasant dream that I stopped and reminded myself (while still asleep) that I would soon have to wake up. I needed to prepare my soul for the cold and hardships of planting.

We worked when the weather suited the two-year-old Douglas fir seedlings. That meant the cold and damp seasons starting in the fall, through winter, and lasting until spring. And of course, our work was right out on the mountain slopes. There, the planter climbed over rocks, tree stumps and branches, past the occasional rattlesnake or bear as he lugged a leaky thirty-pound bag of wet tree seedlings up or down a steep hillside. All that would be challenge enough, but the reason we were there was to put trees in the ground—at least 800 in a day if we wanted to call ourselves average planters. Some, who occupy the pantheon of tree-planting super-heroes, did a lot more. John Jordan reports that he once planted around 2,700 on flat, plowed ground; Larry Jamison's best day was about 1,800.

The operation consisted of swinging a heavy, duck-bill-shaped "hoe-dad" over your head and into the ground as hard as you could, sinking the blade all the way up to the wooden handle. Then you rocked it back and forth, creating a void space in the ground. Next, you pulled backwards on the hoe-dad to open up the hole. Now you could take one of the seedlings and flip the roots down into the hole, remove the hoe-dad and stomp on the side of the hole to close it all up. Takes just seconds—unless there was a root or rock shelf hidden two inches under the topsoil. After you connected with one of those, your hoe-dad and the hands, arms, teeth and body connected to it, would vibrate like a guitar string.

The first fifteen minutes of the day my body would protest like crazy at the punishment I was inflicting on it. Then, it seemed as if I passed through a barrier, and my body surrendered. After that, it was easier, though still not easy. Add to that rain, snow, wind, steep slopes, the guy in front who always took the "gravy" ground (flat, no rocks or roots, dirt softened by logging vehicles) and you get a bit of an idea of what it was like.

Of course, the trials didn't stop there. There was the ever-present danger of committing the worst of all tree-planting sins—planting a "J-root." This happened when the seedling's roots curled up like the letter J in the hole you made with your hoe-dad, instead of pointing straight down towards the bottom. Then the poor tree would die.

After a few days of this kind of work, the mountains had lost their beauty and will power was what got us through. Willpower—and sometimes a little fun, too.

"Zare iz no izcape!"

Once, several different teams were planting together near Cottage Grove, Oregon. The Chicago team (most of them new to the planting brotherhood) was there too, experiencing for the first time the demands on body and soul that planting exacted. The job was typical for tree planting—all the usual trials and tribulations on a cold winter's day.

Our vehicles were pulled off to the side of a logging road as we waited for instructions about our next unit. The whole area had been logged so both sides of the road looked like a battlefield with deep holes, mounds of dirt, and tree stumps thrown up everywhere.

I was wearing a long, army trench coat and standing next to a truck full of Chicago team rookies, talking to them about the hardships of planting. Greg Krumwiede, a good friend and veteran tree planter, was on the Chicago team too, providing experience and help for the newbies. Greg began to walk away from the trucks to answer the call of nature in some trees on the far side of "the battlefield." In mock seriousness, I yelled out to him, "Get back here! You can't quit!"

Greg turned and looked at me and screamed, "I can't take it anymore! I can't take it!" and began to run away over the hills and craters.

I pulled a hoe-dad from the back of the pickup, aimed it at Greg, and using my best twelve-year-old's imitation of a machine gun, shot him. He gave a cry, threw up his arms and disappeared from sight. I turned to the Chicago guys who—at least a couple of them—watched this whole spontaneous performance with a little concern on their faces. In a German accent, I sternly warned them, "Zare iz no izcape!"

To everyone's relief, especially, of course, his own, Greg reappeared. "Zare iz no izcape" became a byword for the Chicago team when things got tough.

"Brother, I Apologize"

Depending on who we worked for—Weyerhaeuser, Scott, Georgia-Pacific, the Forest Service, or whomever, there was always a tree inspector following the path of our planted trees. Wearing warm clothing and carrying a big, green steel thermos full of coffee or hot chocolate, he was (compared to us) never cold or uncomfortable and always seemed able to find every J-root or missed spacing between trees. The crew would get docked for these and if too many occurred, we might even lose the contract.

Which is why each team needed a manager. The manager's job was to make sure we weren't planting J-roots and had the right spacing. He got us our food and water for break times, brought us more trees when we needed them, and made sure we stayed focused on putting trees in the ground instead of getting distracted by deer, rattlesnakes, or whatever. His job wasn't easy. I and the other planters only had to plant trees, but the manager had to make sure the whole thing worked. It could get stressful.

The Germany team was planting for Weyerhaeuser up near Coos Bay, Oregon. The tree planting office sent us a manager who wasn't on the team, but was there to help out.

The different managers had their own ways of dealing with the stress of the job. When something would go wrong—as sometimes happened—our manager would first attempt the reasoned, problem-solving approach. When that didn't work, he would get mad and start yelling. That got everyone's attention, but it didn't work either. It didn't make his job easier when we would do stupid things—like planting on the wrong side of our job's boundary, spending a half hour planting trees on *someone else's property*, for which we would get no pay.

So you could say that there was a little tension between us and our manager. No hard feelings, but a little tension.

One day we were planting on a unit near the ocean. The yellow guide ribbon led us down into a bowl of about four or five acres, which was surrounded by twenty-foot high ledges. We were all down in this bowl when a thick coastal fog rolled in, and we couldn't see more than ten feet in front of us. The tension between team and manager that day was about as thick as the fog. When he yelled at us from the ledge above the bowl, no one answered at first. *More trouble?*

He yelled again, louder this time, "Hey! You guys!"

We were only about fifty feet from him, and his voice came through the fog crystal clear.

Just then I had an inspiration. I knew that fog distorts noise and voices over a distance so I answered back in an indistinct voice that sounded as if I were far away. "Whaa?"

Our manager replied with a tree-planting command, telling us to reverse direction and plant back toward him, "Kick it in the rear!"

I called out—as if from a mile away, "Whaa?"

"I said, 'Kick it in the rear!'"

Me, "Whaga da koo?"

"What?"

Me, "Whaa?" I thought I could see a faint red glow from where he was. He was getting mad.

He repeated, "I said, 'kick it in the rear!'"

By then we had stopped planting and were gathered together, just looking at each other. We started to lose it, but tried hard not to laugh out loud because we knew that we would be dead.

A couple other guys jumped in, "Tada wa wah?" and this went on for a few more minutes.

Now I knew there was a red glow on the horizon, and just before the volcano exploded, one of us called out in a barely distinguishable voice, "To wo cado *in the rear?*"

All of his frustrations came out as he exhaled a huge, "*Yes!*"

We, happily and obediently, answered, "Okay!"

Our laughing made it hard to plant back up to the top of the bowl again, but we made it. I later thought it was a good thing our manager didn't come down into the bowl. Less than fifty feet away, he would've come upon a group of tree planters, leaning on their hoe-dads, laughing, and wiping tears from their eyes as we put one over on him.

Brother, I apologize.

The hard physical demands pushed our bodies to the limits and did the same to our souls. There were only two ways to deal with the stress.

We could complain about not enough drinking water, not enough lunch, the manager, the tree inspector, the guy up front who always took the best ground, the snow, the rain, the cold, the heat, the pain, the bugs, the guy in front of you who was always praising the Lord, or the one behind you who was always griping about something. The brothers who succumbed to complaining were the ones who gave vent to the negative thoughts that we all had to wrestle with in those trying conditions.

The second way of dealing with it was to take to heart the things we had read in the Bible about trials and tribulations. They would come whether we wanted them or not. God wanted to use them to purify us to be servants fit for his use. To some, it was the definition of idiocy, but for those who thanked God for their situation and asked that he use it to change them into his image, the result was peace and victory. This was what Jim called "training your soul" and the benefits extended far into our lives beyond the slopes.

There were some practical ways of dealing with tribulations. One problem was bugs. If the day was hot and there were a lot of bugs flying around, you had to watch out. You would be working hard and fast, sucking in air, when all of the sudden, a bug would fly right into your mouth and straight down the hatch. You would start hacking and coughing, trying to get rid of a critter that was already well on its way down your throat. It was funnier when it happened to someone else.

One day I was planting next to Dan Kler, and every time our planting lines came close to each other, I heard him say, "Swat! Swat!" Just off by himself, no one else around, saying "Swat! Swat!"

I finally got close enough to ask, "Dan, what are you doing?"

"These flies are driving me crazy. If I stop to brush them away, I'll never get any work done, but they hate the sound of 'Swat!'" Worked for him.

If you got cold on a wet winter day in the mountains, the only way to warm up was to work harder. Once, our manager for the day, Brian Augustine, was standing on a tree stump as we planted a hillside. He was yelling all sorts of encouragement to us, cracking jokes and generally being a pest. Then he brought out a verse from the book of Revelation. "Is anyone hot?"

Well, no. It was winter and freezing!

"Is anyone cold?"

No, we're working hard like we're supposed to and that's how you stay warm!

When he replied out of Revelation 3:16 (KJV), "So then because thou art lukewarm, and neither cold nor hot, I will spue thee out of my mouth," we all reached for something to throw at him.

But everyone had a *day* that was memorably worse than all the rest. For me, and I think a few others, it was when we were planting up around Cottage Grove, Oregon. There were a few teams working together planting on a big unit that was walled in by forest. Trees were all around us. The wind came up howling, the temperature dropped, and rain was blowing sideways. The wind and rain were so strong, you couldn't move fast, and the cold penetrated our rain gear so we froze too. I thought, *I hope someone else is putting trees in the ground because I don't think I'm getting hardly anything in.*

The wind in the mountains could be really awesome. You've heard of wind shears. We saw what they can do when they smash the forest—two or three acres of trees just leveled by the wind as if a giant fist hammered them flat. Around them, trees were still standing, but in that one area, every tree was down.

That's the kind of day this was. Every now and then, we heard trees—big trees—being blown down. We would hear a long "craaack!" as the wood of the tree was split by the force of the wind; then a big "BOOM!" when the tree slammed into the ground. One of those giants could crush us and we had to get out of there before it did. But it was so cold, wet and windy, no one could move fast.

Susan Tucker, one of our Germany team members had come with us that morning. A Southern California girl, she was happy to be in the beautiful mountains. She had chosen this day—the weather had been nice down where we were camped—to accompany us to the job. She brought a book, a writing pad, and small lunch and was going to find a nice place under some tree—overlooking, hopefully, a pond or stream—and have some quiet time.

She never left the truck. The wind blasting over the hills kept the truck rocking. The first one of us to make it back when we were done was Jay Hawes. He was so cold and miserable that he wordlessly climbed in, sat down and just stared at the floor. I trudged up the slope, threw my hoe-dad and tree bag in the back of the truck and climbed in. Susan sat against the far door, her eyes wide with surprise and shock at our appearance and how the day had turned out. She couldn't hold back her emotions and exclaimed, "You brothers are so wonderful!" Finally, I had something I could laugh about!

The discomforts of working in trying conditions were a challenge for us all, but on the slopes, just like in life, real tragedy could occur without warning.

In the summer of 1973, just a few months after David Peterson was killed at the Lighthouse Ranch, a tree-planting crew was making its way in the dark down a mountain road near Laytonville, California. The pickup was loaded with equipment and brothers and sisters. Among them were Jim Lane who introduced G. O. to tree planting, his little son Joe, and Fred Simmons, a much-loved musician from the Lighthouse Ranch. As they rounded a curve, a logging truck appeared, taking up most of the road. The brother driving swerved to the right and the tires of the pickup sank into the soft soil next to the road. The soil pulled the truck off and right into the huge limbs of trees next to the road. Jim, his son Joe, and Fred were killed.

Their passing was a loss to us all. Jim was a kind brother who was everyone's friend; he was a disciple committed to serving the Lord and us with his whole heart. Fred's heart for the Lord was an inspiration to everyone. When he expressed it in his music, he sang for all of us. The passing of Jim, young Joe, Fred, as well as David earlier, served to remind us this life was not where we were to be rewarded. We had a job to do on this earth and one day we would be together with them again.

The Fire and the Bear

Tree planters didn't just plant trees; sometimes we cut them down. Trees are really a renewable resource, just like the crops of a field. Like your garden plants or any crop, thick growths of trees need to be thinned so the remaining trees will grow faster and larger. We planted and thinned literally millions of trees in the 1970s and they are close to being harvested today.

So sometimes the tree planters became tree thinners. Most of us liked thinning more than planting. Planting got monotonous. Start the day putting one tree in the ground after another. Stop for a break. Start planting and put one tree in the ground after another. Stop for lunch. Start planting and put one tree in the ground after another. Go back to camp when it got dark. Get up the next day and do it some more.

Thinning, while it could get boring, at least had a powerful, roaring chainsaw instead of a dumb sounding "hoe-dad." Just the kind of thing guys love. Thinning had more of an element of danger too. A chainsaw could bite into a tree trunk with amazing speed and do the same to you if you weren't careful.

Once, Joe Shields was back at camp using his chainsaw to cut a hole in a log. He wasn't as careful as he should have been. Jim and Diane Boutcher remember what happened. "He was cutting a hole in a log so it could be used as a toilet seat. (If you haven't gotten the idea yet—out on the slopes, our lives were pretty primitive.) The log was on the ground and he was using his steel-toed boots to hold it steady. All of a sudden, the saw bucked, came down on his boot, and sawed through leather, flesh, and bone right behind the steel plate. It almost took his foot off; all that was left was a small piece of skin which held the toes and the front of his foot to the rest of it." Joe was rushed down the mountainside to a hospital in Coos Bay, Oregon where his foot was reattached. Miraculously, it worked, and he got the use of his foot back. But that was the end of his career in the mountains.

Falling trees could be a problem if you happened to be in their path. I know of one thinner who got knocked unconscious by the top of a twenty-five foot falling tree. The tip of the tree was the size of your thumb, and he was wearing a hard hat.

Once before almost cutting his foot off, I went to help Joe. His saw had gotten pinched in a tree and I had to cut it out for him. When done, I walked back to my work area over the "slash," the green carpet of trees we had already cut down. It was about two or three feet thick—that is, above the forest floor—so I would walk along the larger trees that seemed to promise steady footing. I was walking on top of one tree, carrying my saw in my left hand, balancing with the right, when I heard a "crack!" behind me. That's the sound a tree makes when it's falling. I turned to look—nothing moving. I continued walking and grabbed the branches of a standing tree to steady myself, when I heard another "crack!" I turned again and there was a tree falling straight toward me. No time to react, I could only watch and see what my fate would be. It sheared to the other side of the tree I was holding on to. Missed me by a couple of feet and my friend, the standing tree, kept me from getting smacked.

There were other dangers too.

We had a thinning job for Potlatch Lumber up near Pierce, Idaho. After an all-day drive from Eureka, we arrived at Headquarters, Idaho, at the Forest Service camp, only to find it deserted. There was a forest fire, and everyone who worked in the woods—loggers, Forest Service people, firefighters and, as it turned out, tree thinners, were out working on the fire. Our supervisor was supposed to arrive from the fire soon, and we were told to wait for him in the mess hall. We walked into a building with a lot of tables and chairs and a buffet full of hot food and desserts off to one side. Behind the counters was a group of local women who, while not on the fire line, were doing a yeoman's job keeping the firefighters filled with good, nutritious food.

Now, if there's anything that a tree thinner, or planter, likes more than not being cold, it's eating. And eating "heaven" for a planter is a smorgasbord or buffet restaurant—all you can eat, for as long as you can stuff it in. Rae Beebe was the president of the "Fork and Spoon Club" formed by a bunch of planters to see who could eat the most at the nearest smorgasbord. (Ask an ex-tree planter about the Samoa Cookhouse in Eureka; he will smile and start salivating.)

So there we were, walking into heaven. One of the ladies, mistaking us for firefighters said, "Oh! You boys are back already! Help yourselves!"

We were embarrassed, thinking, *Oh no! We haven't been out risking our lives fighting the fire. We just got here!* But we didn't say anything.

Then one brother said, "Well, heck, I could use a cup of coffee." *Well, yeah, it's just coffee.* He got his cup and sat down.

Another guy thought that was a good idea and went for a cup too. But there were cookies right next to the coffee . . . and cake and pie. He helped himself. Just like that we lost all self-discipline and everyone loaded plates full of roast beef, chicken, mashed potatoes, and veggies, and everything else that would fill a tree thinner's stomach and make his heart happy.

The next day they put us on the fire. We were working near the bottom of a steep hill, next to a draw that came down from the top. The air was full of smoke as the fire advanced slowly down the hill toward us. Our job was to use shovels, mattocks, and axes to clear shrubs and wood from its path and so deny it fuel. It was burning hot above us and smoldering trees were toppling over and then sliding down the draw past our fire line. One of the supervisors would have us run into the draw and throw dirt on the flaming logs so the fire couldn't get past our line. The falling trees made it dangerous as loosened rocks and boulders would also come hurtling down. I was warned by an experienced logger not to go in, but the supervisor kept sending us out.

Then it happened. Three or four of the guys were in the draw putting out a burning log, when Justin Perlstein came running back screaming that Larry Chambers had gotten hit by a rock. His hardhat and his skull were crushed and he was unconscious.

In our section of the fire, everything stopped as we all worked to get Larry out of there. It was steep, rugged terrain—no roads or paths. We rigged a stretcher and struggled to carry him up the rocky, uneven side of the hill, away from the fire. Rob Anderson remembers that twice the stretcherbearers lost their footing causing Larry to roll around. While we did that, a Caterpillar D-6 created a trail from a flat hilltop to as far down the hillside as he could without tumbling down the slope. We got Larry to the D-6, which took him to the top where a helicopter was waiting. He was flown straight to Deaconess Hospital in

Spokane where he was in a coma for about three weeks. Larry recovered, but his speech was slurred after that.

The fire was finally gotten under control and we tree thinners could start our job. In order to be close to the work, we camped next to Dollar Creek. Jim Wall, our manager, had brought a gold pan with him and spent his time off panning for gold. Sue, his wife, was in charge of the cooking crew, so we named the mess tent "Sue's Gold Dollar Diner."

Bear in the Outhouse

But "they wuzn't just gold in them thar hills, they wuz bears too!" We got up one cold dark morning to get ready for work. (During the wintertime, we never saw our camp in the daylight until the weekend. We left in the dark and returned in the dark.) Rob Anderson went to take care of business at our "one-log" outhouse, which was just a lean-to with a blanket around it. As he parted the blanket to enter he discovered it was already occupied—by a bear! Rob and the bear were both surprised and Rob turned and ran down the hill screaming, "BEAR!" With one leap he cleared our crew-cab pickup and turned, hoping the bear wasn't right behind him. He wasn't. The bear, just as scared as Rob, scampered the other way up the hill.

One of our crew, Don Williams, was a hunter and had brought along a rifle and a shotgun. He knew it was bear season and had gotten a bear hunting tag in case he got the chance to go look for one. When he heard about Rob's encounter, he grabbed his rifle and went looking for the bear while the rest of us had breakfast and loaded up to go to work.

Now I do all my hunting in the Costco meat department. It's daytime and the only danger comes from other shopping carts, not the meat in the bins. Don was walking around the hills in the dark, looking for a bear. I mean, what if he found him? What if the bear found him first? Neither found the other. By the time Don came back to the camp, we had left for work. That meant that, instead of working all day in the cold Idaho woods (it was the end of October) with a bunch of grungy tree thinners, he had to hang out in Sue's Gold Dollar Diner with the womenfolk and drink coffee. Bummer.

Around noontime, our mascot puppy, the brave Caleb, started barking up a storm. Diane Doyle went out of the tent to investigate, and there was the bear not thirty feet away by the creek. "Don, the bear!" she yelled.

Don grabbed his rifle, switched off the safety and stepped outside. Caleb, who wasn't big but could be annoying, had the bear distracted. And, in a moment that had none of the drama of a high-noon shootout, Don shot him down.

The bear's journey didn't end there. We took him into town to some people we knew from a local church. They skinned and butchered him, and we had bear roast for a few days.

This story, while sad for the bear, couldn't have ended any other way. If the bear had gotten into our food supply, he would have suffered not only the wrath of brave Caleb, but all of us tree thinners. You develop a powerful hunger walking around the woods with a roaring chainsaw all day! There are two things you don't want to tell a tree thinner: 1) "You missed a bunch of trees. Go back and do it again." And 2) "Sorry, all the food's gone. We're having cucumber sandwiches for dinner." The bear got off easy.

The Demon

The Germany team was planting redwood seedlings in Mendocino, California and staying on the Lord's Land.

Surprisingly, the redwood seedlings were smaller than the Douglas fir seedlings that we had planted everywhere else. Still, we thought it sounded impressive to say, "We planted redwoods!" and let the listener decide what that meant.

We worked during the short daylight hours in the winter months and would usually end up back at the Land when it was dark. Since the work was hard, we would usually eat, shower, then hit the sack. The men on the team were staying at a house set off from the rest. It was called the "Brothers' House" and had no running water or electricity—at least while we were there. Our sleeping bags were scattered around the living room floor. The only amenity was an outhouse about fifty feet away from the front door.

Many of the nights were as black as the inside of your coat pocket. With no artificial lighting within a half mile, only the moon and stars provided illumination. Since this was wintertime, the sky was usually overcast, so you couldn't see your hand in front of your face.

It was late on one of those nights, when as I slept, I began to dream. I heard a faint wailing sound. It sounded like someone—or something—was saying, "Help! Help me." It was pretty weird. It continued, and slowly, I realized I wasn't sleeping anymore. I was fully awake.

"Help me," the voice pleaded.

This had to be a demon, just like in the movies! It was wailing to announce its presence, and then it was going to get us, just like wolves do out in the deep forest. They howl and carry on, and just when you step outside the door to see what's going on, BLAM, they get you!

I lay in bed, not moving a muscle, praying for the protection of the Almighty. Was I the only one who heard it? Was it coming for *me*?

Then one of the other guys spoke quietly, "What's that?"

Someone else said, "I don't know, it sounds like it's coming from outside."

Taking courage in numbers, we crawled out of our sleeping bags, and walked to the front door. One of us had a flashlight—as if that was going to help against a demon! He switched on the flashlight, and we opened the door, and THAT'S WHEN WE SAW IT!

Well, not really an *it* as much as a *him*. It was Tom, one of our team. He had gotten up to use the outhouse. He had made it out there okay, but coming back, he got lost. Tom never went anywhere without his glasses—big thick ones because he had poor eyesight—except when going to the outhouse on a pitch-black night. He was trying to return to the house, couldn't find it, and was calling for help. We helped him back and showed him to his sleeping bag. Then we closed the door. And locked it.

Advanced Discipleship Training

Most of the men and women had mixed emotions about tree planting. It wasn't for everyone, and in fact, was totally unsuited for some. The work was hard and the living conditions were primitive. Being thrown together in those circumstances would sometimes lead to conflict with one another. But most of us understood that, aside from the financial reasons, tree planting was the ideal setting for what could be called "advanced discipleship training." We knew God was converting us. We knew we had wrong ways of looking at life, ourselves and others, and that to please God, we had to change.

We learned how to be thankful when we froze or when pain showed us new muscles we never knew existed. Because God loved the brothers or sisters who bugged us to death, we loved them too and hoped they loved us in return. We learned we were stronger than we thought when we were able to work up to the lunch break, then to the end of the first day, week, and month. It may seem odd to those who weren't there, but the hardship produced amazing worship when surrendered souls met for a time of praise before the evening meal. Because we saw little of the money we earned but knew it would be used to further the gospel, we learned not to focus on what the world could give us. We knew the reason we planted trees was to spread the gospel. This attitude would dominate our every activity for the rest of our lives.

CHAPTER TWELVE

Alaska

YOU KNEW THAT the Gospel Outreach church planting team to Alaska was going to be special because although no one suspected it, one of the team members wasn't even saved. As the first group was assembled and sent north from Eureka in an old yellow school bus (named "Holy Spirit Skool Bus"), Jim Durkin talked to Werner Welch, who had become involved with G.O. When it was arranged for the team to live on a dairy farm near Anchorage, Jim suggested Werner go and help because he had experience with milk cows and dairies. He did, and got saved. He was the first (and, hopefully, only) person to be sent out on a team before he became a Christian.

It was early 1972. Gale Willy, the Fortuna Christian cowboy who had been so helpful getting the Carlotta Mansion going, knew a Christian mint farmer, Don Turnage, up in Salem, Oregon, who knew a fellow up in Palmer, Alaska, who had a dairy and potato farm. One day, all of them came down to Eureka and met together with Jim,

Lambert Hazelaar, and the other G. O. elders in Jim and Dacie's living room.

Ralph Devilbis, the Alaska dairyman, suggested that G. O. send a team up there. He said the area churches were seeing a lot of young people getting saved, but their idea of discipleship started with giving them a haircut and a new pair of Levi's. He was sure the teaching and discipleship practiced at the Lighthouse Ranch would have a positive impact on the new Christians. They could live on the farm, work it and support their ministry from the dairy proceeds.

Jim sent Ron Juncal and David Leon up with the first few members of the team. They looked at the dairy with eighty cows and decided that it just might work and then visited different churches in the area. They got to know Dick Benjamin, a pastor who headed a church called Abbot Loop, a vibrant congregation that had already established three additional churches in Alaska.

In June, Lambert and his wife Marnie, Susi Schutzle, John Lewis, Mike Becker, David Sorenson, and Barbara Linley packed all their things in the bus donated by the mint farmer and headed north. As they drove, they picked up hitchhikers. Lambert says, "About ten people got saved on the way up to Canada. We had a lot of fun." It must've been a great time, and it would have been hard for any traveler not to want to share the joy, peace and commitment to a goal they saw in that group.

They were stopped at the Canadian border, which is notorious for filtering out anyone who Canada considers undesirable. Next to Skool Bus was a VW bus full of hippies. As it pulled up to the border, the driver slid open the car window and the border agent asked them if they had any dope. As the smell of marijuana rolled out of the car, they answered, "No."

He responded, "Have a nice day."

Then it was the turn of the saved and redeemed, born again, full-of-God's-love Christians. "Do you have any drugs with you?

"No! We used to do that stuff but God saved us. We're driving to Alaska to preach the gospel."

"No you're not. Turn your vehicle around and return to the U.S." Canada wouldn't let anyone in with a police record (who told the truth about it).

The team stayed in Bellingham for a week while things got straightened out. A couple of the hitchhikers who accepted the Lord helped the team by paying airfare from Seattle to Anchorage for those who couldn't cross the border. Marnie's father (she was Canadian) came down and helped to get the others through.

Life in an Ammonia Bottle

They all finally made it to Alaska and the farm. Their living quarters were right over where the cows were kept and, not surprisingly, the place smelled like a barn. Not surprisingly, the brothers and sisters began to smell like a barn too. When they visited different churches, the parishioners would know without turning to look that the Gospel Outreach brethren had arrived.

Bernie Haraldson, who came up for a visit during this time, said, "Living in the barn was like living in an ammonia bottle." Lambert recalled when they went to Abbot Loop church (funny name unless you know that's the part of Anchorage where the church was established), everyone smelled them, but still accepted them like "the King's kids."

The river of God's Spirit that took hold of everyone in California was surging through Alaska too.

The team came to spread the gospel and Marnie remembers the secret of sharing the message with non-believers.

"We all had such child-like faith. We weren't hung up with being politically correct—'I'm not saying it right! I don't look right! Wait a minute, what are they going to think?' We just went out and told people, 'Hey, do you know Jesus loves you?' and they were swept off their feet with his love. People came from every direction. The farm was on a dirt road six miles from the main road, and we would have two or three new visitors at dinner every night. In two months, seventy-five people gave their lives to Christ!"

Since Ralph offered that the income from the cows could be used to support them, the brethren dove into the work. They soon discovered that no one wanted to buy their milk. It wasn't the smell—theirs or the cows—but the barns and the pipes used to move the milk hadn't been kept clean. The cows developed mastitis and the milk was tainted and unsuitable for consumption. Lambert, Werner, and the crew, took the pipes apart, cleaned everything up, and the operation began to hum.

Finally, the first check came in for milk that had been sold and delivered. But, contrary to his promise, Ralph kept all the money and the team got nothing. Lambert couldn't understand why he would do that. He finally concluded, "He was less interested in helping us than in getting a work force."

Without further ado, Lambert decided, "We're out of here." He sent half the brethren to two houses in Anchorage, which became the "Tarwater" and the "Sisters" houses. The other half was sent to a house on a hill outside of Palmer that they called, the "Mountain of the Lord."

One of the houses in Anchorage was to be used as a brothers' house but they found it didn't have enough room for all the new converts. With memories of the Lighthouse Ranch brothers' dorm expansion, they practiced a little urban renewal of their own. The house had a low basement that was almost useless. They jacked the house up a few feet, which raised the basement ceiling, rebuilt the walls and presto! Now they could pack twice as many brothers in.

Before long, G. O. in Anchorage had eight communal houses and was holding Sunday meetings in the Carpenters' Hall.

The team in Palmer found a seven-acre farm, formerly the Lutheran Children's Home, which was turned into another Lighthouse Ranch. It became known as the "Bread of Life Bakery" when Frank Loosli took used bakery equipment that Lambert had bought for $100, and together with Greg Hogue, reassembled it on the farm. Before long, they were baking one thousand loaves a day and sending each off with a Scripture verse in the wrapping. The bread and pastries from the bakery were sold to the stores in the area. The farm population grew to about sixty people and, just like the ranches in California, it became a center of discipleship training.

A ServiceMaster franchise was also acquired. Besides the money needed to support the brothers and sisters in the communal houses, it provided the opportunity to disciple young converts.

Until the work in Anchorage grew enough to justify renting their own meeting hall for Sunday services, the brothers and sisters would visit different churches in the area. A relationship began to grow with the people from Abbot Loop, and soon, that was where they would go on Sundays. It provided a strong church family with many older, experienced Christians who were happy to encourage this band of young, zealous disciples. This was made easier when they moved from the dairy!

Jim Durkin came up to visit the work in late 1972 and met Abbot Loop's leader, Dick Benjamin. Dick says, "Jim and I had a long talk. I quickly began to love, respect and properly relate to him. I invited him to preach in our church. In the months to come, he would preach for us many times. I can truthfully say that his preaching was always excellent."

It was good for the young G. O. disciples to have a church like Abbot Loop around to encourage and support them. But Dick credits Jim with help of a kind that brought enormous change to Abbot Loop and his life.

For some time, Jim had been sensing God speaking to him about the so-called "five-fold ministries" mentioned in Ephesians 4:11. He felt the Lord had put the calling of apostle on his life. Jim felt the same thing about Dick Benjamin. While visiting for a second time in late 1973, Jim broached the subject with Dick. Jim felt impressed by the Holy Spirit that a whole new apostolic ministry awaited Dick's acceptance. What did he think?

Dick got all his elders together and those from the three branch churches they had established in Anchorage. What did they think? They all agreed this was what the Lord wanted, and they threw in their support. Together, Jim and the Abbot Loop elders laid hands on Dick and ordained him as an apostle. While the concept of modern-day apostles is a difficult one for many Christians—even among ex-G. O.ers—no one from Abbot Loop had a problem with it.

Dick wrote me, "Our church had already started three churches. At the time, as best I can recall, we had no immediate plans to plant any other new churches." Together with the ordination, Jim introduced the concept of sending out teams to start churches rather than individuals or married couples. In the next few years, Abbot Loop sent out about thirteen hundred people on teams to plant one hundred churches in the U.S. and eight foreign countries.

Dick and his wife Carol spent the next twenty-five years traveling to minister and shepherd this far-flung family, while their son Richard took over the reins in Anchorage.

Richard remembers, "James Durkin changed all of our lives forever. When he came to Abbott Loop the first time in 1972, he spoke about 'The Purpose of God.' No one could inspire vision in people like James Durkin."

The brothers and sisters from Gospel Outreach would completely agree with that.

A Miracle Now and Then

Planting a new church usually means hard work and sacrifice for those who give themselves to it. A miracle every now and then helps too.

Marnie remembers washing the brothers' clothes at the dairy (which they renamed the "Lord's Land") with the only appliance available—a wringer washer. Since the men also toiled in the farmer's potato field, they would finish the day caked in mud. This meant heavy work for the wringer washer and the sister whose job it was to make everything clean. The washer finally gave up the ghost and the women were reduced to washing clothes with an old-fashioned washboard, the kind used by the pioneers. It was slow, frustrating, and painful.

Finally, after rubbing her knuckles raw, Marnie reached her limit. "I fell down on the floor on my knees and cried out, 'God! I can't do this anymore! We need a washing machine!'

"The next morning, after that crying, shrieking prayer, a brother from Palmer, a pastor, showed up with a brand new, automatic washing machine!"

The new machine did a yeoman's job of keeping everyone in clean clothes until one Sunday, when they piled into their vehicles for a trip to Abbot Loop in Anchorage. Someone tossed in a load of laundry before leaving, and when they returned in the afternoon, there was a foot of water in the basement. Among the items floating about was Marnie's violin. This is a death sentence for a violin. Soaked in water, the glue that holds the instrument together dissolves and it falls apart.

Marnie directed another desperate cry heavenward. "Lord Jesus! My violin!" She took it and hung it up to let it dry—there was nothing else she could do. She said, "I hung it up and it never came apart, and when it was dry, the tone of that violin was more beautiful than it had ever been."

Lambert and Marnie were getting ready to take a new group out to Homer on Alaska Highway 1 at the end of the Kenai Peninsula. Everyone told them it wouldn't work. With the construction of the Alaska pipeline going full bore, it would be impossible to find a house, shack, or anywhere else to live. They were pretty sure that's where the Lord wanted them, so they went down and scouted out the land. The doubters appeared to be right—there were no available houses to be found.

In the center of town, Lambert noticed an empty, boarded-up house that used to be a bank. If the original team could live in a barn above a herd of cows, then this place would be ten times better. He called the county land office to get the name and phone number of the owner. It was a long shot, but maybe he would let them use it for G. O.'s new outreach.

If Lambert needed any more proof that God was ordering their steps (he didn't), then it was given by the land office. The owner turned out to be the same man who rented them the houses in Anchorage! When Lambert called, he was happy to make his building in Homer available.

The work in Alaska grew, and what had begun in the smelly barn above the cows soon included groups of believers in Anchorage, Palmer, Fairbanks, Girdwood, Homer, and Dutch Harbor. People like Scott and Elly Snedeker, Breck Wilson and others, were sent up to help teach, disciple and guide the new converts.

The two years Lambert and Marnie spent in Homer typify the work of God's Spirit up in Alaska. He says, "A lot of genuine, on-fire-for-God people came out of that group. And they're living for Christ today."

CHAPTER THIRTEEN

Big City
Outreaches

New York, Los Angeles, Chicago

IN THE WINTER of 1973, Jim Durkin met with several of the still young leaders of Gospel Outreach in a cabin in the Klamath National Forest, near Orleans, California. The ranches and Eureka were overflowing from an enormous harvest of souls. Many of the new converts stayed to begin their new lives in Christ. Bernie Haraldson remembers Jim telling the brothers, "Eureka is getting too full, and we need to start sending people out on teams." They discussed team composition and setting aside a group of traveling elders or, "mobile ministers" who could visit different churches and provide teaching and support. Up to that point, the team concept was still new and not an established practice.

G. O.'s very first team had gone to Coquille, Oregon, and Jim had sent a team with Lambert and Marnie up to Alaska. More and more teams of tree planters were hitting the slopes of the Northwest. Sending groups of brethren, led by older, tested leaders (which meant they had been

Christians for two or three years but had served as house heads or ranch leaders) was appealing for different reasons.

The fact that we were young meant having a group of our brothers and sisters around us would be an encouragement. We were facing challenges that, as young Christians, were new to us. In some cases, we would be returning to the same world we had left when we met Christ. We would impart the testimony of Jesus in the neighborhoods where before we had done drugs and shared in destructive lifestyles—sometimes with the very people to which we would now be ministering. Rather than tackle this as individual missionaries, or as couples, we would have the support of a large group.

We were still working with the communal house concept. These houses could be effective discipleship centers if there were enough brothers and sisters who were solid in the faith and grounded in the Bible. So it was good for a communal house to have eight or ten team members who could provide a strong spiritual direction. This was especially true when the brethren brought home people from the street.

Rather than each person or married couple finding an apartment, a vehicle or a job, we did it all together. Living and working with one another helped us pool financial and physical resources, which gave us more flexibility to do what we were sent to do—spread the gospel in the cities and neighborhoods where we now found ourselves.

Not the Lighthouse Ranch

The transition from life in Northern California to the "mean streets" of New York or Chicago could be pretty intimidating. Trading the ranch atmosphere of continual focus on God for the hard and fast pace of big city life called for a different mindset. Rather than being surrounded by blue skies and green forests, tall, dirty, buildings seemed to crowd down around us. Some of the communal houses were in the depths of the urban jungle. The people we encountered had been hardened by years of drug use, alcoholism and tragic life experiences.

Dave Sczepanski led the second G. O. team to New York. He had grown up in a middle class family in Midland, Michigan, a modest-sized city. After getting saved he lived at the Lighthouse Ranch and then spent four months in Southern California with the team, making money for the move. Dave was unprepared for what awaited him in the city when he first arrived.

"I remember driving up Atlantic Avenue, the older part, looking at burned out cars sitting on the curb, then riding under the El tracks and seeing stores and businesses with bars covering the windows and doors. There was trash everywhere. I was in culture shock. As a matter of fact, I had a headache for a month. For two months, I wouldn't drive in the city."

Gary Crouthamel compared Brooklyn to a public toilet. "Everyone uses it but no one cleans it."

For West Coasters like Charles and Donna Chambers, Chicago was a whole new world and they had some unusual experiences. Charles remembers one time when he looked in on the brothers' dorm of the communal house where they lived. Single men from the church lived there, and overnight guests—mostly homeless collected off the street—stayed there too. Charles opened the door in time to see some character pouring the blood from a cat he had just killed into a cup and begin drinking it. Of course, this didn't happen every day, but it sure wasn't the Lighthouse Ranch.

Terri Schrater initially felt, "If I wasn't here to share the gospel with these people, I would *walk* back to California!"

Southern California was a different world from those other places. The brethren there had to contend with the carefree, laid back, surfer spirit of the Southland. Life was good and people had difficulty seeing their need for a Savior who could save them for eternity. There were also plenty of solid churches in the Southland. It would have been hard to find someone who hadn't already heard the gospel a few times.

The Sherman Way house was within a mile and a half of the Church on the Way, a mega-church. Bill Ireland says, "We sent a bunch of people to Orange County, which was dominated by Calvary Chapel and other large churches." The fields that were "white unto harvest" seemed to have already been harvested and only the gleanings were left. Still, people got saved and the houses and their Bible study groups grew.

The Macedonian Call

Denny Viehland was a Chicago taxi driver who, together with Chuck Ginther, had a Bible study group of about twenty people. They met in the south part of town and had heard about Gospel Outreach. A relationship with Jim Durkin and the other leaders developed, and Denny and Chuck invited G. O. to send a church planting team to join them. The brethren from the Bible study would provide the seed bed for a new Gospel Outreach church.

This was not uncommon. Small groups of Christians all over the country and even in foreign lands received Radiance publications, cassette tapes or heard about G. O. from others. Small clusters of mostly young believers eagerly consumed the depth, authority and wisdom of Jim's teachings. When they heard of Gospel Outreach's worldwide vision, they understood that its umbrella of spiritual authority and support could cover them too.

A team was assembled in Eureka. Numbering around twenty people (not counting kids) and led by Steve Schrater, Charles Chambers and Gary Zeld, they spent a couple months planting trees in the Pacific Northwest. The team members grew close to each other as they shared the trials of working on the slopes. This was an important time of building unity. As Charles' experience showed, they would be facing many new challenges and would need each other's support. Terri says, "It was one of the happiest times of my life. We were good friends. We really bonded with each other." They finally had enough money for the move, and arrived in Chicago in June of 1975.

Much the same thing happened in New York. A Bible study group including David and Mudgie Dreiling, Randell Jennings, Susan Wishner, Jefferson Duke, John Repp, Ken and Brenda Lomas, and Patty Keighron Esposito were meeting in Brooklyn and began corresponding with G. O. in Eureka. Gregor Chello was back East seeing family and paid a visit. After spending time with them, he called Eureka and told them this group of dedicated brethren was in need of help—couldn't someone be sent?

Jim sent the cavalry—Ron Juncal and the Evangelistic Team. Completing a cross-country road trip (sharing the gospel at gas stations and city parks the whole way), they pulled into Brooklyn. After a short time, Ron suggested the group return with them to Eureka. There they could get training and rest from the forces in New York that threatened to consume them. They all caravanned back west in the fall of 1973 and moved to the different ranches. A few months later, some of them returned with Tom Kennedy (after planting trees). They were the first of three teams that were eventually sent to the Big Apple.

The team decided to return to Brooklyn, a borough that by itself is plenty big. Tommy felt they should go to the part where the need seemed the greatest, even if it was dangerous. After all, we were warriors of the cross; we knew that danger and hardship often were the precursors to a powerful move of God's Spirit. So they chose Park Slope, a middle-class part of Brooklyn that had slid into disrepair and disorder.

Once they moved in, Tommy made a discovery. "It turned out to be rougher than I knew." Drugs and gangs were everywhere, and just a block away was a veritable highway for the heroin trade in Brooklyn.

Spreading the Word

Now that they were away from the ranches and in "real" cities, the team members spread out to share the good news. Instead of a steady stream of wandering youth, the new harvest fields consisted of all classes of society. For the New York group, this meant upper-middle class people from Long Island like George Vaughn and his wife Maria, the sister of Joseph, Francis and Victor Anfuso. Victor was married to a daughter of William Shea after whom the Met's baseball stadium was named. The first communal houses were located in the Fort Greene area. One of them was on Oxford Street, across from Fort Greene Park, which was the old hangout of Nicky Cruz of the *Cross and the Switchblade* fame. The teams reached out to Brooklyn's street people and those who lived in the Puerto Rican part of town.

Dave remembers, "We did a lot more evangelizing in New York than we ever did in California."

Many of those who made the decision to follow Christ joined the church. To buy Shepherd's House, they had to deal with a sharp real estate agent named Jerry Magliulo who was the proto-typical New Yorker. Of Italian extraction, he was "above board," but to Dave's West Coast sensibilities, he seemed just a step away from the well-known, illegal mob of the same ethnicity. The day he met the brethren from Gospel Outreach turned out to be the turning point in Jerry's life, and he eventually accepted the Lord. Jerry became a disciple, and one day would pastor the G. O. church in New Port Richey, Florida.

The experience of the Chicago team was typical for the inner-city evangelistic efforts.

The Wino Ministry

Jim Boutcher initiated what was called the "wino ministry." One of the houses was just a few blocks from Chicago's downtown. Away from the million-dollar glitz and glamour, it was in a different world, bordered by streets full of prostitutes, winos, and drug dealers. Living half their lives on the dirty sidewalks of the city, they sold their bodies or drugs to anyone foolish enough to trade for money. Disease and sickness left faces and bodies twisted and careworn. These were the outward signs of souls and lives wasted by addiction and hopelessness. Close by was a small park where all the transvestites hung out. A lot of the street people were homeless; unlike the prostitutes and drug dealers, they had nothing to offer and could only beg for money.

As Jim walked to the house from the nearby subway station, he would talk to them and share about God's plan of salvation that could set them free. Just like Peter and John in the book of Acts, he told them, "I don't have any money, but if you want to come home with me, we'll feed you." They would follow him home, get a square meal and hear the gospel explained to them. Diane Boutcher remembers, "These guys were hard-core alcoholics and drug addicts and they started getting saved."

They saw lives turned around in remarkable ways. "We saw deliverance of heroin addicts with no withdrawal. We would say to someone who had just prayed to accept the Lord, 'Hey brother, we're going to pray for you so you don't have to go through withdrawals.' We prayed and they wouldn't. Of course, a number of them came only for the food and that was fine. But some of them are still serving the Lord."

The church continued to reach out to the community and once held a Christmas dinner in the downtown house. They invited the sad and battered people who populated the streets and told them to bring their friends too. After sitting down at the table set with dishes, glasses and silverware (who knew the last time they had experienced that?), the guests' plates were loaded with turkey and all the trimmings. The brothers and sisters then took the opportunity to share about God's eternal gift in Jesus. They explained how to become a Christian and invited them to Bible studies and church services. Once the dining room full of guests had been fed, they were ushered out and the house was filled with a new group. The whole thing was repeated until about one hundred lost souls were fed, in both body and spirit.

Visits were also made to shut-ins—those who for one reason or another couldn't get out and mingle with the rest of society. They shared the gospel with residents of a halfway house for ex-mental patients and saw several get saved. They visited and prayed for residents of nursing and retirement homes as well as prisons and schools.

Everyone Needs a Break

Communal living was a once-in-a-lifetime experience for most of us. That means we enjoyed it, but wouldn't want to repeat it.

Being together helped foster the spirit of discipleship that made Gospel Outreach teams so effective. The brothers and sisters were there to pray for and support each other in their labors. There was sacrifice of privacy and family life, but they had come to preach the gospel so that was considered acceptable. They had "counted the cost."

Still, everyone needed a break sometime. Lani and Renee Peck were house heads at one of the big Chicago houses. It seemed as if it had been forever since they had had a free day so they decided to take a Saturday off. They let everyone in the house know beforehand not to bother them. As they relaxed in their room, there was a knock on the door. It was a brother saying, "I know you're taking the day off, but . . ." He had a quick question. Lani sighed, answered the question and then shut the door.

Then there was another knock and, "Sorry to bother you but . . ." It was another request or bit of important news.

After the second visitor left Lani decided, "That's enough!" In frustration he wrote a note in bold letters and taped it to the door for all to see. "DO NOT DISTURB! THIS MEANS YOU!"

There was a knock at the door.

Now Lani was mad! He ripped open the door, ready to give a tongue-lashing to this new offender that would teach him respect. Standing innocently in front of him was the one person in the house who couldn't read; he was illiterate.

Another hallmark of the G. O. church planting teams was that, although we saw ourselves as missionaries, we didn't rely on contributions to support the work. Jim Durkin made sure we had a biblical work ethic, were able to support ourselves and had enough left over to help the needy.

After acquiring housing, the next item on a team's to-do list was to find work by looking for jobs or starting small businesses. In Chicago, Charles Chambers started a vinyl-repair business he had learned back in Eureka from Peter Steimle. He began to train others in the church and soon they had plenty of work repairing vinyl and leather in automobiles. Other small businesses were started and some team members found jobs at the Marshall Field's department store and at other companies.

Are We Missing Something?

Dave Sczepanski was frustrated and a little worried so he wrote Jim a letter. The people in the New York G. O. houses were spending a lot of time on the streets, in parks, and on the job spreading the gospel. In fact, while they were evangelizing more in New York than they did in Eureka, they weren't seeing nearly the same numbers of people getting saved. What were they doing wrong?

Dave wasn't the only one concerned about this. Chicago reported the same. Even L. A., where the Jesus People revival got its start and was the strongest, didn't see the numbers we had all expected. Were we missing something? In New York, Tommy thought he understood. "In California, we knew we could talk to any hippie or counter-culture type." They knew the people, the culture, and the language. Landing in Fort Green, Brooklyn was like landing in a different country. The residents were mostly Puerto Rican who spoke little English and had entirely different life experiences from the ex-hippie Christians who showed up on their doorsteps with gospel tracts and wearing hiking boots.

The teams had arrived in the biggest city of their own country only to find it seemed like a different country with a different culture.

There was no good answer. Formulas and techniques weren't what saved us, and while those things seemed to work for the mega-churches, they never fit Gospel Outreach. We know, because we tried those too.

Maybe the flood of revival was beginning to ebb.

Still, people were getting saved and the churches were training new leaders and sending out teams. Chicago sent groups or individuals to Milwaukee and Madison, Wisconsin, Wayne, New Jersey, France and Germany.

New York opened other houses in Brooklyn and Queens. The group on Long Island did well and turned into its own church. They sent a team down to New Port Richey, Florida and assisted other outreaches.

Son of Lighthouse

Each team dreamed of starting another Lighthouse Ranch as a place of refuge and training for their young converts. New York had a farm up in Delhi for a while. It closed down as the result of misunderstandings between the brother who owned it and the G. O. elders.

Los Angeles did get a ranch out in the desert next to March Air Force Base in the town of Perris. The property, originally built as a horse ranch for Louis B. Mayer (the last M in MGM), consisted of fourteen acres and a cluster of dilapidated, Spanish-style houses grouped around a courtyard. White painted walls and red tile roofs completed the impression of a Spanish mission. G. O. took it over in 1975, a year after the first L. A. teams arrived in Southern California.

Jesse Gift was put in charge in 1979 and work began in earnest to renovate the place. It took longer than expected, but income from a ServiceMaster franchise and vinyl repair more than paid the expenses. Of course, the real work was making disciples. The population there swung from thirty or forty down to a dozen, then back up again. Later, they planted a church in nearby Sunnymead.

Sparks of Light

Back in Eureka, Claudia Jamison was sad. She had just delivered Steve and Irene Barney to the airport to begin their trip to Munich to join the Germany team. It seemed as if everyone was leaving and she felt empty. She went home and cried, then lay down on her bed. Suddenly she saw a map of the world that appeared on the ceiling. From Eureka shone a bright light from which small sparks began to shoot out, landing on different spots on the map. Faster and faster the sparks arched over North America, then the world. The light that was Eureka became dimmer, but in each of the cities and countries where the sparks landed, the lights shone as bright as Eureka's had been.

From Eureka, and then from the original church plants in the big cities, more brethren left to begin new churches: Oswego, New York; Miami and New Port Richey, Florida; Philadelphia and Boston; Manassas, Virginia; Grants Pass, Silverton, Salem, Eugene, Roseburg, Cave Junction and Portland, Oregon; Redding, San Diego, San Francisco and Whittier, California; Phoenix, Arizona; Seattle, Port Orchard, Tacoma, Olympia, and Vancouver, Washington; Denver, Colorado; Honolulu, Hawaii.

Each of the teams was made up of brothers and sisters dedicated to fulfilling Christ's Great Commission. They didn't go to help someone else do the work. In their hearts, they were determined to give all they had to win their new homes for Jesus, to spread "the glory of the Lord as the waters cover the seas."

As we lived at the ranches, witnessed to the lost, or worked in the various G. O. businesses, we all knew that part of our lives was only the beginning of lifelong service to the Lord. We thought the trials we endured and the lessons we learned had been the uphill half of our lives and now that we had stood the test, the rest would be downhill.

Of course, we couldn't have been more wrong.

CHAPTER FOURTEEN

Germany

The Challenge

IT WAS MAY of 1978. I sat alone on a dark-brown wooden bench in a long hallway, holding our passports and other paperwork. I was at the main police headquarters in downtown Munich, seeking to renew Linda's and my residence visas—our permission to stay in the country and continue our work as missionaries with the Gospel Outreach Germany team. The documents were needed to show we were doing productive work and were financially supported.

I looked around at the walls with their coat of tired white paint and the ceilings so high that the hanging lights had lost the illumination battle. The whole effect was dark and gloomy. This added to the gloom I had brought with me.

We had only been in Germany a short time when the Lord began to show me something. If I wanted to do what he had sent me there to do—share God's salvation plan in this foreign society—then the work would start right away—with me.

With every calling from God in our lives, he needs to do some cleaning in order to make us useful "vessels" to do His work. I thought of Abraham who was required to sacrifice his promised son, or Moses who had to endure forty years of humbling before he was ready to lead Israel to the Promised Land. Before God could move them toward their service for him, they had to endure experiences they would never have chosen for themselves—experiences that required exactly what they held in the highest regard. For Abraham it was his son Isaac; for Moses it was his future as the leader of his people. I couldn't exactly put a finger on what quality in my life that God required of me. I do know that, in an important way, a part of me died.

Life in Germany was stressful. German society probably coined the term "over-achiever." If you see the word "über" anywhere, it's German, and it means "over" as in "over the top." A very goal-oriented culture that judged results above all things—much judgment, little grace. If things were done wrong—at work, with government officials, on the bus, in the checkout line, or by not cleaning your sidewalk and curb on Saturday morning—you would often get an icy stare and probably a comment. This happened often until we learned to do it right the first time.

There was also an unspoken sense of the past, as if no one could quite believe his own people were capable of what took place; a past when Germans, not just Nazis, almost exterminated an entire race and caused the death of millions. (How would *you* deal with that if it were *your* people?)

Then, bringing it back to the present, were the Soviet Bloc army divisions sitting across the border in East Germany, poised to attack whenever "the balloon went up." Many people had aunts, uncles, cousins, siblings and grandparents who lived in communist bondage on the other side of the wall. They weren't allowed to see or talk to them.

Thousands of East Germans attempted to escape to freedom in the West. Those who succeeded were immediately helped by the West German government and embraced by their families. Those who failed were either sent to prison or left to bleed to death in no-man's land where they had been shot.

(Germans aren't without humor. When, at the request of the West German government, the U.S. began to station medium-range nuclear missiles in West Germany, the liberals went "ballistic" and demonstrated against it. Older Germans who had experienced the horrors of World War II and knew the unrestrained brutality of Russian soldiers at the end of that conflict claimed, "It's better to have a missile in the garden than a Russian in the kitchen.")

Physically and culturally, we were a world away from the ranches in Northern California or our familiar haunts in Alaska or California. This really was different. If we were going to share the gospel in Germany, God would have to make fundamental changes in how we saw ourselves, the unsaved, and God himself. We all felt the tension and challenge of this new life and had to cope with it in whatever way we could.

After being there for two years, I knew how I wanted to deal with it. I wanted out. I thought I knew how it could happen without making me look like a quitter—which was how I felt.

Every year we had to go to the Munich main police station to get our residence visas renewed. The gloom of the building's interior was reflected in the immigration officials. They were an unfriendly lot who rarely smiled.

Once, Kathi van der Gugten was getting her visa renewed and had a chance to see the folder the immigration office had for her. Her personal file contained a list of every member in our church. They had already told some of our original group their visas wouldn't be renewed and they would have to leave the country within forty-eight hours.

Wow, I thought, *they have to leave and can blame the "anti-Christian" government!*

It turned out our people were allowed to stay. But I hoped the same thing would happen to us, and we wouldn't be allowed to stay. Then I could show humble acceptance, smile, hold my hands up and say, "Oh, well, praise the Lord!"

I waited my turn in the hallway until called, then walked into the office and sat down in front of the official's desk. I handed him my papers and told him I wanted our residence visas renewed. (*Please, Lord, have him say, "Nein!"*)

Wordlessly, he looked at everything, then at me. Then he said, "Ihre Papiere sind nicht in Ordnung." ("Your papers are not in order.") He told me to get them right and bring everything back the next day.

My heart sank, and I felt terrible. Now my torment would be prolonged. I went home and returned the following day with what he wanted.

On the way, I felt tremendously burdened. I had to find somewhere to pray and unload my heart to the Lord. I found a place where I knew I wouldn't be disturbed. It was a huge Catholic church with high ceilings, stained glass windows, and filled with rows of pews and statues. It had been many years since the church had been full of worshipers; now the only visitors were a few tourists and me.

So I had an honest talk with the Lord. I told him, *Lord, I don't want to be here; it's too hard. What's going to happen to me if things get really tough?*

He let me do most of the talking, and as I opened my heart to him, the burden became lighter. Soon it was almost entirely gone. I came to a place where I could honestly say to him, *Lord, it doesn't matter what may come in the future. I want to be where you want me and I know that you'll be right there with me.* The fear and torment left me and were replaced with joy! I didn't dread going to the police station or what might happen there.

A few minutes later I was sitting in front of the same official and handed him my papers. Again, without expression, he looked at everything, then got up and with the papers in hand, left the office. He returned a few minutes later and sat down. Without looking at me or saying a word, he began grabbing official rubber stamps from his "stamp tree." (German officials *love* stamps. They get depressed if they can't stamp and initial a document three or four times.) He began banging away with stamps on our passports and another paper. Then he handed them to me.

I was a little confused and wasn't sure what had just happened. "Did I get it?" I asked.

"Ja," he said, *and he smiled!* Now tell me God doesn't do miracles. The last time anyone in that building smiled was probably in 1913.

We stayed in Germany, and with a break in between, ministered there for twelve years.

"Yay! I Get to Go to Germany!"

My own path to Germany probably started with the way God made me. I spent two years in college in Fullerton, California with a vague goal of working for the U.S. State Department in the Foreign Service. It felt like a natural fit for me. In school my interests were political science, English and foreign languages. After my first year of college, I spent the summer of 1969 traveling through Europe with friends, and then later, in the army, I was stationed in West Berlin. I enjoyed living and moving in a foreign society.

God speaks to us all in different ways, and I have rarely gotten a "thunderbolt" from the skies to tell me what to do. Gospel Outreach was putting together the Germany team, which would join those already sent over to prepare the way. I prayed and fasted, seeking to hear from God if I should join them. I guess I can say I did hear distinctly from the Lord, but he didn't tell me specifically to go to Germany. What he impressed clearly on me was, *I don't care where you go, as long as you love me.*

My response? *Yay! I get to go to Germany!*

I remember sitting on a picnic table in the garden at Carlotta praying. With no one else around, it was just me and the Lord, and it felt like a special time of closeness. As I got ready to return to the house, I had one last request. *Lord, can you give me a couple of eagles soaring up over that hill, on the wind currents? I would love that!*

I sat there and watched in anticipation—waiting to see if the Lord would give me what was really just a light-hearted request. I got two crows (which was still pretty cool)!

The G. O. outreach to Germany resulted from widely separated threads coming together and being spliced into a single cord. The threads originated in Ireland, West Berlin, Hanover, West Germany and the Lighthouse Ranch.

Ireland

Alan Conroy was an Irish lad who got himself a forged passport and used it to travel around the U.S. in 1971. As in so many of our lives, he thought he was in control of his plans. God used his steps and missteps to fulfill his purposes. This Irish boy, who wasn't supposed to be in the States, ended up at the Lighthouse Ranch, heard the gospel and got saved. One of the first orders of business for him was to get his passport straightened out. Jim Durkin took him down to the Irish Consulate in San Francisco where he received the proper papers but still had to leave the country within the next few months.

Hannover, West Germany; the Lighthouse Ranch

An American couple, Loren and Laurie Snider, were active with church outreaches in the northern German city of Hannover. They had originally gone to Germany with Youth With a Mission (YWAM) to work in the 1972 Olympic Outreach. There they helped to secure a small castle outside of Munich as a base of operations for YWAM. This later became one of YWAM's Discipleship Training Schools.

After the Olympics, they returned to the U.S. for a short time and Loren and the pregnant Laurie visited family in the Eureka area. Laurie began to experience difficulties and had to be admitted to the hospital for treatment. Things got worse, and then she lost the baby. Infection kept her in the hospital and Loren was left to sort things out for himself. *Why did God allow this to happen? Was Laurie going to be okay?* He needed to find someplace where he could pray and look for comfort and wisdom from God.

Loren drove out to the ocean south of Eureka and found a beach beneath a bluff that stretched for several miles. With few people around he could walk the beach with only the wind, waves and God to hear his prayers. As he walked, he happened to look up and saw something that surprised him and made his heart jump. A big cross stood above him at the top of the cliff. For this man who had just lost a child, and whose wife was in danger, it symbolized hope and help from a compassionate God. Loren climbed the steep slope.

As he crested the hill, he was surprised to see a collection of buildings behind the cross, gardens, and men and women walking around doing various jobs. It was the Lighthouse Ranch.

The ranchers were used to visitors dropping in from the road or the beach and welcomed him. Before long Loren was learning more about the Ranch and the extraordinary commitment of these Christians who called themselves disciples.

After Laurie recovered and was released from the hospital, he brought her out to see for herself. Loren had been raised in the church—his father was a Baptist minister, and Laurie grew up in Hollywood—a relative of the Bridges acting family. They were unprepared for the stories the brothers and sisters told of the powerful move of God they were experiencing. What they heard excited them and gave them a vision for another Lighthouse Ranch in Germany.

The Sniders were getting ready to return to Germany and met with Jim and Dacie to discuss the possibilities. Nothing was decided, but Jim took the opportunity to introduce Loren to Alan Conroy. Alan had already spent time at the Ranch, was returning to Ireland and Jim felt he could make a positive contribution to what Loren and Laurie wanted to do.

West Berlin

Thomas van Dooren, born and raised in West Berlin, was the son of a band leader/musician and grandson of a concert pianist. He met his future wife, Kristine, in the summer of 1970 when she and her sister were traveling though Europe and included Berlin as one of their stops.

Their stay lasted longer than planned after Kristine's sister was taken to a hospital with injuries suffered escaping from a couple of attackers. Through mutual acquaintances, Thomas and Kristine got to know each other and found that they had similar interests. The extended visit allowed them to spend more time with each other, and before they knew it, they had fallen in love. Rather than return home to San Francisco, Kristine decided to stay in Berlin with Thomas when her sister flew back.

The city of West Berlin was located one hundred miles inside Communist East Germany and was surrounded by the Berlin Wall. Special permission was needed to pass through East Germany to the West; entry into East Berlin was just as difficult.

The open spaces of California must have beckoned, and after a year and a half, Thomas and Kristine decided to move to the States. They stayed with Kristine's parents in the San Francisco area for a while and then struck out on their own, diving wholeheartedly into the hippie/back-to-the-land scene. During this time they were married and shortly thereafter, Kristine became pregnant. Their idea of moving out on their own meant sewing an Indian teepee together that they set up in a field overlooking the ocean in Mendocino County. When they awoke one morning to hear a hammer pounding nearby, Thomas got up and investigated. He found signs saying "Hunting by Permission Only" nailed to some of the trees. Time to move.

They heard of different communes nearby so Thomas hitchhiked through the area looking for a suitable place for him, Kristine, and the soon-to-arrive baby. One ride took him to a commune just west of Garberville, called Living Waters. He saw the big cross with the words, "Whosoever Will May Come" written on it and immediately felt welcome. He talked with some of the residents, who said he and Kristine could move there.

Thomas returned to the teepee and told of his find. After mulling it over, they decided to wait because they weren't sure they were ready to live with a bunch of Jesus Freaks. The next day, Thomas hit the road again and was picked up by a fellow who had given him a ride months before and had invited him to his commune. He repeated the invitation and this time they picked up Kristine and drove to the Lord's Land. Impressed with the obvious joy, love, and care of the brothers and sisters, they were deeply moved as Tomas Dertner shared the gospel message with them.

Thomas had figured out his own life philosophy, which included everything under the sun, except for the Christian God. Kristine was raised in the church, and although her faith obviously wasn't the kind that shaped her life, she believed that Jesus was the Son of God.

Tomas told them things they had never heard before—at least not from someone who was full of the Holy Spirit. Kristine tells the story, "I had never heard about Jesus like this before. My heart was pounding in my chest. What really affected me was when he said, 'Your lives will be changed forever when you take this step. You will feel different and will know without a doubt that God really is near.'"

Tomas and the others invited the couple to pray and accept the Lord, but Thomas wasn't ready to take the step and put them off.

They spent the night there in their sleeping bags on the wooden floor of the dining room. They talked about the commune, the brothers and sisters, and most of all, the excitement they were beginning to feel in their hearts that, at last, they had found the truth. They asked each other, "Is this possibly the end of our search? Is this the chance for a new life, a life lived close to God?"

Kristine says, "There seemed to be no more doubt that Jesus was the answer to our longing."

They had nothing to lose and if they were really searching for the truth, then they at least had to give Jesus a try. Before they fell asleep, they prayed. "God, forgive us of our sin. We believe you sent your Son Jesus to save us."

Tomas had promised them the night before that they would know they were saved once they gave their lives to God. The next morning Kristine got the proof.

The sisters were preparing breakfast in the kitchen and she offered a bag of softened soybeans to add to the meal. This was gladly accepted and Kristine put them in the oven to toast. Before she knew it, they burned and she pulled out a tray of what were now black beans instead of soybeans. She swore. That wasn't a surprise; up to that moment it had been a normal part of her everyday speech. But now she experienced something new.

"I felt very awkward. As soon as I said that word, it became clear to me I never wanted to speak words like that again. I knew immediately God heard me, and that it wasn't pleasing to him. I also knew this new feeling was the answer to our questions. Yes, I was new; I was different, and I didn't have the slightest doubt! God was real."

The brothers and sisters rejoiced to hear of Thomas and Kristine's prayer the night before and invited them to stay at the Land. But Thomas had felt that Living Waters was the place where they belonged.

They headed out to the highway to hitchhike back down to their teepee. As Kristine (very pregnant) sat on their stuff and Thomas stood with his thumb out, they discussed this change in their lives.

Thomas told her, "Well, I guess this means we're Christians now. But we're not going to be like all the others who go around preaching to everyone. You know, like missionaries."

God immediately began his work in their lives, changing them into his son and daughter and eventually—missionaries who shared their faith with everyone.

Things happened quickly, very quickly. Within a twenty-four hour period, they had turned their lives over to God and began to experience his transforming power. After returning to the teepee, Thomas ran a quick errand and coming back, took a shortcut along the beach. He was almost washed out to sea in a spot where the locals reported several people had been lost to fast moving tides. Caught by the swirling waters, he was beyond exhaustion but saved in a way he couldn't explain.

Then when Kristine gave birth to their daughter Nomtini (later changed to Naomi), she popped out into Thomas' arms, looking straight into his eyes.

They moved to Living Waters and under the guidance and teaching of the brethren, they committed their whole lives to God and began to grow into the kind of disciples that were the hallmark of Gospel Outreach.

Some Sundays, the people from Living Waters would ride the old school bus one hundred miles up Highway 101 to Eureka to attend church at Vet's Hall, with all the other people from Gospel Outreach. These were always fun times of fellowship, a shared midday meal between the two Sunday services, and a time of strolling around town.

Jim Durkin often preached in the first service. One Sunday, as Thomas and Kristine listened, he implored the young disciples saying, "Jesus is calling you! Follow him to the ends of the earth and preach the gospel! It won't be easy, and you will be persecuted, but you will receive an eternal reward." He finished the message with the questions God asks in Isaiah 6:8 (NKJV), and Isaiah's reply. "Whom shall I send? And who will go for Us? Then I said, 'Here am I. Send me!'"

Something was stirring in Thomas and Kristine's hearts. They added a new prayer to the requests and petitions they brought to the Lord: "Lord, we want to serve you with our whole life and are ready to go where you want us to go. Send us."

A still, small voice replied, *Return to Germany*.

They understood. It might take a few years of preparation. There were financial matters to sort out and probably more training before they left California, but now they had direction.

They were surprised during another visit to Eureka when Jim and Dacie invited them to lunch after the morning service. Jim said he had heard many good things about them from the elders at Living Waters. He told them there was a married couple who had visited the Lighthouse Ranch a short time before, Loren and Laurie Snider, who were interested in starting a Gospel Outreach church in Germany. "Would you be interested in joining them?"

Thomas and Kristine were a little taken aback. They had been Christians for less than a year and weren't sure they were ready for such an important step, but they said, "Yes, we can see ourselves returning to Germany."

Jim was glad to hear that. He couldn't tell them when it would happen but told them they needed to get ready.

As the summer of 1974 approached, Tony Tuck decided to sell the property at Living Waters and the van Doorens were to help David and Rosemary Hatton close it down. The brethren still living there were sent to the other ranches, to the in-town Eureka houses or down to the teams in Los Angeles. The job was done by the end of November, and

Thomas and Kristine moved into one of the Eureka houses. That same day they attended a G. O. church service. As they walked into the building, they were surprised when someone told them that a church planting team was to be sent out to Germany during that service.

Jim explained to the assembled brethren that he never had a goal of building a mega-church with the young people who came to believe in Jesus at the ranches. Rather, his vision was that we would all fulfill the Great Commission to take the gospel into all the world. Now the Lord was showing him to send a team of three married couples to Germany to join the Sniders and Alan Conroy and his new wife Elly. He named them: Gregor and Linda Chello, Peter and Jackie DePalmo, and Thomas and Kristine van Dooren. Carlos Ramirez, sitting behind them, leaned forward and asked, "How long have you known about this?" Their surprised expressions gave the answer. Along with everyone else—they had just found out!

They were all called to the front of the church for prayer, which gave the van Doorens their first opportunity to meet the Chellos and DePalmos. As surprising and unsettling as this may feel to us today, the Spirit of God was moving. It seemed as though daily or weekly, important events were unfolding, great plans were being made, and we were in the middle of it all. Thomas and Kristine knew God was calling them. In spite of the confusing circumstances, they were confident he was behind it all.

Both Gregor and Peter were ordained elders in Gospel Outreach and had served in various positions of leadership in the church. Together with Loren, Alan, Thomas, and their wives, they would begin building the new church in Germany. In a way, the new arrivals already had a start on a new church. The Sniders and Peter and Jackie had two small children, and both the van Doorens and Chellos had one child and were expecting another.

This initial group was intended to prepare the way for a second, larger team. It was much better for a small band of missionaries to learn the lay of the land, which included making mistakes and learning how to do things correctly, before the larger team showed up.

Potatoes and Peanut Butter

Loren had shared his vision for a German Lighthouse Ranch with a local pastor near the city of Hannover, Germany. The pastor had then offered him the use of a large house with land. It was ideal. The Sniders and Conroys were working hard to get it ready for the new team, when the pastor came to Loren with bad news. He had changed his mind; the house was no longer available.

Now things got really interesting. The three families from Eureka were already on their way and there was no place to put them.

The Lord stepped in. Elly tells of a middle-aged Christian couple from a local church who heard of their plight. The couple owned a farmhouse in a nearby town that was empty. They could use it but it needed lots of work. Elly says, "The new Christian landlord was a very kind man and helped us as much as he could with the repairs and even started to build out the attic for us. His wife used to bring us food. After weeks of hard labor to get the old house in shape, it was time to collect the couples from Holland."

The three families had traveled to the East Coast of the U.S. The Chellos flew directly to Germany while the DePalmos and van Doorens took a train to Quebec. There they boarded a Polish steamer sailing for Rotterdam,

Holland. Loren met them and everyone piled into his Volkswagen bus with all their gear.

The end of December 1974, they finally arrived at their new home in Nienburg, a small town in northern Germany, midway between Bremen and Hannover. In the land of castles and palaces, their new home appeared to Peter to be "older than the United States of America."

Five families with six kids (there was also one single brother) were stuffed into a house that was half as big as it appeared—the other half was a barn with animal stalls and rooms for equipment. Originally built for a farmer, his family, and his animals, it wasn't designed for comfort or four additional families.

The four rooms on the ground floor were arranged in a line; three were used as bedrooms. If your bedroom was the last one, you had to go through the first two to get to yours.

The upstairs living space was even tighter. The sloped roof of the house meant the walls were slanted, which made it hard to place furniture or even stand next to the walls. Narrow stairs led up to the top floor. When you opened the door, a small refrigerator, stove, and sink stood directly in front. The rest of the space was divided up into a small dining/living room with a wood heating stove, and two more bedrooms.

Having a bedroom upstairs didn't offer its occupants more privacy than the arrangement downstairs—the one bathroom in the house for the sixteen inhabitants was between the rooms. All the traffic went past the bed and dresser. Still, it would have been even busier if the house had a shower or bathtub—which it didn't. Everyone heated water on the stove and bathed in their rooms—when there wasn't traffic going through.

The cramped, ancient, and inadequate living space might have been a little more tolerable if only the food were decent. It wasn't; it was terrible. Before the team arrived, Loren had a great idea. He knew finances would be tight so he filled the basement with potatoes. After all, he reasoned, the Irish lived on potatoes and thrived (to which Elly commented, "Did he realize that a million died of starvation?"). Added to that, they had cabbage, huge turnips, enormous tubs of peanut butter bought in Amsterdam, and fresh bread from a local baker. If their fare was not appetizing, at least they wouldn't starve.

They came to preach the gospel, but the very first item of business was to make the house more livable, or at least, less uncomfortable. Gregor and Peter got busy adding heating stoves to each of the bedrooms and installed a shower in the small laundry room on the first floor.

The nice thing about being young and full of faith is, when you have big plans, you assume the details will take care of themselves.

This team with the goal of bringing the gospel to Germany had one major weakness. While Loren and Alan had some grasp of the German language, Thomas and Elly were the only ones who could communicate in every situation. While the others looked on, Thomas handled most of the translation of their requests and messages to the grocer, public officials, other pastors, doctors, and anyone else who provided a needed service.

The men started a leather business just like the ones that Peter had in Eureka, Living Waters, and with the Evangelistic Team. They sold leather key chains, belts, and other small items at flea markets from Hamburg in the north to Munich in the south. This, together with a monthly amount sent from Eureka helped to cover the basic costs, but just barely.

Going out on a limb like this for the Lord necessitated a miracle or two and according to Kristine, "He always came through!"

Peter remembers, "There were times when the women told us there was no food (aside from the now rotten potatoes) or the money to buy any. All we could do was pray. Before too long, there would be a knock on the door. When we went to see who was there, there was no one, just a basket of food on the doorstep loaded with cheeses, sausage, fruit and bread."

While they were living at a subsistence level in Nienburg, a bigger challenge was being prepared in Eureka. The second Germany team, this one seventeen members strong, was coming together. Now they would need an even bigger miracle. It was obvious that a farmhouse in northern Germany that was barely big enough for the first group would be way too small for the rest. The decision was made to search for a new place and at the same time, leave the countryside and relocate in a major city. It was felt that this would provide better opportunities to reach the greatest number of people.

Thomas and Alan were sent to look at Berlin and Munich and after they reported back, Munich was chosen.

Sometimes the Lord just does amazing things. They found a house in Munich that was everything the farmhouse wasn't. They traded their small cramped quarters for a residence that was built by the German Airline, Lufthansa, as layover housing for aircrews flying in and out of the nearby airport. Including a basement with living quarters, there were four floors divided into bedrooms, bathrooms (with showers!), a living room, dining room, and kitchen. The families could even have separate rooms for the children.

Negotiations were tough—not many landlords would want to lease a house to a group of people who called themselves Christians and, what would be troubling for a German, professed to be neither Lutheran nor Catholic. (German society is very ordered. Everything has to fit in the box that was made for it. For many Germans of that time, there were three Christian religion boxes: Catholic, Lutheran and Weird. We were put in the latter box.) Still, the lease was signed, with G. O. in Eureka paying the deposit and the first few months' lease.

The Team Assembles

The new team was assembled in November of 1975. John Jordan led the seventeen people—all single men and women with just one engaged couple—Linda and me.

The changes that Linda and I experienced as a result of being missionaries to Germany started before we joined the team, before we really knew each other and even before she could speak one word of German.

A meeting was held in the summer of 1975 in the living room of Carlotta—as well as at the Lighthouse and other G. O. ranches and houses. People were asked to pray about joining the different teams being sent out. I had already signed up for Germany. As Jim Durkin Jr. explained the choices to the brethren sitting around on the old furniture, Linda's hand shot up. She later told me, "The Lord did it. I didn't raise my hand, but suddenly, I had this big desire to go to Germany."

After the meeting, I talked to her and asked if she knew any German. She didn't, so I offered to help. This was very nice of me but then, she was a cute, blonde sister with a bubbly personality who loved to laugh, and that may have helped. We spent an hour each afternoon practicing. While her progress with the language was slow, the growth of our friendship was fast.

One day I noticed a subtle change in the teacher/student relationship. It was something in her eyes. "Are you falling in love with your teacher?" I asked. Now, not only Linda's German, but her English failed her; she looked down and mumbled something. Her embarrassment and smile told it all. It looked as if I might not be going to Germany as a single brother.

A couple months later we got engaged. In January of 1976, we got married during the time the Germany Team was planting trees. We honeymooned in Honeydew (of course!) south of Eureka. Then our first home was a tent up in Coos Bay, Oregon, where we joined the others.

The tree planting provided money for the team's move and gave us a financial cushion once we arrived. We worked in the forests of Mendocino, staying on the Lord's Land, which was now empty of the disciples who had once witnessed to Thomas and Kristine. From there we moved on to other jobs throughout the Pacific Northwest.

While planting in Coos Bay, Oregon, we were joined by a newly saved young man from Switzerland, Peter van der Gugten. He had been traveling throughout the U.S. and Canada when he showed up at the Lighthouse, and turned his life over to Jesus. Peter was an enthusiastic young believer who made a great contribution to the team, as he was its only German-speaking member, and he had experience living in Europe. Among other things, he taught us how to eat correctly, keeping our fork in our left hand, and knife in our right. He taught us Swiss German—which was of limited value in Bavaria where they speak (surprise!) the Bavarian dialect. Still, he was a big help.

This had to be loads of fun for Peter, a young Swiss guy traveling around the U.S. Like every European tourist, he hoped to get an idea what life in the New World was all about. Now he was plopped down in the middle of a bunch of Christian disciples and roaming the rugged mountains of the Pacific Northwest, where he learned about Jesus, planted trees, and became a part of God's family.

We planted together for eight months. Part way through, we sent some of the team ahead to Munich. Kathi, Vernita Robinson, Randy Cole, Tom Nesmith, John Lewis, Roger Dusatko, Ron Gloeckler, and Peter, made the trip first. They joined the families who had already moved into the house in Munich.

The rest of us (John Jordan, Suzi Schutzle, Chris Funnell, Dan Kler, Mike Stopp, Jay Hawes, Susan Tucker, Greg Hogue, Linda and I) finished our last job in Colorado, on a mile-high butte. When done, we were too tired for much celebration but we posed for a team photo in front of a tent with our hoe-dads and worn boots on the ground in front of us.

After the photo, we packed our gear, threw our boots away, and headed for New York. Flying Icelandic Air from New York to Frankfurt, we all arrived in our new home by the end of June 1976.

The first team had done its job. The Chellos, the DePalmos, Sniders, Conroys, and van Doorens had truly broken ground for this Gospel Outreach effort in Germany. Without having a clue as to what they were getting into, they volunteered to be the planted seed that had to "die" in order for a healthy plant and crop to grow. They endured the initial deprivations, confusions, and trials of a new work in a foreign land.

With the move down to Munich, Loren and Laurie elected to stay in northern Germany. After the second team arrived and had gotten established, Gregor and Peter and their families planned their return to the U.S. Alan and Elly moved to Ireland, settling down near Dublin.

Thomas and John Jordan now took over the leadership of the church. We were still a little shaky as three years was the longest any of us had been Christians. Jim sent over Steve and Terri Schrater to help out. Peter and Jackie agreed to stay awhile longer to help the transition to the new leadership team.

Strangers in a Strange Land

We loved our new home, especially considering we just spent the last eight months living in tents in the mountains. It was located on a quiet street in the Munich suburb of Trudering. A three-story affair, it was nicely divided into apartments with shared bathrooms and showers. There was a common kitchen, living, and dining room on the ground floor. Compared to the Lighthouse, Carlotta, or any of the other ranches, this was luxury.

We noticed a few differences. Unlike the houses of the American West, which were built of wood from the abundant forests, homes in Germany were mostly constructed of the readily available stone and brick, and all the roofs were tile. As a result the houses were loud. Stone stairways and floors amplified voices and sounds throughout the house.

Munich lies on the same parallel as Seattle and New York City, which means that most of Germany is as far north as Canada. It could get really cold. All the windows were double paned in the old style, that is, each window opening actually had two windows that could be opened and closed separately. In the wintertime, the sill between the windows provided a handy refrigerator for the individual rooms where milk, yogurt, fruit, or chocolate could be kept fresh. In addition, every window had what was called "Rolladen" or interlocking outside shades installed in the wall above the window. When closed, they added extra protection from the cold and also shut off all light from the outside, making that room totally dark.

We grew accustomed to different style light switches, electric outlets, small refrigerators, (Germans shopped several times a week; they didn't need large refrigerators because they were always buying fresh food) clothes washers and dryers. Gasoline and coffee were expensive. At a time in the U.S. when twenty-five cents would buy you unlimited cups of weak restaurant coffee—a dollar would buy you one cup in Germany. Two cups cost two dollars. But it was *really* good coffee! Clothing and shoe sizes were different. In the States my shoe size was 10 ½, in Germany, 44. In innumerable ways, both large and small, we were now living in a different world.

One custom that almost all of us appreciated was the "day of rest" that was observed every Sunday. It actually started on Saturday around two in the afternoon when shops began closing, and they didn't open again until Monday morning. Big semi-trucks were forbidden to drive on the Autobahn and in general, except for restaurants, all business came to a halt. The result was a real sense of rest. When we returned to the U.S., we immediately noticed that the hectic lifestyle here never let up; we missed the day of rest that German society embraced.

"I'm Going to Throw Up in Five Minutes"

Of course, the biggest adjustment was with the language. In North America, you can travel from the West Coast to the East, from the Rio Grande to the Arctic Circle and almost everyone speaks and understands English. In that same area in Europe you will find people speaking twenty different languages and a hundred different dialects. And no one understands all the others.

Peter's Swiss German got us started, and after we arrived, we attended language classes offered to foreigners at the local high school. The learning process included our attempts on the street to understand and be understood. We were never far from being embarrassed or getting a good laugh.

A friend who belonged to the Bavarian Alpine Club arranged for Linda and me to spend a week up in the Alps in one of the club's huts. These two-room log cabins, placed throughout the mountains roughly a day's walk from each other, were cozy and had enormous wood-burning kitchen stoves for heat and cooking. Since it was between the skiing and hiking seasons, we had the whole place to ourselves and enjoyed it tremendously. We couldn't wait to tell our friends.

Now, the German word for hut is pronounced "hoota." This is dangerously close to the word for hat, which is pronounced "hoot." Hoota = hut; hoot = hat.

Linda, who understood this new language but didn't speak it as well, got the words mixed up. She excitedly told everyone we had just spent a whole week in a Alpine hat.

The Munich church started a work project that would both raise money and provide discipleship training for new converts called "die Glasblume" (the Glass Flower). The brethren made glass-framed flower pictures that were sold to gift and flower shops. John Langsev managed it for a while and with his first delivery, faced a language problem. Many transactions at that time were done with cash, as credit cards were relatively rare. When receiving cash, the seller—in this case John—was required to note the payment on a receipt by writing, *"Betrag dankend erhalten"* ("Payment gratefully received"). With a start, he realized he didn't know what he was supposed to write or how to write it. Trying to keep his cool, he calmly took his pen and wrote some squiggles, loops and lines. With a blank expression the German shop owner looked at the receipt and asked, "What is this, Turkish?"

Judy Jordan hadn't been long enough in Germany to have mastered the language, but a couple days at the Trudering house gave her all the confidence she needed. At breakfast one morning in a house full of people, one of them was looking for margarine for his bread.

"Wo ist die Margarina?" he asked.

Judy volunteered to help. "I'll go get her!" She ran up to the sisters' dorm asking everyone where Margarina was—she was needed down at breakfast.

Of course, we were able to embarrass ourselves in other languages too. Before I learned German, I had a couple years of school Spanish. We picked up three visitors from Argentina once, and just like at the Lighthouse, allowed them to stay for a few days with us. That was a help for them in their travels, and it gave us the opportunity to share the gospel with them. One spoke Spanish and English, another spoke French and Spanish, and the third, Jorge, only spoke Spanish.

He was my guy; I would try to share the salvation message with him. He had to work as hard at understanding as I did speaking. This was actually an advantage in sharing the gospel. If we didn't speak well, people really had to pay attention to understand what we were trying to say. Every time I thought of what to say to Jorge in Spanish, German wanted to come out. In the middle of it all, we were interrupted when someone told me I had a phone call. I excused myself and told Jorge I would be back in five minutes. His eyes got real big and he looked very surprised. I thought, *Oh great, what did I just say?*

Fortunately, when I returned, Saul, the English speaker, was there too. As I walked in they both started laughing. "Marc," Saul asked, "What did you say to Jorge?"

"I just told him to wait here, and in five minutes, I will return."

He laughed, "Well, what you really told him was, 'Wait here, and in five minutes, I'm going to throw up!'"

The type of German that almost everyone speaks is called High German. In addition, the different parts of the country each have their own dialects; often, people from other areas can't understand them. We spoke High German with our friends and brethren. We understood them; they understood us. Then, one day I was listening to Dagmar, one of the sisters in the Trudering house, speaking to her mother who lived across town. She was speaking Bavarian, and suddenly, I couldn't understand a single word.

For the first several months, Thomas, Peter, and some of the German brethren who spoke English were our main translators. Slowly, more of us became proficient and confident with the language. This didn't happen to everyone. Some people were obviously more gifted to learn foreign languages than others. John Lewis, our oldest team member (I don't think anyone knew how old he was—probably in his fifties), never went past a rudimentary grasp of the language. But his friendliness, ready smile and laugh opened plenty of doors for him.

Those of us who had spent time planting trees had a good idea of what physical effort and fatigue felt like. For me, speaking German all day long introduced me to a new kind of tired: mental. For the first couple of years, until I became more or less fluent, I always had to think about everything I was going to say. I needed to make sure it was grammatically correct and that I was using the right words. This was especially important since I was sharing the gospel. I'd pray, "Lord, let this be what you would say, without the errors, but use them too." I was mentally worn out at the end of the day.

Changing Our Gypsy Look

Before we hit the streets with our guitars, tracts, and gospel message, one more thing had to change. When we packed our suitcases for the move, we threw in the clothes that we wore at home. In the States we were Christian hippies, Jesus Freaks, and tree planters. In Germany, when people saw how we were dressed, they thought we looked like Gypsies. That had to change because, whatever romantic image we Americans had of Gypsies from the movies, Europeans saw them largely as thieves that were not to be trusted. While things may have changed since then, that attitude was based largely on experience.

Linda and I visited the Italy team once. Linda was walking with Linda Costa as she pushed a baby stroller down a sidewalk when four Gypsy girls approached. The others held back as one came to the stroller to admire the baby. In no uncertain terms, Linda Costa strictly ordered her to stay away. She later explained it was common for one of them to first get your attention; then the others would crowd around, and before you knew it, things were missing from your purse or stroller.

We couldn't look like Gypsies, and we couldn't expect to share the gospel in Germany the same way we had in the States.

It was not uncommon at home to meet people for the first time, witness to them, then pray with them to accept the Lord. It was a time of revival and the Holy Spirit and other Christians had often done a lot of the groundwork. Walter Burbank had never met Kim van den Plas when the second statement Kim ever made to him was an invitation to accept Jesus. Walter did. I didn't know Sou Sou Knife when she witnessed to me at Carlotta, and I got saved.

Our experience in Germany was different, and it had something to do with the character of the people. It's typical for Americans to be open to new ideas. Germans aren't, necessarily. They are taught to examine things, test them, and evaluate the benefits, disadvantages, and usefulness of new ideas or products. Once they're satisfied with the value of something, they accept it.

The dominant church in Bavaria is the Roman Catholic Church, so the religion question was already taken care of. People asked, "What is this new thing these Americans are bringing?" People would point out all the obvious problems in the U.S. and ask, "Why don't you stay home? There's a big need there." We would approach someone in the city square, in a park, or at a lake and strike up a conversation. Eventually, we would ask, "Are you a Christian?"

The usual answer was, "No, I'm Catholic."

From people we spoke with, I learned that in 1976 America had three hundred different (what they called) cults. In the minds of the people, this meant Baptists, Methodists, Pentecostals, Assembly of God and so on. Sharing the gospel was going to be more work than we had experienced in the States.

The purpose of moving from Nienburg to Munich was to be closer to large concentrations of people, so we looked for the best areas to do that. Many years before, the city of Munich had turned its main downtown street into a pedestrian zone that stretched for over a mile past restaurants and cafés with sidewalk seating, ice cream parlors, and stores of every description, from tobacco shops to high-end clothing stores. During all the daylight hours, and especially on Saturdays and in the summer, the street was packed with shoppers, tourists, and others who just wanted to enjoy a cup of coffee and slice of cake and watch the crowds.

Within a couple of weeks of arriving, and after recovering from jetlag, we made our plans to start sharing the gospel. After a time of prayer and worship at the house, we would pile into our vehicles, a VW bus and a couple of flimsy, little Citroen cars nicknamed "ducks" because they were so ugly. They looked like they were built from a 1930s design, had a canvas roof that could be rolled back, side windows that swung out on a hinge and a two-cylinder engine. Their top speed with only the driver, was about sixty miles per hour; with each passenger the speed dropped. Once, four or five sisters (no names) took a duck on a tour of Bavaria. As they tried to drive up a steep hill, the poor little thing tried its best but just couldn't make it with the load. Except for the driver, they all had to get out and hike to the top.

We would drive downtown and park near the city center then walk through the narrow streets of old-town Munich. In front of the Munich Rathaus (I know that sounds funny, but it's the city hall—not a political statement) with its famous Glockenspiel, we gathered and unpacked our guitars. We had several musicians in our group, including Thomas, Randy Cole, Steve Barney, Hervé Parsy and Antos Bogacki. Standing in a semi-circle, we began singing and worshipping the Lord, mostly with German songs, but sometimes a couple English ones too. The singing had two purposes: it attracted a crowd and it encouraged us.

As we closed our eyes, lifted our hands and worshipped, it helped to move our focus from ourselves, and the intimidation we might feel standing in front of hundreds of people. We became aware of the presence of God, who loved all these people and earnestly desired that his salvation message be shared with them. This was why we had traveled thousands of miles and placed ourselves in a foreign land. Whatever trepidation we felt was replaced by confidence that the God of creation stood with us. We had nothing to fear; these people needed to hear what we had to say. Then we preached the gospel.

After a crowd had gathered, a brother or sister would step forward and begin sharing the message the Lord had put on his or her heart. This really wasn't a hit or miss thing. Often, we felt the Holy Spirit was supplying a specific topic to talk about. It might be our personal testimony, a story from the Bible illustrating mankind's need for God, current events, a telling of the sacrifice of Jesus, or something else. We knew we were sowing seeds. Each of the different stories, while maybe not making sense to some, were exactly what others needed to hear.

It wasn't unusual to get crowds of dozens and even a hundred people.

There wasn't a great deal of opposition, but there were plenty of scoffers, and we learned how to deal with them. They might yell out comments meant to make fun of us or to distract the crowd. Sometimes onlookers tried to take control of the situation by engaging the speaker in an argument. One of us would get this person's attention and debate him, so he would leave the speaker alone.

At Englischer Garten—a huge city park like New York's Central Park—we were sharing the gospel, like we did in downtown Munich, when a man came up loudly denouncing us, interrupting the speakers, and causing a real distraction. I was able to get his attention so the brother sharing could go on with his story. The man was very passionate and was angry at God and anyone foolish enough to call himself a Christian. We had a loud debate, and his anger and intolerance were plain for all to see.

All of a sudden, a screaming woman, who turned out to be his wife, plunged through the gathered crowd. "What are you doing here?" she loudly demanded. "Don't you have better things to do than trouble these people? Leave them alone and get back to your family!"

His whole demeanor changed, and he looked like a whipped puppy as he slunk away. I stood there with my mouth open, suppressing a laugh, and in awe at how God handled this scoffer.

We didn't see the same results in Germany we had come to expect in the States. This was a different society and people approached what we shared differently. Some engaged us in serious conversations as God's Spirit spoke to them. When they walked away, we knew we might never see them again, but we had a secret—the Holy Spirit wouldn't leave them and would continue his conversation with them.

Munich is a crossroads of Europe and many people from different countries live in the city or travel through it. We shared the gospel with anyone who would listen. Sometimes we found non-Germans were open in a way that Germans weren't. This was probably because, being far from home, familiar places, and people, they were more aware of their own personal needs. They didn't have to deal with peer pressure if they stopped to listen to a bunch of Christians.

Among the people who became Christians through our ministry, or joined us, were, besides Bavarians and other Germans, people from England, Ireland, Austria, Switzerland, Portugal, France, Romania, New Zealand, Iran, Norway, Ghana, Greece, Czechoslovakia, Argentina, and Serbia. Oh, and the U.S. too.

I tell people the gospel message that changed our lives wasn't an American or G. O. brand of Christianity because each of the people from those countries had the same experience we did. A compassionate God showed them their need for him and the obstacles that stood in the way. When they turned from their sins and accepted Jesus as their Savior, they experienced the same transformation we did. It would be difficult for the sister from Serbia to relate to the life the brother from Argentina lived, but now that we were brothers and sisters in Christ, we had something in common that would last much longer than our cultural differences.

Spiritual Rulers

Being transplanted from one country to another, from one culture to another, can be an eye-opening experience. As we grow up in our own homes and towns we often aren't able to "see" the spirits that rule the land and influence our lives. When we arrived in Germany, those spiritual rulers became very obvious to us.

Thomas stated that, "The spirit in the States is one of affluence and materialism, which is not really attacking as much as saturating you. But there is a very heavy and obvious kind of spirit over Europe and specifically over Germany that people easily sense. Everyone who travels from Germany to America, for instance, immediately feels like they are taking a breath of fresh air.

"Specifically, in Germany, there is a spirit of condemnation and a spirit of fear. Those two are very influential. There is also a spirit of sensuality, which is very heavy all over Europe. At times we have been led to break the power of these spirits, to bind the strong man. After these times, we experienced much more freedom and liberty in the Spirit, and much less fear."

We had to recognize these were special needs for the Munich church, so we made sure they were areas of prayer and teaching. While no doubt some of our mannerisms were a little off-putting to our German brethren—things like spontaneous shows of affection or starting new projects before sufficient preparation—they genuinely enjoyed our sense of freedom.

Things began to roll, and before too long, the house in Trudering was too small for the growing church. Young disciples like Werner Stoll, Dagmar Schneider, Michael Attenberger, Monika Botzang, Evi Blaha and others moved into the house. Others like Helmut Felzman, Hans Stoll and Regina Schmidt joined the group while living at home.

The official name of the church was "Christliche Hausgemeinde" (Christian House Fellowship) or "CHG" for short. A new house was found in the area of Munich called Schwabing, a fairly upscale neighborhood close to the city center. It was designated our Evangelistic House and Linda and I were the house heads for a couple of years. We brought in the homeless from the "highways and byways" to have a hot meal, a warm bed and to hear the gospel. We had plenty of room just like the Trudering house, so new converts were encouraged to stay. If they didn't already have jobs, we got them busy working in the Glasblume. This gave them something to do with their hands and gave us the opportunity to use work as a discipleship training ground.

Additional houses were opened up on the pedestrian zone in downtown Munich and in other areas of the city. These either served as evangelistic houses, which brought in the homeless and travelers, or as brothers' or sisters' houses.

The task of bringing souls to Christ was only part of our job. Jesus commanded us to "go into all the world and make disciples." Once a person got saved, God began his job of converting him or her to their new life and we assumed our roles as teachers and trainers.

Part of our focus was to identify those who could eventually assume leadership in the church. There were many who had the potential. Werner Stoll, and his brother Hans, Helmut Felzman, Louis Moinet (a French brother who had gotten saved in northern Germany), and Antos Bogacki, a New Zealander who gave his life to the Lord at the Evangelistic House in Schwabing, were all early disciples we saw as future leaders.

As Gospel Outreach, our vision was that each local work—especially a foundational church like the one in Munich—be a launching pad for other church planting teams. For a time, plans were made for a group to go to Ludwigshafen, roughly in the middle of the country on the Rhine River, but these were dropped. When a farmer and world-renowned agriculturalist, who was also a born-again Christian, invited us to send a group to his farm in Austria, we envisioned another Lighthouse Ranch. After a short while, we found it couldn't be sustained and the group returned to Munich.

The Munich church had success as the catalyst for others who shared the burden to bring the gospel to Europe. We got to know an English Christian couple, Brian and Christine Martin, who lived in Munich. He was a scientist, a virologist, who worked for the Max Planck Institute in Munich. We were able to help Christine during a difficult pregnancy, and a close relationship with them developed. Upon their return to England, they expressed the desire to continue to work with Gospel Outreach. From this relationship, the G. O. England team was born. Soon, the Elsaessers and Hewats joined them in Birmingham, England.

Andy Costa's Italian roots drew him back to the land of his ancestors, and he brought a team over to Florence. His initial contact in Italy was through the Munich church.

Jim and Diane Boutcher and Mark and Mary Richards, left the G. O. church in the Midwest to plant a team in France, near the Swiss border. They made a couple of scouting trips through the country, speaking with church leaders in various cities, looking for the place God had for them. Nothing seemed to click until, encouraged by a Portuguese brother in the Munich church (who lived in Switzerland), they moved to a small city on the border of France and Switzerland.

With all of these efforts, the brethren in the Munich church, led by Thomas and John Jordan, facilitated exploratory trips and the big move when the time arrived. We were able to offer our experience and prayers as they began to discover what it meant when Jesus said to take the good news into all the world.

Linda Costa says, "Our experience was made so much better by the love and encouragement of the G. O. Germany team. Thomas, Kristine, and the team there truly blessed us in many ways." They knew we were nearby, had already been through what they were facing and understood their challenges and trials.

Three Things

Three things stand out in my mind about our experience in Germany and I think every missionary can relate to them.

First, God brought an extraordinary group of young disciples to us—those I mentioned earlier and many others. We came confident of God's salvation plan and our ability to share it in Germany. Actually, we were overconfident. We were unaware of the many assumptions we brought with us, based on our cultural backgrounds, first as Americans, then as American Christians. The simple act of hugging each other—something American Christians take for granted—was awkward familiarity for many Germans and proved an obstacle to opening their hearts and minds to what we had to share. Where Americans are ready to make friends, Germans are slower to build relationships. We had to understand this wasn't because of any spiritual deficiency but a cultural fact that was neither good nor bad. It's just how they did it. Our German brethren showed patience and love toward us. At the same time they were eager to receive what God had given us.

Second, when we seek to serve the Lord in a more meaningful and effective way, he puts us through experiences that cause us to yield more of our self-reliance and self-will to him. There is a cost to be paid in serving the Lord, and it is not to be taken lightly. But the reward for doing so can only be described as glorious: a deeper relationship with God and the brethren and knowing we have stood the test.

Third, Hebrews 11:13-15, talks about those who have gone before us who admitted they were "strangers and pilgrims on earth." Instead, they longed for a better country—a heavenly one. Although we loved being there, we never felt at home in Germany. The circumstances forced us to see what God wants us to understand. This world isn't our home.

CHAPTER FIFTEEN

Guatemala

CARLOS RAMIREZ, A G. O. elder living in Eureka, was wondering where "into all the world" he would take the gospel that had saved him and his wife, Linda. It wouldn't have been too hard to guess. Carlos was born and raised in Colombia and had a good understanding of the Latin culture, and of course, the Spanish language. He had talks with Jim DeGolyer, James Jankowiak and LeRoy Nidever who were all interested in the countries south of the border.

On February 4, 1976, at 3:01 a.m., the list of possible locations was suddenly reduced to one—Guatemala. An earthquake with a magnitude of 7.5 on the Richter scale struck north of the capital city, just below the surface of the earth. The devastation was enormous. Those who could free themselves from the wreckage of collapsed houses and buildings peered through the darkness of the night and the dust to see entire neighborhoods where not a single house remained standing. The morning light, accompanied by terrifying aftershocks, revealed a new world to the survivors. Their homes, neighborhoods, and towns ceased to exist and had been turned into piles of adobe bricks, wood, and smashed furniture. That's what the survivors saw.

Other victims either lay injured, trapped, or dead in the rubble. Many were rescued; many more would die where they lay. The final toll was 23,000 dead and over 70,000 injured. Help was a long time coming for many of them. Numerous bridges and roads were destroyed or damaged by the quake as were 40 percent of the hospitals in the country. In an earthquake that lasted less time than it takes to read this paragraph, over 250,000 homes in the country had been destroyed and a million people became homeless.

Carlos and Linda were visiting his parents down in L.A. where they watched TV news reports of the tragedy. The reports mentioned that a local musician was flying a planeload of relief supplies down to help. Linda remembers, "Carlos saw that and said, 'We should do that.' He caught the vision immediately."

He and Leroy drove down to Guatemala with a financial gift donated by G. O. Eureka and to see what else could be done.

Carlos was walking down a street in Guatemala City one day when a man he didn't know approached him. The man addressed him in Spanish and asked, "Do you want to help Guatemala?"

"*Si*," said Carlos.

"Then build houses!" the man replied.

Carlos understood this wasn't a chance meeting; God was speaking to him through this man. He called Jim Durkin and told him. Jim asked, "Where are you going to get the money?"

Carlos said, "I don't know—God will have to provide."

There was so much devastation and loss that a team could be kept busy helping for a long time. The men returned to Eureka and shared their burden with Jim

Durkin, Steve Schrater, and Bernie Haraldson, and they all supported it. But the question was repeated: "How are you going to get the money to support it?"

They discussed getting jobs and saving their money—G. O. standard operating procedure. Then LeRoy stepped in and said, "No, we're going to do fundraising for this team." So for the first time in G. O., an outreach team did fundraising instead of planting trees or finding jobs. They got busy asking for donations from different churches, and at the same time, the team and vehicles were assembled.

While the army of God travels with more authority and power than any earthly force, its mode of transportation is often a chance collection of unmatched, non-descript, overworked and under-maintained conveyances. The team had an Airstream trailer, a U.S. Postal Service truck that Jim DeGolyer converted into a camper ("Pretty nice," according to Linda), a couple of vans, campers, pickups, and two other trailers.

Once they had the money and the vehicles ready, they got the team together. Coming from Eureka and Los Angeles G. O., Arcata First Baptist, and the Prince of Peace church in Portland, the team included Carlos and Linda, Jim and Mary DeGolyer, James and Lynn Jankowiak, Tony and Jane Tuck, Bob Smith and Carolyn Sprague (who were already engaged to one another), Susan Insko, Bob Trolese, Tom Becotte, Paul Boright, Iliana Ada Benach Ireland, and Dick Funnell. They loaded up their gear, and within two months of the earthquake, the G. O. Guatemala team set out.

The officially-christened "Love Lift" team's journey took them down California, across Arizona and New Mexico, and finally into Texas, heading for the Mexican border. The entire trip from Eureka to Guatemala City took almost three weeks. They spent an entire week just trying to get through the Lone Star State.

That's where the trouble started—in Texas. One vehicle after another broke down. Linda says, "It seemed like if anything was going to happen to them, it was going to happen there. It was crazy; we were constantly pulling over—the whole caravan." Bob Smith said, "If it hadn't been for Dick Funnell working on everything, we never would have made it. He was in his coveralls the whole time. We were the Beverly Hillbillies."

This didn't bode well. It wasn't that difficult to get things fixed in the States. What were they going to do once they were deep into Mexico? They need not have worried. Linda reports that, after they entered Mexico, they didn't suffer so much as a flat tire. The rest of the way to Guatemala the vehicles ran perfectly.

They arrived on the outskirts of Guatemala City, at a one-time Bible school called Los Alamos. This only worked for a short time because next door was a chicken ranch. Along with the noise and stink of squawking hens, came the odor of burning feathers when dead chickens were cremated. Everyone got breathing problems from that. They next moved to Dos Alicias, a piece of property used by missionaries who left after the earthquake.

For the first six months, the married couples of the Love Lift team lived in the trailer and campers, and the single men lived in small storage rooms on the property. The single women lived in the house.

Linda describes the local church they attended. "It was the kind of church where the men and women sat on opposite sides of the room. The brethren there were so precious. Most of us didn't speak a word of Spanish but they just welcomed us in. The women took the team's sisters to the market and showed us how to buy food."

If they hadn't yet mastered the art of haggling for purchases, at least they could learn how not to be taken advantage of. The women also taught them how to make a staple of their new diet—tamales. Linda says when Bob and Carolyn Smith got married the Love Lift women spent an entire day making enough tamales for the celebration.

So there they were in a country where a huge earthquake had shaken both the physical and spiritual foundations. The team came to share the message of God's salvation, which transcends this life with its trials and sufferings, but they had to do something to help those who had lost homes and loved ones.

Among their connections were several pastors who asked the team to help rebuild their churches. After working on a couple buildings, the team looked around at all of the people who were still homeless, and decided, "We've got to help these people get homes."

Gringos Eat People

While the four main leaders, Carlos, Jim, James, and Tony, began making contacts with the government, aid agencies, and church leaders, the other men began to branch out. Bob Smith said, "There was an explosion of direction." Bob Trolese managed a building project in the old shantytown of Colonia Carolinga. There, in an effort that eventually replaced destroyed shacks with 3,000 brick homes, Bob had the duties of general contractor. They weren't alone; Christians from the Church of Norway, the Church World Service, Mennonites and other evangelistic groups also labored with them. Tom Becotte, Dick Funnell and Paul Boright assisted with other projects.

Bob and Carolyn began to work with the poor Mayan Indians in the mile-high village of Cerro Alto about an hour north of Guatemala City. This was an eye-opening experience for them. Guatemala City was settled and built in the style of the homeland of its Spanish settlers. Its streets, buildings, cars, trucks and people looked European, but were still familiar to American eyes. Carolyn remembers the homes at Cerro Alto were just "sticks." Bob said that after the earthquake, the town looked like a bomb hit it. "The richest man in town had an old 1948 pickup, one cow, and a kerosene-powered refrigerator." The people were Mayan Indians, short, illiterate and spoke the local Indian language but only a little Spanish, if any at all.

The team came to build houses and started looking for the people with the greatest need—widows with no family to help. The brothers enlisted the aid of locals. Linda remembers, "It reminded me of a *National Geographic* article. The people would carry loads of wood on their heads, up the hillsides, around bushes and trees." Starting with houses for the ten widows they found, they eventually built around ninety new homes. A year later they added concrete foundations to the houses.

A ministry called CEMEC donated all the wood for the 10' x 16' houses. It was precut and only required a simple system to assemble. The Love Lift team, with the help of the locals, was able to build two a day. Each structure had two rooms, a door and two windows.

Besides being more stable than the original dwellings, they had another huge, added safety factor. The huts of Cerro Alto all had roofs made of loosely laid, heavy tiles supported by wooden beams laid across the walls. When the earth shook, these roofs simply collapsed, killing or maiming those underneath. The builders secured corrugated tin roofs to the new houses. As Bob said, the roofs probably sounded like tin drums when it rained, but no one would be hurt when the next earthquake hit.

The team became close friends with their helpers as they worked together. Once Bob invited a man named Juan and his wife Emelia to spend a night with him and Carolyn in their house near the city. This was a whole new world for the two Mayans. Toilets were unheard of in Cerro Alto so the trees and bushes around the house served their usual purpose. The next morning, Bob greeted Juan and noticed that he looked a little ragged, as if he didn't get much sleep. He asked, "What's the matter? Didn't you sleep well?"

"No," Juan answered, "My wife didn't get any sleep and she kept me awake."

Bob was surprised, "Why?"

"Because she believes, '*Gringos comen gente*' ("White people eat people")." It was a myth in the mountains—white people were so big because they ate people. Some Mayans, clueless about God's love which brought the brethren to help, thought the team was building houses in exchange for small children—who would then be consumed. Carolyn remembers driving the dusty road up to the village and seeing people dive off the road into the bushes when they saw them coming.

The work progressed. Floors were being laid, walls raised, and houses covered with roofs, but Bob began to realize something. "One day it dawned on me that just building houses, praising the Lord, and mentioning his name during the day wasn't enough." They weren't seeing God move because while they were talking about God, they weren't inviting people to actually meet him.

"Then one day, after we finished a house and prayed for it, we shared the gospel with a very poor man and his family. We asked them if they would like to receive Jesus. The father said, '*Si*,' and then his two shy boys and a neighbor boy also received the Lord." Bob and the others went home rejoicing that four people had given their lives to God. A day later, fifteen more children prayed to accept Jesus. While they enjoyed building houses together with the people of Cerro

Alto, leading people to the Lord is what they were really there for, and they began to pray for more souls.

They took scraps left over from completed houses and built a new home for another widow. It was only a 10' x 12' shed, but in her life she had never had anything nicer. The pain Bob had first seen on her face was replaced by thankfulness as they finished the job and she could only say, "Gracias! Gracias!" As with every house they finished, they prayed, blessed her, and left. Two months later, they saw the widow again, and she was transformed. When she saw Bob and the brethren, her face lit up. She told them that on the night they finished the house and prayed for it and her, she had given her life to the Lord. She was a new person.

The team hoped to experience physical healings—the kind that "wowed" those who witnessed them—but were disappointed. Instead, they saw the miracles of transformed lives. Linda remembers like it was yesterday: "There was a family that Bob and Carolyn were reaching out to. They had a daughter who could have been in her teens or twenties. It was hard to tell because her body was deformed and she spent her entire life curled up in a hole next to the fire and never spoke. The girl was also spastic. Bob wanted us to pray for her. Team member Iliana, originally from Cuba, shared with the mother, and tried to communicate with her daughter about God's love, mercy and power.

"Bob said, 'Let's pray for her and worship. I think she really wants to praise the Lord with us.' We did and all of the sudden her body became calm. There was a moment when our eyes locked, and I know that she was looking at me." It was the beginning of a new life for this girl. Bob made a wheelchair for her. Soon, she was up and, though limited in movement and the ability to communicate, she began to have a life.

After Sunday church services down in Guatemala City, Bob and Carolyn and other team members would drive up to Cerro Alto and hold Bible studies and prayer services. For a time, Jim DeGolyer, Carlos and Steve Fish, who spent a year in Guatemala with Layne and family, alternated in giving pastoral care to the young flock.

Still, Bob says, "We weren't seeing as much fruit as we expected." They couldn't get around the fact that, while the Mayans were grateful for the help they received, these gringos might just as well have come from a different planet. The cultural differences were pretty big, and this proved a barrier to effective communication for many of them.

This was not a problem the church in the capital was having.

Middle and Upper Classes Respond

The brothers were working hard at the project at Carolinga. Just like at Cerro Alto and another outreach near the town of Huehuetenango, the gospel was being preached to the poor.

But, in the metropolitan capital of Guatemala City, something else began to happen. People from another level of society responded to the message, and at first, the brethren were a little surprised by this. When most of us in Gospel Outreach got saved, we were young and poor. The Bible told us that the poor are "rich in faith," and that the rich are guilty of oppressing those less fortunate than themselves. We asked ourselves, "Why waste time on the rich when the poor are ready for the message?"

It turns out that the middle and upper classes of Guatemala were ready and waiting for what the Love Lift team really had to offer. The brethren began holding church meetings at Dos Alicias for the team, their neighbors, and those they had witnessed to on the job. The word began to spread.

People noticed that these Christians were working hard to build houses and said, "God sent them." The teaching from the Bible wasn't what anyone had ever heard from a priest. They heard, "God has a purpose for your life and wants you to be a whole-hearted follower of Jesus." Soon, government and office workers, businessmen, the wealthy, and even a retired army general came to hear this new message. They started getting saved.

The team rented a house that used to be a girl's school. It had several rooms plus a large hall where sixty to seventy people could meet together. That quickly became too small and the church moved to a big circus tent. The first Sunday service saw 800 attendees and soon they moved to two services.

Jesus commanded us to make disciples. The Love Lift team had no intention of creating a church just for themselves. The plan was to reach the lost for Christ and train the new converts to be disciples and to assume church leadership.

Alfred Kaltschmitt and his wife Patricia were among the first and they brought in a steady stream of friends and relatives. Alvaro Contreras, Francisco Bianchi, and their families soon followed. The spread of the gospel was aided by the close-knit structure of Latin American families. When one person got saved, they evangelized the rest of the family and inevitably, more relatives followed.

With a growing congregation and a core of leaders in training, a name needed to be chosen that fit the culture and expressed the group's ideals. They decided on "Verbo" which means "Word," or Logos, the living Word, who is Jesus. It was a choice that would show reverence to the Bible. Not content to rest on their laurels, the brethren launched into a burst of activity that became the envy of the rest of us in G. O.

In 1979, when the communist Sandinistas overthrew the government of Nicaragua, most Christian missionaries cleared out. Communism and organized Christianity generally didn't get along well, and Christians always got the short end of the stick.

In 1980, after the Verbo elders visited the country to look at the situation, Bob and Myra Trolese took a team of Americans and Guatemalans and moved to Managua, into the lion's den. Showing much courage, wisdom, and faith, Bob led the team and then a congregation through the difficult twists and turns of sharing the gospel and making disciples in a country whose government was hostile to God and his people. They completed public work projects, established churches among the Miskito Indians on the east coast and elsewhere in the country.

In a nice, nose-tweaking move, Bob took advantage of an offer by the communist government of Cuba. They would pay for Nicaraguans to visit Cuba to see how the better half lived. Bob gladly accepted and used the opportunity to visit churches on the island.

Tom and Guisella Becotte took a team to Quito, Ecuador. Jim DeGolyer had been an exchange student there and soon joined them with his family. The church saw the same phenomenal growth that Guatemala was experiencing, and soon had the largest evangelical congregation in that country. Like their brethren in Guatemala and Nicaragua, they planted other churches in the country. Today there are around thirty churches.

Dick and Gladys Funnell led a group of brethren to Quetzaltenango, the second largest city in Guatemala. Their church became the hub for more congregations and schools along the border with Mexico.

Alvaro Contreras was in the very first group of Guatemalans to be ordained as Verbo ministers. He and his family did something a little different—but just as needed. They took a team to the U.S. In Miami, Florida they established Verbo Miami among the Spanish-speaking populace.

In 1985, James and Lynn took a team down to Brazil, setting up in Rio de Janeiro. They intended to establish a beachhead for the Portuguese-speaking world. Eventually they counted five congregations as the fruit of their team's labors.

Those of us in the other G. O. outreaches—in the States or in Europe were proud and happy for our brethren who responded to Guatemala's need. We knew the fruit they saw was the result of the foundation and teachings of Jim Durkin that we had all been given as well as faith and hard work. They were on their own now and had gone beyond even Jim's experience, learning the answers to entirely new problems and circumstances.

School Director/President of the Country

A circumstance that could never have been foreseen was when Verbo's school director was made president of Guatemala.

NEWSFLASH (Associated Press, March 24, 1982)
Rightist army officers ousted Guatemala's military President Romeo Lucas Garcia yesterday in a coup backed by tanks, planes and hundreds of soldiers who seized control of the capital, rebel spokesmen said . . .
The rebels appointed a three-man army junta led by retired General Efrain Rios Montt.

General Rios Montt was, at the time of the coup, sitting in his Verbo school office having parent-teacher meetings. Life in Guatemala was falling apart, which was not uncommon. Finally, a group of junior army officers had had enough and decided to overthrow the government. *Time* magazine reported that almost every detail of the coup was carefully planned. As helicopters flew over the presidential palace, tank gun and cannon barrels were trained on the building. Rebel troops took up positions, ready for a fight. A few hundred curious citizens watched from rooftops and neighboring windows to see what would happen next. At the first shot of a rifle or tank gun, they would instantly disappear.

A voice from a loud speaker filled the square as the coup leaders addressed the quiet palace. "Come out with your hands up, one by one. We don't want to hurt you."

There was no fight, no shooting, and General Garcia, the now deposed strongman president, exited the building and was led away.

Now the young officers were faced with a dilemma. Garcia was gone; they knew they weren't ready to run a country. Who could they get to do it?

General Rios Montt came to mind. Every officer in the army knew him. While the army's chief of staff, then head of the military academy, he had a reputation for integrity and honesty. That was exactly the kind of leader they needed now.

But, there had been some changes. Guatemala was one of those countries often dismissed as a "banana republic," where the words "coup" and "election" got equal use in describing transfers of power.

Rios Montt had actually run for president before—and won. But those in power didn't let him ascend to the office that every observer, both foreign and domestic, knew was his.

Fortunately, that didn't mean that Rios Montt's life was in danger—as long as he accepted the post of military attaché in Spain. This he did, and later returned to Guatemala.

General with a Servant's Heart

After Verbo began having meetings in the big tent, a distinguished-looking gentleman with dark hair and gray mustache walked in to have a look. He had heard from people about this group of Christians—not just Catholics—who were doing so much to rebuild devastated Guatemala and broken lives too. He liked what he saw and heard, and he gave his life to the Lord. Efrain Rios Montt became a born-again Christian.

He had a servant's heart and looked for any way to help his new brothers and sisters. Jim DeGolyer said it was common to see him with broom in hand, sweeping out the big green and yellow meeting tent.

Helena Moreno Loberg was a Guatemalan living in Eureka at the time. She was interviewed by the *Los Angeles Times* after the coup and asked about Efrain. "When I first met him," she said, "he was sweeping the church, then later painting it. I thought he was a janitor. Then I found out he was Gen. Efrain Rios. He has the respect of the cross-section of Guatemalan society."

Marta Pacheo, also of Eureka said, "He was my Sunday school teacher. He was a general, yet he is a humble man."

Before the coup and before the rigged election that brought it on, Rios and the leaders at Verbo fasted and prayed about him running for the presidency. They didn't have peace that this is what the Lord had for him. It was his decision—nobody tells a general what to do unless you're a higher-ranking general—or God. Then one of the brothers had a specific word for Efrain. "Your time will come, but it is not yet."

So he wasn't altogether surprised when he got the call from the coup leaders. They wanted him to join two other senior officers to lead the government. It quickly became apparent to Efrain and the others that, with his senior rank, integrity, and experience, the people of Guatemala would be best served with him as president.

He knew this wasn't his opportunity to be the big chief— it was God's. He would lead the country like King David, with respect, fairness, and looking to the Lord for guidance and grace. In the history of nations it can probably be said that it is very rare to have a leader like Rios Montt. On a NBC-TV news story, Rios Montt is quoted as saying, "I am trusting God, my Lord and King, to enlighten me, because he is the only one who gives or takes away authority."

Change came immediately to Guatemala. One of his first acts was to clear the government of men who had directed the killing squads that nightly shot up cars and people on the streets of the capital. Almost overnight, peace returned. An activist from one of the political parties told reporters, "I don't carry a gun with me anymore." The streets came alive again at night, as lovers and strollers could enjoy warm evenings, unafraid of violence.

The U.S. embassy wasn't completely happy with this turn of events. Not only did they not understand the character of this new president, they were clueless that the coup was coming. Still, they admitted that the difference from the previous regime was like night and day.

Rios Montt was a leader and had a good idea how to run a country, but he also brought in Francisco Bianchi and Alvaro Contreras from the church as spiritual support.

Carlos Ramirez served as his trusted translator when he made the occasional trip to Washington D. C.

There were others who had their own agendas who weren't pleased. Evangelist Luis Palau quoted a U.S. embassy analysis of complaints about Rios Montt and Guatemala's human rights record. It concluded, "We find a concerted disinformation campaign is being waged in the United States against the Guatemalan government by groups supporting the communist insurgency in Guatemala. This has enlisted the support of conscientious human rights and church organizations which may not fully appreciate that they are being used. This is a campaign in which guerrilla mayhem and violations of human rights are ignored."

There wasn't just a little "disinformation," there was a lot. One embassy official began his report with an easy-to-understand analogy. In addressing false claims and downright lies, he said, "My problem is like that of a mosquito on opening day at the beach. It's not that I don't know what to do, I just have to decide where to start."

Amnesty International, liberation theologians, and an organization with the acronym WOLA/NISGUA were all groups that flooded the news services with claims of murder and massacre ordered by the new president. The U.S. government found the reported incidents to have been actually committed by communist insurgents or not to have taken place at all.

President Rios Montt did his best to steer his country away from the things that harmed and toward the things that healed and built stable, strong societies. He restored discipline and order to the military, and required oaths of honesty from his officials. Weekly he would share a homily on the radio, encouraging the listeners with the Word of God.

He started a program for the poor Indians in the interior of the country who were plagued equally by poverty and the communists. Called "Beans and Rifles," it gave them both food and weapons to defend themselves from raids.

But, on August 8, 1983, Rios Montt was overthrown in a coup led by his defense minister. I asked Bob Smith about it. Rios Montt was exactly what Guatemala needed, why did he get removed? Bob said he didn't have enough support. "He wasn't left wing enough and he wasn't right wing enough." Rather than push the agenda of a particular political group, he was sincerely committed to bettering the lot of all Guatemalans.

Verbo Goes On

Anyone from Gospel Outreach who visits Verbo's website today will feel right at home. Purpose and Vision, Discipleship, Go Into All the World, Practicing the Word, etc.—are all there. Verbo is living out these principles and teaching them in thirteen countries with tens of thousands of brethren. Wherever Verbo has gone, they have labored to fulfill the Great Commission. They have shared the gospel with the lost, introduced the saved to God's family and showed them the way of discipleship. They have built schools, universities, and orphanages. Then they prayed for teams of brothers and sisters and sent them out to new places to do the same. It's a process that began many years ago at an old lighthouse station in Eureka, California.

Linda Ramirez (now Davisson) visited the church in Guatemala City not too long ago. "Many people came up to me and said that they had been in Verbo for thirty years and thanked me for leaving my home and my people and bringing the gospel to them."

Remembering the early days when they lived in trailers and campers, Linda thought of the first Guatemalan converts. Alfred and Patricia Kaltschmitt were attracted to the Love Lift team. In spite of their wealth, Patricia (they called her Pat) came to wash clothing with the women in an old wringer washer. Of course, they were happy for her friendship and to see her accept Jesus as her Savior. Still, they were curious. Why did she come to them?

Patricia answered, "The thing that is drawing me here is the love that you have for one another."

CHAPTER SIXTEEN

England, Italy and France

IN FOREIGN COUNTRIES, they don't do it like we do it. In Germany, when conversing, people will stand uncomfortably close as they talk to you. If you back up, they move closer. When entering a room, you shake hands with the men first, then with the women. Don't hug anyone! Learn how Germans shake hands—they do it aggressively. If you don't know how, you'll be embarrassed when some woman shakes your hand and throws it around like she's fly casting. That's what happened to me.

In Italy, learn how to use your hands when talking, but you better find out what the offensive gestures are first. Honking your horn to hurry traffic along isn't considered rude; it's communication.

In England, when first visiting in a home, stay seated until you leave; don't walk around. A "boot" is a car trunk, a "bonnet" is the hood, and a "lorry" is a truck. They drive on the "wrong" side of the road and then have to shift gears with their left hand instead of their right. It's thought that because everyone in the U. K. lives cheek-to-jowl on an island, they developed the habit of speaking nicely to each other. Unless they are on opposing football (we call it soccer) teams, then everything is allowed.

Every Christian everywhere has to learn the qualities of love, faith, and patience. Starting a new church in a foreign country requires those traits in an even greater measure, plus a lot more. The ways of a new society—how the people relate to each other, speak to each other, treat strangers, shop, drive, live in their homes—it's all different. It all has to be learned if a missionary wants to be able to share his or her message effectively. What's considered offensive? What's considered polite, funny, rude, sad, normal, or even wrong? Much will be different from the way they did it back home. The missionary needs to learn and adapt because he has come to share God's message. He doesn't want what he says to be discounted by habits he has brought from his own country, so that people who hear or see him think, "Oh yeah, well, he's an American. That's why he says that."

Gospel Outreach sent two families to England and even though the U.S. and England (or the United Kingdom) share a common heritage and language—we got most of ours from them—there are enough differences that the team still had plenty of adjusting to do.

The G. O. England team got its start in Germany. The Germany team got to know an English Christian couple, Brian and Christine Martin. He was a scientist working for a lab in Munich. When Christine had problems with her pregnancy she was advised to spend the final months before delivery in bed. That, of course, was a nearly impossible thing to bring off, except that the brethren at the Trudering house in Munich offered to help. They set aside a room for the couple and helped care for Christine until her due date, when she delivered a healthy boy.

As a result, a close relationship developed. After Brian's work at the lab was finished, they moved back to Birmingham, England. Jim Durkin visited the G. O. church in Germany and on his way home, he stopped by the Martins'. Jim discussed with them the possibility of a G. O. group coming there to start a church. They were open to the idea.

In the States, the call went out.

Alex Elsaesser was at a G. O. elder's conference in Santa Cruz, California and watched as Peter DePalmo, recently returned from Munich, showed slides of his travels in Europe. Alex describes what happened. "When a picture of the London City Mission appeared on the screen, the Holy Spirit came on me, and I began to shake." He knew the Lord was calling him and his family to go.

After the meeting, he signed up, along with several others, to join what was anticipated to be a team along the lines of the Germany or Guatemala teams, which each had fifteen to twenty members. Both the other big teams were organized and sent out in a period of a few months, but the Birmingham group didn't leave until three years later. By that time, the number of people had dwindled down to four adults, plus kids.

Alex and Renie, and Harry and Sandy Hewat, prepared for the move. They both had small businesses in Eureka, and worked hard to save the money for the move.

Even though Tony Tuck and Steve Schrater, two of the main G. O. leaders, spent time with the Elsaessers and Hewats, Gospel Outreach never had a missions board to supervise foreign outreach. There are probably two reasons for this. Jim was very busy with the churches and groups in the U.S. He had never worked with foreign missions, and no one in the church had the background to be able to implement that concept. Secondly, we all saw ourselves as missionaries whether we went to Arcata, Seattle, Los Angeles, Chicago, Germany, Guatemala, or wherever. We didn't feel it was someone else's responsibility to send us money. Our success depended on the Lord and our own efforts, not those of others.

The plan was Gospel Outreach standard operation procedure: find places to live, find jobs, or start businesses, then start sharing the gospel.

While still in the States, they applied to British authorities for permission to come to the country and start a ServiceMaster carpet cleaning business. With the help of Brian Martin, they engaged a solicitor (lawyer) in Birmingham to help them with all the paperwork and then waited to get the okay. The process took longer than expected, but finally their solicitor told them it was all going to work out. They could go ahead and come; everything would be wrapped up once they were on English soil.

You Can't Stay

After visiting family on the East Coast, in February of 1980, Alex and Harry flew over to prepare for their families' arrival. While the wheels of bureaucracy were slowly turning, they went ahead and took a one-week ServiceMaster training course, in anticipation of starting the business that would support them financially. After a week and a half, Renie, who was very pregnant and traveling with two boys and suitcases, and Sandy arrived.

Then they got a call from their solicitor. The application had been denied. What had looked like a sure thing when begun, was shot down by an English law that had just been changed. They couldn't start a business, they couldn't have a wage-earning job, and they couldn't stay in England. The government told them to leave. This turn of events was made immensely more interesting since they only had money for the move over and getting settled. They didn't have enough money to go back to the States.

Sometimes, it seems as if the Lord doesn't use our well-laid plans as much as our half-baked ones. With little money and no possibility of earning any, the Elsaessers and Hewats turned to the only help they could—the Lord. Harry and Sandy had found a house to rent, and Alex and Renie were offered a one-bedroom flat (apartment) at the Birmingham Bible College. The head of the school had spent time in Canada and had a soft spot for Americans. He now came to their aid and let the Elsaessers stay rent-free. Alex and Harry applied for residence permits to remain in the country as Bible students and the permits were granted. While getting the kind of education that no one else in G. O. got, Alex and Renie traded their labor around the college grounds for the Bible training and the rent-free flat. (This was probably the first, and maybe the only time, someone in G. O. studied at a real Bible school!)

This proved beneficial to the work in England that Alex and Harry wanted to do. Not only was their knowledge of the Bible expanded, but a certificate from the college gave them more credibility as they associated with other leaders. Harry studied for three years, and Alex continued for one more, finally receiving a Cambridge diploma in religious studies.

Word got out about their dire situation—they could stay in England, but couldn't work, or earn an income. People in both the U.S. and England began sending them money. As they became known in the Birmingham area, people would drop off bags of food. This helped, but not so much that they could neglect praying for God's provision.

They began holding meetings in Brian and Christine's home, and as people joined the church, they rented a community center. Unlike the Munich G. O. church, which did a lot of street and park evangelism, the brethren in Birmingham canvassed neighborhoods and passed out invitations to their meetings.

Friends in High Places

As the church began to grow, they saw that two services a week weren't enough for young people who had been plucked off the streets, and for whom conversion meant a drastic change from habits that were destroying them. The drugs and loose living had affected them as much as it had us; removing them from that atmosphere would increase their chances of success.

Alex, Harry, and the other church leaders were sure that a place like the Lighthouse Ranch would be ideal. Much prayer, thought, and research went into the idea, and a group of Christian project managers was enlisted to help. These men aided churches and Christian organizations in finding facilities that matched their needs and goals.

They discovered the ideal place. It was called the Forhill House and at one time was owned by the Cadbury family, a well-known name in the U. K. The Cadburys were Quakers who built a chocolate empire similar to Hershey's here in the States. They donated much to Christian and social causes and turned over the house and adjoining property to the Bournville Village Trust, outside of Birmingham. Before it became a target for the G. O. church, it was used as a youth reformatory. You could say that the church would use it for a similar type of activity—but with a different spirit. Just like the other Gospel Outreach ranches—like Carlotta, the Land, the Lighthouse—it was a real fixer-upper. Sitting unused for three years, it had been vandalized. Fixtures were missing, windows were broken, and the whole place was a mess.

But that was okay; Alex and Harry had been through that before and wanted to go ahead. The project managers helped put together an offer for the town council. The trust was willing to let the property go for one English pound a year—about three U.S. dollars—a terrific deal. Then they realized that included in the lease was the requirement to fix the property, bringing it up to building codes and making it livable. That would cost a good deal of money and labor, but everyone was sure God was behind this and waited for the trust's approval.

The council met to decide and then gave it to another organization.

Alex and Harry were bewildered when they learned that a group, which admittedly had plenty of experience with these kinds of properties, had been given the lease to the Forhill House. Then they got really upset when that group turned around and sublet the house to a Moslem organization. Not only had God's promise been taken from them, but it had been given to a group that was antagonistic to God and his people! How could that happen? They *had* heard the Lord properly, hadn't they? It appeared as if this was one dream fated to die, and they were devastated.

When Alex next talked to Peter, the head project manager, he told him of this depressing turn of events. Peter was very surprised and not happy with the decision. He promised to talk to one of the town council members who was a Christian.

Later, Alex got a phone call from the manager of the Bournville Trust. "I wonder if you'd like to visit the Windmill House," he asked. Like the Forhill House, it used to be a summer place for the Cadburys. Alex was given the address and told to meet with the trust afterwards.

When he got his first look at it, Alex was stunned. He says, "It was a seventy-bed conference center, all "kitted" up [that's English for "fixed up"]." It had a caretaker's house as well as other small buildings on the property and needed no renovation. They could have it for about $500 *a year* plus taxes. (The trust was practically giving it to them.) It had a new furnace, a fully-stocked kitchen, bedding—everything ready as if a conference would start the next day.

Alex went with Peter to the trust manager's office. The manager asked, "So what do you think of the Windmill House?"

Alex answered, "It's fantastic! Amazing!"

Then, as if to remind Alex that while our plans may sometimes coincide with God's plans, we can never outdo him, the manager said, "You have friends in high places."

Alex knew what that meant. He says, "It was the Lord. It was the old story of 'death of a vision.' God had a better plan than ours. We were so glad we didn't get the Forhill House. The Moslem group put a lot of money into renovating it, but could never get approval from the local council's planning department, and they ended up being kicked out."

The only stipulation with the Windmill House was that someone had to move in immediately to discourage the vandalism that had made the Forhill house unlivable. The next day Alex moved in with three of his boys. Not too much later, the rest of the family followed and others from the church joined them.

The Windmill House had many uses and purposes. Besides providing housing for church families, it became a training center for new converts. People who had gotten saved off the streets or hard cases from other churches found a place of refuge, just like Elsaessers and Hewats had experienced at the Lord's Land and the Lighthouse Ranch. It provided the home base for a ServiceMaster business. (Alex says, whereas a free franchise had been offered when they first arrived in England, four years later, he had to pay for it!) Other church groups also used it for meetings and conferences.

Alex took over the leadership of the Windmill House as well as a small congregation the Birmingham church started. Harry pastored the original congregation that eventually numbered around 120. Their efforts, and the efforts of those whom the Lord added, bore fruit as many people got saved and a cadre of leadership was developed.

Most missionaries will spend from two to thirty years on the mission field, always keeping in mind where they came from—"home." The Elsaessers and Hewats have made England their home. Harry says, "Right from the start, we were coming here long-term. We knew we were going to stay and we burnt our bridges behind us. We've become British citizens and now, this is home. There is missiological term; we are called 'bi-cultural migrant missionaries.' Someone who makes their mission field their home. We've adopted it, and it has adopted us. Still, you're neither one nor the other completely. Neither fully American nor fully British. Instead, it helps you to focus your mind—your citizenship is with God. Our citizenship is in heaven."

Italy

In the late 1970s, an Italian Christian who lived in northern Italy contacted the G. O. Munich church. From income earned by a couple of language schools he owned, Tony Tomaselli was able to buy a farm with a vineyard near the town of Acqui Terme, halfway between Genoa and Turin.

With the relative scarcity of "on-fire" Christian groups in Europe at that time, we all either knew or knew about each other. Christ is the Answer was a traveling evangelistic group from the U.S. that was staying at the big Munich house when the Germany team arrived to join the Chellos, DePalmos and van Doorens. Tony later hosted them at his farm and learned about their stay in Munich. Aside from growing grapes, Tony saw the potential to turn his farm into a Teen Challenge Center.

American sensibilities may have trouble with a drug rehabilitation center selling grapes to wineries. While Italy—and Germany for that matter—has problems with alcoholism, drinking wine or beer with meals is as common as drinking soda in the U.S. and considered just as harmless. In many areas, the water really is unhealthy.

Italy was flooded with heroin and other drugs, and the youth were being decimated by its ravages. Tony and his wife, Charito, wanted to help. To that end, G. O. Munich offered to send down labor to help renovate the old farm buildings.

Linda and I traveled to northern Italy in the good, old-fashioned way that missionaries with no money often traveled. We hitchhiked. With thousands of hitchhiking miles behind me, I can attest that doing it with a female companion is easier than without one. We made it to Tony's farm in one day. The two brothers who accompanied us traveled separately and were on the road two days.

While riding with a businessman in his big Mercedes, I learned that speed is relative. Traveling at an average speed (including stops) 120 miles per hour, I could barely read the road signs we flew past for the first ten or fifteen minutes. Then everything began to slow down and start to feel normal, but I still couldn't read the signs. Next we caught a ride in a big gas tanker truck—the kind with the driver's cab over the front wheels. After dark, when the villages were empty of farm traffic, we swept down streets where two-story houses were built right up to the curb.

The headlights reflected off the fronts of the houses and it seemed as if we were taking up the whole road without leaving room for so much as a stray dog.

Tony's place was old—from the previous century—and needed a lot of work. It was on a hill surrounded by his vineyards. For a month we helped get rid of junk and scraped out old mortar from between the ancient bricks which made up the walls. Tony cautioned us to not be too zealous—if we removed too much mortar, the walls might collapse!

When Tony learned that G. O. was sending a team to Italy, he invited them to stay at the farm until they got their bearings.

Andy Finds His Tribe

Led by Andy and Linda Costa, the outreach to Italy had been in Andy's thoughts for some time. After accepting the Lord in 1972, he searched for a church whose zeal matched the evangelistic fire that God had ignited in his heart. Until he learned better, even the Children of God—one of the larger and better-known cults of the Jesus People movement—looked good.

Through the Christian grapevine, Andy heard of the Lighthouse Ranch and went to Eureka to pay a visit. He saw a group of people who were "living the gospel at all levels" of their lives. They approached the work of the gospel with the same passion he felt and knew these were the disciples he wanted to be with. Since he was from Southern California and had commitments there—his family owned Italian (of course) restaurants the leaders at the Ranch directed him to Carmello Bazanno, then the head G. O. elder in Southern California.

With Gospel Outreach, Andy had found his "tribe" and began to share his burden to take a team to Italy. He made a couple of exploratory trips first, one with Linda, and through the Munich church made contact with Tony. On December 2, 1980, the G. O. Italy team—the Costas, Andy's cousin, Cathy Vinci, Harold Bailey, Larry Lapmarado, and Barbara Nichols arrived in Acqui Terme.

The farm was up and running as a Teen Challenge Center, and there were already young men there turning their lives around. The team stayed for nine months, helping Tony and the staff minister to the residents. This time was invaluable for them. Andy and Cathy were already fluent in Italian; the others still had much to learn. It provided them the opportunity to become acquainted with Italian culture and minister to the youth without having the burden of actually leading a church. They also traveled throughout the country, visiting different ministries and praying. They didn't yet know specifically where the Lord would plant them.

Teen Challenge has just about the best success rate for drug rehabilitation of any organization, and Tony's farm, now called L'Arca, was the best in Italy. One of the young men there, Luca, needed to make a trip back to his home in Florence to register for the Italian military. Since he wasn't that far removed from his drug lifestyle, Andy accompanied him to give support. Luca, who was only eighteen years old, had already used heroin for two years and had a brother who was still an addict. They met up with his brother, and traveled around to Luca's old haunts. Andy's eyes were opened to a world he didn't know existed. "I'd never seen Florence from the eyes of a kid doing drugs. I'd seen it as a tourist. When I saw the part tourists don't see, it blew my mind. The epidemic of drug abuse was huge in all of Italy, and Florence was pretty bad. The underground was huge."

They were there for three days. When they returned to L'Arca, Andy told the team, "Guys, let's pray. I think God is going to open up Florence to us, and that's where we're going to go next." They took an exploratory trip there and all the team felt confirmation that this was where the Lord was sending them to start their own church.

The rolling hill country full of vineyards southwest of Florence is where the Brethren Church had a conference center. Near the town of Poggio Ubertini, this is where Andy and the team landed. In exchange for helping around the center and in its vineyard (it seemed like everyone in northern Italy had a vineyard!), they got free room and board. This served as their base of operations until they had a better idea of where they would be ministering in the city of about a million inhabitants.

The team often rode the train into Florence to take prayer walks, asking God to show them where they should begin their work. Doors began to open. Near the center of Florence, not far from Michelangelo's famous David statue, they discovered a Christian bookstore run by Dany and Carmelina Aversano. A relationship developed and Dany and his wife proved to be a great help. The team found a meeting hall not too far from the bookstore. They also got to know Salvatore and Maria Zaccariello. Salvatore was a leader in a Pentecostal church who had taken a break from leadership. When he met the team, he and Maria joined them. Andy remembers, "They had a gift of hospitality; any time we had a need, they were there. Money, food, a place to stay, they were always so giving." Both couples became pillars of the church.

L'Arca fed a continual stream of rehabilitated young men to the church where the work of conversion to disciples of Jesus continued.

A religious spirit has ruled over Italy for centuries, but of course, has done nothing to bring its people closer to God. Instead, it convinced them that religion was a sometimes-useful tool to gain position or acquire riches in this life. At other times, it was of no use at all. A result was many Italians were skeptical and felt they knew everything there was to know about God. Linda Costa says many were agnostics or atheists.

Still, people started getting saved. They got saved through street evangelism and meetings held in their hall. First the team, and then the church, sponsored concerts and served meals to the needy. Others would come from different parts of Italy, having heard about this group of people who taught that the God of the Bible desired a relationship with them—not blind obedience to the rules of men.

In Germany, France, and England, hard work had been needed to bring a few souls to the Lord and the church. Something different began to happen in Italy. Linda says, "We had many people give their lives to Christ. Our 'harvest' was a mixture of new converts, seekers, travelers, and visitors from other churches. Many seekers would come from all areas of Italy out of curiosity because of the novelty of our fellowship, and they made decisions to follow Jesus."

At one point, the Sunday attendance of the new group, named Cantico Nuovo, was close to 400. On the continent that had been so deeply affected by the gospel, the traditions of Christianity were still evident, but the experience was almost non-existent. Four hundred attendees on a Sunday was pretty good, especially for a young church.

The Italy team also got its own Lighthouse Ranch. A lady from the church had a villa with a producing vineyard and olive grove just outside of Florence. The maintenance of the grapes and olives had been contracted out, but the villa had room for between six to fifteen young men at a time.

Original team member Larry was assisted by Pino Squillace in discipling the young brothers. Many of the residents were graduates from L'Arca who wanted more teaching and training in the Christian life.

They were kept busy tending a large vegetable garden, and working in a church-run business that assembled and took down trade show displays in Florence. Brethren from the States came—some on short-term mission trips and others who joined the team. Jim and Cathy Scapparotti, Denny and Maureen Hurst, and David and Debbie Alexander were some who came to join in the work. Andy and Linda returned to the U.S. in 1986 and left the church in the hands of Salvatore and Maria, who continued to lead it for many years.

France

Jim and Diane Boutcher and I were sitting around talking about life in a foreign country and the special challenge speaking a new language all day presented. I told them of being mentally tired after a day of speaking only German. They agreed. Jim said, "Yeah, after a day of speaking French, my lips were sore." He explained that together with the mouth, teeth, and tongue, the lips had a big job producing the sounds needed to buy a loaf of bread or find a bathroom. Unlike Germans, many who prided themselves on their knowledge of English, the French saw no need to learn any other earthly language. When the world came to their doorstep, it had better be ready to speak the native tongue; nothing else would do.

The Boutchers had originally moved to Chicago, via the Lighthouse Ranch. After a few years there, they felt led by the Lord to plant a G. O. church in France. Mark and Mary Richards, from the G. O. Milwaukee church, joined them.

The Boutchers moved to Milwaukee so the couples could get to know each other better.

Jim made an exploratory trip to France. He planned to prayerfully visit different cities, seeking the Lord for guidance and confirmation as to where they should start the work. He met up with two French brothers who were a part of the G. O. Munich church, Louis Monet and Hervé Parsy, and traveled with them to their hometowns—Louis in Cannes, France, and Hervé from north of Paris, as well as visiting with YWAM in Paris. Jim returned home with inconclusive results—he still had no solid idea where the new church should be planted.

Missionaries Not Wanted or Needed

Next, the Boutchers and Richards all made the trip and again roamed the country, looking for the town or city that felt right. What they discovered surprised them—it seemed like no place was right.

Their experience in Lyon was typical. Jim related, "When we got to Lyon, we met with different churches there, and I was struck with how unwelcoming they were." Diane interjected, "And that's where we were the *most* welcome!" Jim says, "I remember sitting in a room where they had a map of the city on the wall, and it was divided up into different areas for the different churches. They pointed out which area was theirs and which areas "belonged" to other churches. They showed us a tiny little spot off to the side and said, 'If you want to come, you can go there. But don't expect us to support or help you.'"

They got the same story from the government when they applied for visas. France didn't need or want missionaries. They reapplied and were turned down again, this time with a warning. If they asked again and were denied, they would be blacklisted with no hope of staying in the country.

It was pretty discouraging. They were ready to leave their homes, plop down in a foreign country and preach the gospel. It's just that the churches and the government didn't want them.

Not sure what to do next, as an afterthought they stopped in Geneva, Switzerland to visit a man who was a member of the Munich church. Manuel Diaz was a Portuguese citizen, living and working in Geneva. He had talked to Jim during his first visit. This time, when they told him of the cold reception they had received, he asked, "Why go to France? Come to Switzerland; we have such a need here and you would be welcomed!"

The Boutchers and Richards met with the Bible study group that Manuel was a part of, and everyone seemed open and excited to have the missionaries come and minister in their midst. While some worked and lived in Geneva, most were French and lived just across the border in the small town of Collonges sous Salevè.

The openness and enthusiasm of this group of around thirty French and Swiss Christians couldn't be ignored. It was concluded that God had indeed shown them where they would spend the next few years of their lives.

Before the final decision was made to join with them, Jim decided to visit Manuel and the group one more time. He brought with him a couple heavy hitters of the G. O. foreign outreaches: Thomas van Dooren from Germany and Carlos Ramirez with other elders from Guatemala. Both Thomas and Carlos were men of faith and authority and the Bible study members were duly impressed. It seemed like G. O. itself was going to make a major push in their part of France. They were excited and expectant to see what these mighty men of God were going to do.

On May 1, 1986, Jim and the pregnant Diane made the move with four children in tow. The Richards followed a few weeks later. They didn't want to bring a ready-made program that would essentially be a prepackaged American-style church plant. Instead, the two couples planned to spend the first year getting to know the language and how the French lived their lives. Then, as they became familiar with the people and the culture, they could begin to minister.

The brethren in the Bible study had different ideas.

Diane says, "The visit [of Thomas and Carlos] really impressed them. They thought we were miracle workers. I don't think that's an exaggeration. Some of the people looked at us as being way bigger than we were. As if, now that we were there, 'things were going to explode.' They started bringing us all sorts of sick people for prayer. There were a lot who had serious emotional and mental problems—bi-polar and so on. There would be prayer going on in our house for hours."

They didn't see the same rich harvest of souls like they did at the ranches, but people began to get saved.

Feast of the Holy Beard

Gospel Outreach never embraced the idea of church leadership as a unique group of ministers separate from the rest of the church. We were all called to be ministers. Any one of us could be used powerfully by the Holy Spirit to share the gospel. So when church planting teams like the France team were sent out they immediately began to look for brethren who could share and eventually assume the mantle of responsibility for the flock. Jim and Mark began to work with Abel Felix and Michel Bidot as two men who could eventually take over leadership of the church.

At the same time, they found a more positive reception from the area churches than they had in the rest of the country. Jim recalls that, "We developed some good relationships with local pastors."

Besides teaching and encouraging the brethren to share the gospel with neighbors, co-workers and families, organized outreaches were an important way of sharing God's message with the locals. After the new families got established, the G. O. Munich church sent over an evangelism team to hit the streets with the French brothers and sisters. This provided the Munich brethren a valuable experience of sharing the gospel in a foreign country and was an encouragement for the French church.

The French church had several members who were trained musicians, and they helped teach the youth to sing and perform street theater. Another joint G. O. effort was carried out in Dunkirk, France. The youth groups from Birmingham, Munich, and France all got together for a several-day effort. One of the families in the church started a YWAM King's Kids chapter in Geneva. Once it was up and running, they counted as many as eighty kids from many different churches.

Sometimes the local community provided the occasion and crowds for evangelization. In anticipation of a yearly festival, the church designed posters and exhibits for the townspeople who, it was hoped, would visit their building and so be exposed to God's message. They were happy with the steady stream of visitors and didn't care that the celebration was in honor of Saint Bard, or, as the locals called it, Feast of the Holy Beard.

In 1984, after eight years of service, the Boutchers returned to the U.S. with two more kids than they had arrived with. But they didn't completely leave France. Like all missionaries who give their lives to the people of another land, they left part of their hearts with the brethren, and continued their friendship and communication with them. The Richards elected to stay in France, getting jobs with international organizations in Geneva.

More outreaches to foreign peoples followed: Chris and Cindi Raymond and Ron and Diane Easley left Alaska to labor in Japan, and Ed and Sue Kearney moved from Vancouver, Washington to Tashkent, Uzbekistan. Mike and Mary Lou Bryan planted a church in Russia and Brad and Andrea Snow went with their family to Croatia.

Almost all of us G. O. brethren who went to foreign countries arrived in our new homes with the intention of spending the rest of our lives there sharing the gospel. We had read of the extraordinary commitment of our brothers and sisters in places like China who, in spite of incredible hardship and privation, stayed true to their calling. We wanted to do that too. We were also aware that if we stepped off the plane with a return date in mind, our effectiveness would be limited.

Most of us discovered that the "grace" to minister in a foreign land had an expiration date. At some point, the burden diminished and couldn't be brought back to the same level. Whatever the reason: family, finances, or just being weary, we found that prayer, fasting, "faith confessions," or even breaks were not enough to fuel up the engine again. The grace had run out.

Because of our initial commitment, we sometimes had to deal with condemnation and feeling like failures. Then we got another lesson in how truly loving and gracious our Lord is. It was okay. He understood. He loved us and was proud of what we had been able to do. We weren't moving "back," we were moving on.

CHAPTER SEVENTEEN

Their Fame Continues

THE TITLE OF this chapter may seem a little presumptuous, but it ties together some loose strings—and in our eyes, the fame of our brothers and sisters does continue.

Leon Umweg/David Leon

The word *Umweg*? Doesn't that mean "detour" in German? (Yes, it does.) According to Bill Ireland, that was David Leon's real last name, and his first name was Leon. I can't tell you why he changed it; I only have guesses.

David was . . . strange? Different? Yes, according to everyone who knew him. He evidently got saved through Youth for Truth, or as they became better known, the Children of God. They were a cult in every sense of the word that got started in Seattle. Still, people met Jesus through them. Those who stayed with the group eventually lost sight of Jesus and focused on David Berg, their leader and "messiah." Some, like David Leon, left the group and followed the Lord instead.

At first David spoke mostly King James English because, with its "thees" and "thous," that was the language of his Bible. The Scripture verses on his clothing showed his obedience to God's command to the priests of the Old Testament. He was quick with a reproof, or if needed, a rebuke, when brethren engaged in "unprofitable" talk about things like politics, sports, movies, etc. He was extremely dogmatic and legalistic. Lambert remembers up in cold Alaska when brothers would pray wearing stocking caps. David would insist they remove them because we're not supposed to pray with our heads covered. Tommy Kennedy had to send him from Mendocino back to Eureka after he rebuked the devil in Brother Webb's Foursquare church in Casper near the Lord's Land.

But God used him. He opened the coffee shop at Clark and B that pulled Jim Durkin out into the current of the revival. He introduced Ron Juncal to street evangelism. As it became obvious that something was happening with Jim and the Ranch, David approached Ron about his coffee shop in Fortuna. He told him, "We're here, you're there, and Jim has the Lighthouse Ranch. Are we the body of Christ or not?"

They decided to join up with Jim and Gospel Outreach.

He was passionate about sharing the gospel. Bill Wheeler remembers David fondly. "So many might not have known Jesus if it wasn't for David."

David certainly didn't have a lot of friends—maybe none, really—except that Tom Kennedy considered him a friend. He says David got married, but it didn't last. Then one day in 2008, he was out riding a bike. He pulled to the side of the road, got off, sat down and died.

As Tom said, "It's not a bad way to go."

Richard Twiss

Richard Twiss was an enrolled member of the Rosebud Sioux Tribe of South Dakota whose life mirrored that of many other youth of the 1970s.

He became involved in the American Indian Movement and participated in the armed occupation of the Bureau of Indian Affairs offices in Washington D. C., in 1972. After that, he wandered about the country searching for purpose and doing drugs. In the middle of a bad drug experience on Maui, Richard called out to God for help. The paranoia that held him tightly suddenly disappeared, and he was filled with new life and the peace of God.

He found his way up to Alaska and became involved with Gospel Outreach there. In 1975, at the Bread of Life Bakery, outside Wasilla, he met Katherine Kroshus of Vancouver, Washington, and six months later they married. In what Katherine calls "our formative years," Richard grew in knowledge and maturity and soon became a leader in G. O. Alaska.

In 1981, he and Katherine accompanied Jim and Sue Wall to Vancouver, Washington to assume the leadership duties of the church started by Adrian Simila and his evangelistic team. They ministered there for thirteen years with Richard becoming the pastor. At the same time, working together with Joseph Anfuso and Forward Edge, Richard began taking groups of Christians to the Rosebud reservation in South Dakota and to the Crow Agency in Montana for short-term mission trips.

The burden grew to see his people freed of both the spiritual and societal bondage that kept them poor in every sense of the word. Katherine says, "Richard had a desire to see Native and Indigenous believers become co-equal partners and contributors in the life, work and health of the church. He did not want them continue as a perpetual mission field."

Richard resigned as pastor of G. O. Vancouver. He worked for a period as the director of the Native American Department for the American Bible Society on the Couer d' Alene reservation in Plummer, Idaho.

Then in 1997, Richard and Katherine launched Wiconi International, which means "life" in the Lakota/Sioux language. Through this non-profit ministry, Richard and Katherine have touched the lives of many thousands of people.

Richard also co-founded NAIITS (North American Institute for Indigenous Theological Studies), was chairman of the board for My People International, a member of the CCDA (Christian Community Development Association), and co-founder of Evangelicals4Justice. In 2011, Richard earned his doctorate, a D.Miss., from Asbury Theological Seminary. Until his passing, Richard continued his teaching career through the NAIITS program, Portland State University, and other institutions of higher education.

Richard authored a number of books, pamphlets and articles over the years. His first book, *One Church, Many Tribes*, reached many people with the message of an inculturated faith in Jesus.

Richard left his labors in the hands of faithful brethren, when he passed away on February 9, 2013 at age fifty-eight after a heart attack, while attending the National Prayer Breakfast in Washington D. C.

Wiconi International is today an important ministry that reaches out to native peoples on every continent. It brings the message of Christ together with the education and encouragement that will improve their present lives and give them hope of a better future.

More G. O. Music

We all remember the amazing worship we experienced in Gospel Outreach. For Christians in many church settings, the experience of God's presence is special and rare. For us, as the chapter about worship shows, it was the norm. We were blessed beyond measure.

While some of our musicians and worship leaders may have thought about careers in music—and some of them could've certainly gone far—they were too busy preaching the gospel to spend the time and effort needed.

Still, the talent couldn't be denied. Rebecca composed and performed songs that made it easy to enter into the Lord's presence. Her song "Let Us Go Unto the House of the Lord" was published by Scripture in Song and Vineyard Music and continues to be sung.

Paul Johnson still appears in Southern California, playing the surf music that he helped introduce to the world as well as worship music.

Thomas van Dooren, of G. O. Munich, came from a line of talented artists, and passed it on. His grandmother was a concert pianist, his father a bandleader, and his mother a dancer.

Thomas continued the tradition and became a respected worship leader as well as speaker for Christian meetings and conferences in Germany. He translated English language worship songs into German, and he and Kristine produced several worship events in the country called, "Fest zur Ehre Gottes" or "Celebration in Honor of God." He wrote a song, "Worthy is the Lamb" which Kristine says is still sung in German churches. Some songs draw attention to what God has done for us, and others tell about how we feel about the Lord. Like the worship we had in G. O., Thomas' song only points to Jesus and the honor he is due. It's a beautiful song and is often used as the introduction for communion services.

His five daughters are all talented. For many years they sang together as a group, focusing on Christian themes. The oldest, Naomi, and the youngest, Debbie, are still involved. Their zeal for the Lord gives them many opportunities to share their faith, both in the secular and Christian music worlds. When the first Disney *Little Mermaid* appeared, Naomi sang songs for the main character. Years later, the second *Little Mermaid* was made, and this time Debbie sang Ariel's part, and Naomi sang the part of her mother. Debbie has a career as a singer and Naomi is a singing coach for the German version of the singing talent show *The Voice*.

In Italy, Andy Costa formed a record company La Sorgente that produced contemporary Italian Christian music for the church. It was one of the first to do so in Italy, and had two platinum albums. Andy sold the company when the Costas returned to the U.S.

Verbo also started a music publishing company that continues the rich tradition of worship they have enjoyed since the early days.

Rios Montt

After the coup in 1983, Rios Montt returned to his duties at Verbo. Starting in 1989, he became involved with politics again when he formed a political party. He was elected to several terms as a legislator and tried to run again for president but was prevented from doing that.

A life in politics is sure to produce enemies, and Rios Montt has his share of them. He has had to defend himself from unceasing claims of genocide against the Mayans and other Indians of Guatemala. He was once found guilty; he appealed, was found not guilty, and now is being tried again.

This time the courts have decided that, if found guilty, he won't have to serve any sentence because of his age and failing health. It's hard to imagine a scheming, power-hungry general joining a bunch of American missionaries, sweeping the church, and becoming the head of the school. Without exception, no one from the Love Lift Team or Verbo who knows Rios Montt believes the accusations against him.

Festival of the Son

Ron Juncal had a lot of good ideas and the Festival of the Son was one of them. It was actually a Christian version of a rock concert with a difference. It was primarily a time of worship for the body of Christ with teaching by Jim, Ron, Ern Baxter, Dennis Peacock, and others. The first one was held at the Lighthouse Ranch in the summer of 1971, and at Living Waters in 1972. After that, for the next few years, the hills of Santa Cruz provided the venue for crowds that numbered up to three thousand or more.

The Evangelistic Team

As if being a reborn, whole-hearted, sacrificial, committed disciple of Jesus wasn't enough, Ron Juncal took it a step further. In early 1973, he, Peter DePalmo, and Bob Gormin showed up at the Lord's Land and pitched an idea that would take the Gospel Outreach experience even further. It would be called the Evangelistic Team and would emphasize Bible study, prayer, evangelism, and something that was especially close to Ron's heart, the friendship and support that believers could provide each other in their journey on God's path. They visited the ranches and soon enlisted a core of brothers and sisters who were excited about the promise of a still deeper experience with the Lord and one another.

The operative model was intensity. Every day was filled with the activities mentioned above, in addition to working for support. (Jim Durkin was never in favor of soliciting donations for Gospel Outreach.) They had foreign language lessons and made evangelistic road trips.

The team rented a large house about forty-five miles south of Eureka in the small town of Weott. One source of finances was the old Gospel Outreach standby—a leather shop that made belts, Bible covers, and purses, etc., with Ron designing most of the articles. Others, like Peter DePalmo, who had had a shop in Eureka and at Living Waters, would cut out and assemble everything. The brothers would then load the goods in a van and head up to Eureka or down to San Francisco to sell them. Tree planting rounded out the money-making activities for the Evangelistic Team.

The team did a lot of traveling—down to Los Angeles for the G. O. "Invasion," up to Portland, and Vancouver, B. C., and then across the country to New York City. There they met up with a group of struggling young believers in Brooklyn living at St. Marks Place. It was, according to Bill Ireland, "A tough neighborhood." He said, "We packed them up and brought them back to California with us."

As a team led by an evangelist, they shared the good news wherever they went. Chris Funnell remembers, "It was easy to witness. Whoever you shared the Lord with, they were open, at least to listen." They would stop in city parks, sing songs, and share the good news. If deep enough water was near—a pond, lake or stream—they'd baptize the new believers. New converts were either directed to local churches or encouraged to head back to the Lighthouse Ranch.

Ron worked with the team for year and then sent them on their way to work with G. O. teams in different cities and countries. With the help of some of the original members, he got another group together and repeated the whole thing. After that, Adrian Simila, together with his wife, Debbie, put together a third Evangelistic Team which followed in the footsteps of the first two.

The Evangelistic Teams did what was advertised. They produced mature, faithful brethren who continued the work of the gospel and brought a solid commitment to the local congregations wherever they went.

Sabine Ball

Sabine returned to Germany in 1992 to begin a youth outreach in Dresden. She set up a coffee shop and second-hand store and the income supported two communal houses. The outreach she created grew and soon attracted national attention. Sabine was the subject of magazine and television stories. Her whole-hearted evangelistic efforts to help the lost youth of Dresden and Germany drew comparisons to Corrie ten Boom and Mother Teresa. Two elementary schools in Germany have been named after her. Sabine passed into the presence of the Lord on July 9, 2009.

Forward Edge

In 1983, a vision began to grow in the heart of Joseph Anfuso, one of the G. O. elders in Eureka. Through contact with Verbo in Guatemala, he saw countless needs that could be met by short-term mission teams. Joseph envisioned a ministry that would enlist Christians to both evangelize and provide material aid to people and churches around the world.

After pitching the idea to Jim Durkin and the other leaders, Forward Edge was launched.

The first Forward Edge team was assembled to join the G. O. Italy team in an evangelization effort in Florence, Italy. More teams were organized, and more projects adopted until the services provided by Forward Edge included sharing the gospel, building orphanages, churches, and bringing disaster relief to places from Nicaragua to Sri Lanka.

By 2005, Forward Edge had sent out over 10,000 workers to thirty-three countries and numerous U.S. states and cities. Based in Vancouver, Washington, Forward Edge is now a full-fledged disaster relief and development organization that continues to provide Christians opportunities to share their faith, and assist needy people all over the world.

Other Revival Groups

Beside the relationships the different G. O. churches built wherever teams went, we also worked with groups like Prince of Peace in Portland, Oregon. POP sent brethren to plant trees with us, and some of their members joined teams heading out to start churches. Among others, Randy Cole and Ron Gloeckler went to Germany with the team and Kathy Dowd Griffith joined the Chicago team; Myra Cromwell Trolese, whose father was pastor at POP, was a Guatemala team member. Whenever tree-planting crews worked near Portland, we always enjoyed attending Prince of Peace services and having fellowship with the brethren.

We were pretty busy, so opportunities to get to know other ministries were limited, but we knew they were out there and were serving the Lord too.

Shiloh Ministries of Oregon had several communal houses. God's Army was located in Fresno, California. Christ is the Answer was a traveling evangelistic group that held tent meetings all over the country and in Europe. Youth with a Mission (YWAM) preached discipleship to young Christians and opened Discipleship Training Schools (DTS) all over the world. Sabine donated the Lord's Land to YWAM, and it continues to serve as a retreat and training center. Jesus People USA (JPUSA) and Jews for Jesus were two more groups that had a strong, positive influence on the saved and the lost.

Of course, there was Dick Benjamin and our good friends up in Anchorage at Abbot Loop, Dennis Peacocke, Dick Iverson of Bible Temple in Portland, and Jerry Russell from Smartsville, California. They were anointed and tested leaders who never failed to give us encouragement and solid teaching.

The Jesus People Revival probably had its roots in the charismatic movement, which preceded it by a few years. This was the outpouring of the Holy Spirit that swept through mainline churches as well as the Catholic Church. The revival surfaced in 1968 when Lonnie Frisbee began working with Chuck Smith and Calvary Chapel, preaching the gospel and baptizing people on the beaches of Southern California. Thousands got saved and baptized, and created an explosion of new Christians for Calvary and other churches in the area. From there, it spread throughout California, up the West Coast, the U.S. and the rest of the world.

Jesus said the Holy Spirit is like the wind—no one can tell where it comes from or where it is going. It took a while to realize it and even longer to admit it, but sometime after the mid-'70s we began to notice the wind had turned into a gentle breeze. The Jesus People Revival—at least in the U.S. and Europe—had passed.

Fasting in Bridgeport

There was an episode in the life of Gospel Outreach that left everyone confused. In the fall of 1974, after crews from G. O. completed a contract picking apples for a large orchard in Bridgeport, Washington, Jim Durkin approached the owners with a proposal. He would have people do winter maintenance on the trees—pruning and so forth—if G. O. could use the large bunkhouse facility for church purposes. He wanted to get G. O.ers together for a time of fasting and prayer. The orchard was away from town, the buildings were more than adequate and the brothers and sisters would be undistracted.

That was fine with the owners. Soon a stream of "older" brothers and sisters made their way to apple-growing country. Most of them had served in leadership in one form or another and could be expected to both work in the orchard and sustain a period of fasting and seeking the Lord. By this time the tree planters' school had fizzled, so Jim invited them to come too.

It turned out that climbing ten-foot, three-legged, fruit-picking ladders in freezing rain, and fasting to hear from the Lord, were not very compatible. Besides weakening the body, fasting exerts an unhappy influence on attitudes. So, brethren really had to work on their "faith confessions" to keep an even keel. They followed a fasting plan that led to progressively longer fasts. It was up to each person how long he or she wanted to do it. While some went for longer, most settled for a week-long fast. Jim personally had a desire to see miracles and healings in the church and was beating at the gates of heaven during a forty-day fast.

The most notable result from this time was that a group of brothers who felt a prophetic calling warned Jim that the direction of G. O. needed to change, or the Lord was going to change it himself.

Bridgeport was a good try, but no one felt that much was accomplished.

Jim and Dacie Durkin

Jim and Dacie's lives were suddenly transformed the day David Leon walked into Sequoia Realty. What had seemed like the "typical" life of a businessman and part-time pastor turned into a worldwide ministry that spread the name and message of Jesus to thousands. Jim was finally able to rest from his cares and labors on January 12, 1996 when he entered into the presence of his Savior. Dacie joined him on March 23, 2011.

Good-bye Lighthouse Ranch

Gospel Outreach of Humboldt County sold the Lighthouse Ranch buildings and property to the U.S. government in 2005. The buildings were old and full of asbestos. Any attempt to renovate them would have cost more money and resolve than anyone was willing to spend. The lighthouse lens was sent to the Smithsonian Institute in 1974 and the lighthouse itself was relocated as a monument in Eureka's boat marina. The government tore down the buildings and seeded Table Bluff with grass. All that remained were the tall, dark Cypress trees that enclosed the property and the square cement foundation of the lighthouse itself.

There was one last event before that happened.

Two Russian Orthodox monks, Father Herman and Father Seraphim, were leaders of a monastery on Highway 36 on the other side of the coastal range from Carlotta. Gary

Todoroff got to know them through Mary Mansur, a onetime G. O.er who was a part of that community.

They enjoyed meeting and getting to know Gary, and loved hearing his stories about the Lighthouse Ranch and communal living. After all, that was how they lived too. They were planning a conference and asked Gary if the Ranch was available for that sort of thing. It was. It had been some time since the Ranch had been a discipleship center that trained and sent out teams to share the gospel and plant churches.

Harry Hewat was on the Ranch leadership team in the late 1970s and felt the beginnings of a subtle shift in the atmosphere. According to Jim Durkin (the son) more and more young people who came to the Ranch were no longer open or transparent. "They were seeking a place to stay and a free meal." Within a few years it became a parking spot for troubled youth. Some of their parents—ex-ranchers themselves—hoped the experience that had given them new life would change their children's lives for the better.

Gary got busy with a crew who painted the inside of the main building and cleaned the place up. When the monks and other attendees arrived, Father Herman led a procession around the land and buildings, sprinkling holy water and blessing everything.

The brothers loved it and after the meetings, Gary found Father Herman. He asked him, "So, Father Herman, what do you think about this place?"

"Oh, Gary," he replied, "this is holy ground. You just sense that God changed thousands of lives here."

CHAPTER EIGHTEEN

Stamped by God's Seal

I WAS TALKING TO a brother who had been there at the beginning. He was telling me of the focus, vision, and joy, of serving the Lord together with the brothers and sisters. We knew we were in the middle of a powerful move of the Holy Spirit.

He also told of sharp disagreements with Jim. They became so strong that eventually they led to separation. The brother left, and G. O. continued on its way.

While I was listening, I began talking to the Lord. *Lord, you knew Jim had shortcomings. You knew we would have problems that would limit us and lead to G. O. shutting down.*

Thinking of all the good that had happened in our lives, of the love, joy, challenges, and trials we all shared, I demanded of him, *How could you let that happen?*

His tone wasn't strident like mine, but I sensed the Lord saying to me, *I will use anyone who is willing to the limit of their willingness and ability.* He wasn't looking for perfection. That was his job.

Two things stand out. We didn't understand it then, but Jim was limited and so were we. We were willing instruments in God's hands and thought we had this Holy Spirit movement thing down. We saw what produced fruit in our lives and in the lives of those God brought to us and never thought it would be otherwise.

As teams left the protective umbrella of the ranches and Jim's direct input, we were suddenly on our own, and that's when our lack of life experience and maturity began to tell. While several churches and individuals had success—think Eureka, Alaska, Silverton, England, or Guatemala—most grew to a certain point and then stagnated.

Perhaps Jesus' parable of the sown seeds is appropriate—the seed that was cast on shallow ground grew quickly and then withered because, "it had no root."

Awkward efforts to continue the movement became forced. Instead of reproducing what we had personally experienced, we drove people from our churches.

But a difference needs to be pointed out. What God did in each of us individually, and as a family, was real and a miracle. We were once lost and now knew Jesus. Our experience was just like what we read in the Gospels, the book of Acts and the rest of the New Testament. But different gifts and abilities were needed to build congregations of believers. For most of us (though not all) those needed time and experience before they could become effective. By the time we had that experience, Gospel Outreach was gone.

I think every one of us today still endorses the things that Jim taught us: Purpose and Vision, Training Your Soul, Bold Confession, Going Into All the World, and Discipleship, etc. But if we were to find ourselves—as we are now—in the same situation as at the ranches in the 1970s, our application of those truths would be much different than how we did it back then.

To me, this means that God's revelation to Jim was timeless; it held power, and it still lives in us today. We've changed, and the implementation has changed, but those truths are still there. "For the gifts and calling of God are without repentance" (Rom. 11:29 KJV). What God has given us he will not take back.

Our lives don't in the least resemble what they were back then, but we were stamped with God's seal, wielded by Jim Durkin.

We're still disciples.

CHAPTER NINETEEN

The Spring

WHAT STARTED IN Jim Durkin's life as a small spring began to grow. First the Lord told him to help David Leon and the brothers open their coffee shop at Clark and B. They began attending services at Deliverance Temple, and Ron Juncal and his group joined them. The spring became a small stream.

Then the people at the Lighthouse Ranch came to hear Jim's message. Jim acquired the Ranch, moved out there with Dacie, and the stream grew to a river.

The Holy Spirit moved powerfully up and down the West Coast, all across North America and the world. Dozens, then hundreds, then thousands of people showed up at the Lighthouse Ranch, Carlotta, Living Waters, the Lord's Land, the houses in Eureka, and at all the different cities and countries where Gospel Outreach teams went.

They heard the voice of God, felt his touch, and yielded their lives to him. The stream of new believers became a strong river.

A powerful river coursing through gorges and valleys leaves the mountains and enters the broad plains. The exhilaration of the rapids crashing against rocks and boulders and changing the landscape is traded for a calmer, smoother flow. Some of the excitement is gone, but the river has become more useful to those who need its life-giving qualities. It begins to widen, covering a greater area and bringing its richness to many.

Finally, the river approaches the flat land of the coast. There it spreads out into many smaller parts, streams again, really. What was once a mighty river has become numerous waterways, still nourishing, still moving toward the sea. It reaches its goal; the force of its current meets the vast body of water, and before long, is indistinguishable from the sea itself.

Is that the end of the river? No. The God of springs, streams, and rivers is also the Lord of the seas. The winds and waves and ocean currents are at his command and he sends them where he wills.

And besides, "This gospel of the kingdom shall be preached in all the world for a witness unto all the nations; and *then* shall the end come" (Matt. 24:14 KJV).

Go ye therefore, and make disciples of all nations . . .
and lo, I am with you always, even to the end of the age.
(Matt. 28:19–20 NKJV)

References

van Dooren, Kristine. 2007. *Das Lied Meines Lebens* (*The Song of My Life*). Gerth Medien, GmbH, Asslar. pp 110, 212-216

Radiance Media. Jim Durkin message quotes are courtesy of Radiance Media.

www.jim-durkin.tlchrist.info/radiance.htm.

www.goalumni.homestead.com by Joan Pritchard shows many photographs from the early years of Gospel Outreach.

Resources

Al Jenke has done a great job collecting and making available Jim Durkin's teachings. Below are the links as well as other Gospel Outreach oriented sites like Paul Johnson's "Radiance Music Restoration Project," and Joseph Anfuso's "Forward Edge" missions outreach organization, etc. Al's site will lead you to those and more.

Jim Durkin:
www.jim-durkin.tlchrist.info/index.htm.
Radiance tapes:
www.jim-durkin.tlchrist.info/radiance.htm.
Websites:
www.jim-durkin.tlchrist.info/books/jd_books.htm.
Anfuso, Joseph. 2010. *Message in a Body*. Pediment, 2010.
Fallon, D'Arcy. 2004. *So Late, So Soon/A Memoir*. Hawthorne Books.
Means, Bob. 2015. *My Soul to Keep /Picking up the Pieces*.

Contact Information

To order additional copies of this book, please visit
www.redemption-press.com.
Also available on Amazon.com and BarnesandNoble.com
Or by calling toll free 1-844-2REDEEM.

CPSIA information can be obtained
at www.ICGtesting.com
Printed in the USA
JSHW011042040423
39817JS00003B/148